A Lyn

Lynne Sharon Schwartz

The Bread Loaf Series of Contemporary Writers

LYNNE SHARON SCHWARTZ

A Lynne Sharon
Schwartz READER

SELECTED

PROSE AND POETRY

Middlebury College Press
Published by University Press of New England
Hanover and London

MIDDLEBURY COLLEGE PRESS
Published by University Press of New England,
Hanover, NH 03755
© 1992 by Lynne Sharon Schwartz
Printed in the United States of America   5   4   3   2   1
CIP data appear at the end of the book

Acknowledgments appear on p. 255.

TO TED SOLOTAROFF,

for seeing and believing,

for patience and concentration

Contents

A Bread Loaf Contemporary

A T   A   T I M E   when the literary world is increasingly dominated by commercial formulas and concentrated financial power, there is a clear need to restore the simple pleasures of reading: the experience of opening a book by an author you know and being delighted by a completely new dimension of her or his art, the joy of seeing an author break free of any formula to reveal the power of the well-written word. The best writing, many authors affirm, comes as a gift; the best reading comes when the author passes that gift to the reader, a gift the author could imagine only by taking risks in a variety of genres including short stories, poetry, and essays.

As editors of The Bread Loaf Series of Contemporary Writers we subscribe to no single viewpoint. Our singular goal is to publish writing that moves the reader: by the beauty and lucidity of its language, by its underlying argument, by its force of vision. These values are celebrated each summer at the Writers' Conference on Bread Loaf Mountain in Vermont and in each of these books.

We offer you the Bread Loaf Contemporary Writers series and the treasures with which these authors have surprised us.

Robert Pack
Jay Parini

A Lynne Sharon Schwartz Reader

Introduction

I B E G A N writing at seven, before I knew about the strictures of literary genres: poem, story, essay. I had read quite a bit—essays in *The Reader's Digest*, poems by Robert Louis Stevenson, novels by Louisa May Alcott—but I didn't distinguish my reading in terms of genre. If I made any distinctions, they were probably along the lines of: daily world or dream world; meandering or giving information or problem solving; charmed flight or dull trudge. And so my own writing was not hampered by any considerations of form. Those early efforts, now unfortunately lost, I believe to be among my best work. (Did some fit of intellectual condescension make me throw them out, I wonder? Or did they go the sad way of other childhood memorabilia?)

What I wrote was poetic speculation, partaking of all the genres and bounded by none. One piece was about how the world began (created by a kind scientist). Another was about setting prisoners free, another about the inner life of flowers. Now that I see the themes set down so baldly, I think maybe it's just as well that they no longer exist, for I might be sentimentally tempted to include them here and embarrass myself publicly. Certainly I have been embarrassed on behalf of dead writers, imagining them shifting uneasily, betrayed in the grave, by the publication of their juvenilia. Though for all I know they welcome it as one more blow against the devouring wolf, oblivion.

Whatever the literary merit, those were difficult subjects I took on, subjects I might think twice about broaching today, for a variety of educated self-doubts. School teaches us to undermine our own aspirations, a lesson we labor all our lives to unlearn. But as a child writer I didn't know they were difficult subjects; they were simply the subjects of my reverie.

In my teens and twenties I wrote stories, rarely finished and rarely submitted to magazines, for the reasons given in the opening essay here, "Taking It Seriously." When I finally did begin to take "it" seriously I wrote a novel, not that I particularly wanted to, I felt happy writing stories, but a novel was a mark of seriousness. Because it was bigger, a novel was tacitly considered a grown-up short story. (This novel was never published, for which I am now grateful.) Of course, a novel is not a grown-up story any more than an epic is a grown-up sonnet. I think I suspected that all along.

In the fullness of time I wrote and published stories and novels and even a few poems. I couldn't help noticing that my novels were out of step with most of their fellows. Show, don't tell, was the command to young writers. Even though I never attended a writing program (something else for which I am grateful), such commands trickled down, as it were. But I liked to tell. I especially liked to tell what the characters were thinking and, even more radically—or retrogressively—I liked to tell what I was thinking about what they were thinking. Given such unfashionable tendencies, I was very fortunate to find an editor (or rather to be found by him), Ted Solotaroff at Harper & Row, who encouraged and published my writing.

So I was labeled a novelist. But I noticed further that my novels were coming to sound more and more essayistic, with leisurely musing passages about how I saw and felt things. One novel, *Leaving Brooklyn*, actually grew out of an essay that wouldn't stay within the confines of fact but kept wilfully veering off into fancy. I had never planned to be a novelist in the first place. I had planned, from the age of seven, to be a writer. A writer writes anything and everything, just as a composer composes anything—not only sonatas or only nocturnes or only symphonies.

I was glad to be recognized as any sort of writer—it came late and in modest measure—but I felt limited by that label, novelist. I could see from my own work, as well as from the best examples in literary history, that the inner process of writing paid no heed to genres, so why must my notion of what sort of writer I was? "They" might call me a novelist, but I began to write essays that occasionally sounded like fiction, just as my novels occasionally sounded like essays. When I found myself daydreaming about a person or incident from the past, I would harness my waywardness before it galloped off without me. Why not write out the daydreaming itself, as I had as a child?

The essays included here are not, obviously, pure daydream but a special sort of daydream subjected to the rigor of language and occasion. A couple sprang from the extemporaneous spoken word, which I then expanded in a written form of musing. At a memorial service for Tom Victor, the photographer of writers, so many friends went forward to speak their impromptu piece that I felt it would be shameful to hang back even though I hadn't yet shaped my strong feelings into words. When I opened my mouth I liked the words I heard and vowed I would write them down. It was a year before I could do so, but they still felt genuine, they had held up, as had the feelings that impelled them.

Another time, as I was telling a friend about the person I call Mattie in the essay "Help," he said, You ought to write that down. I don't usually write anything on the friendly suggestions of others: while the story may be one they want to read, it is seldom one I want to tell. But now and then the suggestion strikes a sensitive chord; the prospect of telling that story feels like an adventure that might take me someplace I need to go, as happened in this case.

During the Watergate hearings of 1973 I was teaching freshman composition at Hunter College in New York City, a summer session course that met four nights a week. I would arrive home late, hot and enervated, and resuscitate to TV reruns of the day's proceedings of the Senate investigating committee. I came to know the situation and the characters involved very well indeed and wished I could write about them, but I couldn't find a handle, as they say—until the following spring, when Richard Nixon's secret tapes of inner-circle confabulations were transcribed and published in the *New York Times*. I read them with fervor. Here was my handle: the tapes were theatre.

"True Confessions of a Reader" was written in a time of despair over writing. I was convinced I knew very little, and that little had been used up in my fiction, so how could I write anything more? The only abiding thing I knew was utterly commonplace: how to read. I had done enough of that to be an expert. Very well then, I would write about reading. Since reading leads to many other things, the piece took the form of a meandering, going places I could never have anticipated.

The poems erupted haphazardly over the years, sometimes in a clump and sometimes at wide intervals. Even when I had written quite a few, starting from high school, I never had the temerity to call myself a poet or take my endeavors seriously. Having been raised amid labels and hierarchies, I always thought a poet was the highest kind of writer, and that some special, ineffable attribute was required to deserve the name, like having ESP or being double-jointed. I often wrote the poems in old blue exam books I must have purloined while teaching freshman composition at Hunter College, as if they were timid student efforts. Then I would forget them, only to find them months or years later, lying in wait in a drawer, half-furtive and half-petulant, begging to be noticed, bashful yet craving release. Now that I know better about the puerility of labels and hierarchies and now that I have written several dozen poems, maybe I am a poet. Or maybe it is better to avoid labels altogether, as well as not to stifle the poems but set them free, like the prisoners I wrote of long ago, onto the airiness of the printed page.

All of the essays in this volume and some of the poems have appeared in periodicals, but to novelists (and when it is convenient I do call myself a novelist), writing is never quite real or solid unless it has a life in hard covers, just as only a brick house, and not straw or wood, will protect the three little pigs from the annihilating breath of the wolf. So I am pleased that these writings, disparate only in superficial, formal ways, are joined together here. Bringing them into the shelter of one book is the closest I can come to recapturing the free and wandering spirit of the seven-year-old dreamer I was.

ESSAYS

Taking It Seriously

FOR EIGHT years I worked under a bed. There I wrote two novels, three halves of novels, twenty-odd stories, several dozen reviews, a few translations, and other odds and ends. It was a loft bed, so I was not writing lying on my stomach in the dark with the pen between my teeth. Nonetheless it was limiting. The space was about five feet four inches high (I could just stand up without crouching) and its length and width were equivalent to those of a double bed— the size of an ungenerous cell. Not a bad image, actually, since a writer is a prisoner of her own desire to write, captive audience to her own fantasies. At night I slept on top of my work, like a hen, and dreamed of space.

A few months ago I went out and rented the proverbial room of one's own; since I was jailer as well as prisoner, why not provide the best quarters I could afford? I furnished this room to make it resemble the room I had dreamed about up in the loft bed, so that now I am not sure whether it is a fantasy room or a real room. When I shut the door and go home it may vanish, springing into material existence the next day at the sound of my key in the lock. No one close to me has ever seen it, and perhaps no one ever will. I pay the rent and I pay the electric bills; I buy my dream, month by month. I wonder if anyone can understand what serious business that is. When I receive a check for my work I immediately calculate how much rent it will pay, how much longer I can maintain that dream by selling off my fantasies one by one. Serious business indeed.

On cork boards above my desk I have hung pictures and sentences that reverberate in my mind when I look at them, reminding me of certain essentials: I want to keep the essentials before my eyes at all times. Some are beautiful, some frivolous, some austere. I find that my favorites share a distinct tone of defiance: Willa Cather saying,

7

"Whatever is felt upon the page without being specifically named there—that, one might say, is created." I can imagine her shaking her head sternly as if to add, "And nothing else, don't pretend otherwise." Jean Cocteau saying, "Whatever the public blames you for, cultivate it—it is yourself." So much for the critics. And a potent dare for someone brought up to be, in the eyes of the world, a good girl.

The most potent, though, is a small black and white War Resisters League poster of the late Dorothy Day, obviously at a protest demonstration. The photo is taken from a low angle: you see Dorothy Day seated on one of those portable folding aluminum stools, with legs crossed and bumpy veined hands clasped implacably on her knees, wearing a nondescript dress and a big straw hat—perhaps it was a gruelingly hot day—her jaw tilted upward and her mouth set in immutable resistance, her face bony and wrinkled with eyes barely visible yet fiery behind thick glasses, while surrounding her like columns are the thick legs of policemen hung with clubs and holsters. Dorothy Day is taking her life and her work very seriously; somehow you know she will not be moved from that stool, she will have to be dragged. Below, her comment reads, "Our problems stem from our acceptance of this filthy, rotten system." That, above all, is what I want to remember, because it took such a long and muddled time to learn.

I wrote my first story when I was seven. It was about the creation of humanity by a "kind scientist." Probably at no other age would I have dared attempt such a mighty theme. I completed it at about eight o'clock one morning and immediately brought it to show my father, who was shaving. To his eternal credit, he put down his razor and, standing in the steamy bathroom wearing a towel, his face covered with lather, read the two pages through, then gave them the sober praise writers so badly need. I came away feeling I had achieved one of the few things in the world whose importance was transcendent and beyond question—not merely the writing of the story, but having had it read and comprehended.

A couple of years later I was so enthralled by *Little Women* that I began copying it in order to take possession of its magic: " 'Christmas won't be Christmas without any presents' "—words that unsealed an incorporeal universe mirroring our own, only better, because all the feelings and sensations were miraculously articulated and transformed: ink on the page set off vibrations in the blood. That was the universe I wanted; I felt it was mine by instinctive right. When the time came, presumably adulthood, surely it would gather me in.

So for the first thirty-odd years of my life I secretly hoped and expected that being a writer would happen to me one day, descending rather like a state of grace. (At least something of the sort must have been in my head: my outlook then seems as distant and benighted as the attitudes of prehistoric man.) Meanwhile I dabbled on the respectable peripheries of writing—translating, producing spoken records, editing. Even more respectably, I married and had children. Not until I was about to embark on a Ph.D. thesis in comparative literature did I grasp that being a writer required more than being a good girl and waiting; it required action, labor, and a certain daring vis-à-vis the truths of the heart. Unfortunately, nothing in my past had prepared me for such a quiet but mighty revolution. Quite the contrary. The 1940s and '50s were hardly a breeding ground for originality.

Of course in any generation the world conspires—in all innocence, perhaps—to make its children feel insignificant and powerless. Clogged by the detritus of tradition and habit, it teaches that acceptance of many "filthy, rotten" systems is the easiest and wisest path. My twelve years in the New York City public schools, for example, were a pungent lesson in passivity—I was quite a good girl there. But acceptance is not the easiest path, especially not if attended by frustration and eventual atrophy of the spirit.

Back then the notion of inventing a life and a life's work, rather than accepting those given us, required first a certain vision of possibilities, which we lacked, and second, taking ourselves very seriously indeed. And taking oneself seriously was a failing to be mocked: worse than fatuous and inaccurate in the light of world events (we were still reeling from Hiroshima and retching at Joe McCarthy), it was unsophisticated. Far more chic to lean back and roll with the inevitable punches, wallowing in irony like pigs in mud. Irony was our cardinal virtue; looking back, it is not hard to see why. At college we listened to many speeches on our future, particularly on the theme of combining marriage and "career"; the advice might have been good or bad—again, I don't remember. I do remember that we laughed, with affectionate irony, at the earnestness of the speakers: they took it all so seriously!

Unprepared as I thus was, when I grasped what I needed to do in order to be a writer, I tried to yank my life out of its accustomed path. With a sense of recklessness I became an activist: I wrote.

I put aside the notes for the Ph.D. thesis that I had come to regard with fear and loathing. "A *novel!*" sputtered my adviser at NYU, a well-known literary critic. "But you can do *that* sort of thing any time!" I claimed for my virtues many of those qualities I had been taught were vice: dropping out, selfishness, aggression, stubbornness. I stopped trying to be a generous person and tried instead to learn a little ruthlessness; it was eminently clear, all at once, that I could be a writer or I could be a good girl, but never both together. And I resolved to take my work seriously somewhat in the manner that Pascal advises skeptics to risk believing in God: there is everything to be gained and nothing much to lose. A writer's life is built on this sort of pretense; some might prefer to call it faith. It was when my pretenses became too large for that space under the bed that I rented this room. Here they have so many square feet to fill: with some awe I watch them grow, and try to suppress the sense of irony—but not entirely.

(1981)

True Confessions of a Reader

R A R E L Y D O E S the daily paper move me to reexamine my life. But a recent *New York Times* piece quoted a Chinese scholar whose "belief in Buddhism . . . has curbed his appetite for books." Mr. Cha says, "To read more is a handicap. It is better to keep your own mind free and to not let the thinking of others interfere with your own free thinking." I clipped his statement and placed it on the bedside table, next to a pile of books I was reading or planned to read or thought I ought to read. The clipping is about two square inches and almost weightless, the pile of books some nine inches high, weighing a few pounds. Yet they face each other in perfect balance. I am the scale on which they rest.

Lying in the shadow of the books, I brood on my reading habit. Mr. Cha's serenity and independence of mind are enviable. I would like to be equally independent, but I'm not sure my mind could be free without reading, or that the action books have on it is properly termed "interference." I suspect the interaction of the mind and the book is something more complex. But perhaps that only shows how enslaved I am. Buddhism aside, there is no Readers Anonymous, so far, to help curb this appetite.

Luckily I am not prey to every kind of reading, for there are many kinds, as there are many kinds of love, not all of them intoxicating. There is pure and specific curiosity: how would an Israeli Arab regard growing up in an inhospitable state, or who was Albertine, really, or what is it like to be brilliantly gifted and in love and desperately ill at twenty-three years old? Then we don't read directly for the "high," though we may find it, in Anton Shammas's *Arabesques* or Keats's letters, but to satisfy the mind. Or less specific curiosity: What is anthropology, I used to wonder—the enterprise itself, not the exotic data, since ordinary urban life provides enough exotic data. How do you approach the study of "man" or "culture"? How do you tilt your head, what angle of vision? I read enough to find out how the discipline works, which is by accumulation and accretion, making a mosaic. You gather and place enough pieces, then step back and look. I saw the pattern and stopped.

We may read for facts alone: the eye skims along, alert for key words, and when they appear, like red lights on a highway, it slides deftly to a halt. That kind of reading propelled me out of graduate school. However useful, it does not feel like true reading but more like shopping, riffling through racks for the precise shade of blue. I would have made a poor and ludicrous scholar, like a diva singing ditties in TV commercials, or a pastry chef condemned to macrobiotic menus.

My addiction is to works of the imagination, and even if I became a Buddhist, I think I couldn't renounce them cold turkey. Not after a lifetime, the better part of which was spent reading. Was it actually the better part, though? Did I choose or was I chosen, shepherded into it like those children caught out early on with a talent for the violin or ballet, baseball or gymnastics, and tethered forever to bows and barres, bats and mats? We didn't know any alternatives; there was no chance to find them out. Reading, of all these, does not win huge sums of money or applause, or give joy and solace to others. I don't even remember much of it.

When my younger daughter made disparaging remarks about *Billy Budd* I rushed to Melville's defense with a speech on the conflict between the rule of law applied generically and the merits of individual cases. Billy Budd struck a superior officer, I reminded her; according to the letter of the law, he must hang. And yet, and yet, we cannot quite swallow it . . . I ended in a glow of ambivalence. "It wasn't that he struck him," she murmured. "He killed him." I had totally forgotten, which was appalling. And yet, I consoled myself, I had remembered the conflict, and the dark malice of Claggart, and Billy's faltering speech, and the terrible earnestness of Captain Vere, and the wry world-weariness of the old Dansker—modes of being swirling and contending like gases in the primeval void, to coalesce into a particular universe, a configuration of events. Wasn't that enough? Not quite. What happens is important too. What do I have, then, after years of indulgence? A feel, a texture, an aura: the fragrance of Shakespeare, the crisp breeze of Tolstoi, the carnal stench of the great Euripides. Are they worth the investment of a life? Would my mind be more free without them?

In truth I have made some tentative steps towards freedom. Over the last five years or so, I have managed not to finish certain books. With barely a twinge of conscience, I hurl down what bores me or doesn't give what I crave: ecstasy, transcendence, a thrill of mysterious connection. For, more than anything else, readers are thrill-seekers, though I don't read thrillers, not the kind sold under that label, anyway. They don't thrill; only language thrills.

I had put aside books before, naturally, but with guilt, sneaking them back to the shelves in the dark. It seemed a rudeness of the worst sort. A voice was attempting to speak to me and I refused to listen. A spiritual rudeness. Since childhood I had thought of reading as holy, and like all sacraments, it had acquired a stiff halo of duty. My cavalier throwing over a book midway may arise from the same general desacralization as does the notable increase in divorce, marriage also being a sacrament and, once entered upon, a duty. Every day joy and duty pull farther apart, like Siamese twins undergoing an excruciating but salutary operation: they were never meant to share a skin, they may look alike but their souls are different.

So, like recidivist marryers, I take up the new book in good faith, planning to accompany it, for better or for worse, till the last page do us part, but . . . it stops being fun. Other, more intriguing, books send out pheromones. There are after all so many delectable books in the world. Why linger with one that doesn't offer new delights, take me somewhere I've never been? I feel detached from the book on my lap much as the disaffected husband or wife feels detached from the body alongside and asks, why am I here, in this state of withness? In a marriage, one hopes it may be a transient feeling—there may be extenuating circumstances, although these lately do not seem to possess great force—but in the case of a book, why not be abandoned, and abandon?

This is a far cry from my idealism at age twenty, when I longed to read everything, simply because it was written, like adventurers who climb Mount Everest because it is there. Other sensationalists must sample everything edible or try every feasible sexual posture, however slimy or arduous, respectively. Thus do they assure themselves they have truly lived. No experience has passed them by, as if exhaustiveness were the measure of the good life.

Gradually I lost, or shed, the Mount Everest syndrome. Book-shelves still tease and tantalize, but like a woman with a divining rod, I know now where the water will be, I do not have to scrape earth and dig holes seeking, only there where the rod begins to tremble. The unfinished or unread books languish on my shelves, some bought because friends said I must read them (but it was they who had to read them), or because the reviews throbbed with largesse of spirit (but it was the reviewer I loved, just as Priscilla loves John Alden, or Roxane Cyrano. I should have bought the reviewer's book.). Others were just too gorgeously packaged to resist. I am in fact coming to distrust book jackets calculated to prick desire like a Bloomingdale's window, as if you could wear what you read. The great French novels used to come in plain shiny yellow jackets, and the drab Modern Library uniforms hid the most lavish loot.

Once in a while I take these castoffs down and turn their pages for exercise, stroke them a bit. They have the slightly dusty, for-lorn patina of people seldom held or loved, while their neighbors stand upright with self-esteem, for having been known, partaken of intimacies. I am regretful, but my heart is hardened.

I can face myself, abandoning even the most sanctified or stylish books, but there is forever the world to face, world without end. I envision a scenario: a group of writers sits around talking of the for-mative books, the great themes, let's say man grappling with nature, with death. Perhaps they are women writers, musing on men's com-pulsion to view everything in terms of struggle and mastery. One turns to me, saying, Well, for instance, *Moby Dick*?

I cannot lie about reading. A remnant of holiness still clings. It would be tantamount to a devout Catholic's claiming falsely to be in a state of grace. So I blush, confess I never finished it, and though they remain courteous, repressed shock and disapproval permeate the room (or could it be that the women find me daring, the Emma Goldman of reading?).

I puzzled for years over how a friend, frantically busy at a pub-lishing job, where manuscripts are thrust at you daily for overnight perusal, had read every book ever mentioned. Colossal erudition, I thought in my innocence, and speedy too. Till it struck me, as it might a child suddenly seeing through Santa Claus: it can't be. She lies. I wasn't filled with indignation, didn't even banish her from the

ranks of the trustworthy. Simply: Aha, so that's what's done, a help-
ful currency of social exchange like the white lie, and equally easy.
You read reviews and jacket copy, and listen carefully. If you are
reasonably *au courant*, who knows?, you may come up with criti-
cal judgments no less plausible or even valid than had you read the
book. What has been lost, after all? Only the actual experience, the
long slow being with the book, feeling the shape of the words, their
roll and tumble in the ear.

Still, lying about reading feels too risky, as risky as saying you
have seen God or drunk the milk of Paradise when you haven't—the
kind of lie that might dilute the milk of Paradise should it ever be
offered you.

Nor can I throw a book away. I have given many away and ripped
a few in half, but as with warring nations, destruction shows regard:
the enemy is a power to reckon with. Throwing a book out shows
contempt for an effort of the spirit. Not that I haven't tried. Among
some tossed-out books of my daughters' which I rescued, to shelter
until a foster home could be arranged, was one too awful to live. I
returned it to the trash, resisting the urge to say a few parting words.
All day long the thought of its mingling with chicken bones and olive
pits nagged at me. Half a dozen times I removed it and replaced it,
like an executioner with scruples about capital punishment. Finally
I put it on a high shelf where I wouldn't have to see it. Life imprison-
ment. Someday my children, going through my effects, will say,
"Why did she keep this wretched thing? She hated it." "Oh, you
know what she was like. It was a book, after all."

To tell the truth, I had begun to think about reading before coming
upon Mr. Cha. It was the spring of 1986, an uneasy time for me
but a magnificent season for the New York Mets. As often happens
with a new love or addiction, I didn't know I cared until it was too
late. I had never followed baseball and felt safe from television, the
devil's latest ploy to buy our souls. But alas we are never safe; in
the midst of life we are in death, and so forth. My family watched
the Mets. At first I would drift through the living room and glance,
with faint contempt, at the screen. Gradually I would stand there
for longer and longer spells, until I came to know the players by
name and disposition and personal idiosyncrasies: how they spit and
how they chewed, how they reacted to a failed at-bat—with impas-

sivity or miming the ritual "darn-it" gestures—how their uniforms fit and which folds they tugged in moments of stress. The game itself I already knew in rudimentary form, having played punch ball on the summer evening streets of Brooklyn as the light fell behind the low brick houses and the pink Spaulding grew dimmer with each hopeful arc through the twilit air. All that remained was for the finer points to be explained to me. I was surprised and touched by the element of sacrifice, as in the sacrifice fly (the adjective evoking *esprit de corps* and a tenuous religiosity) and the bunt, a silly-looking play, several grown men converging to creep after a slowly and imperturbably rolling ball. I was impressed by the intricate comparative philosophy of relief pitching, and shocked by the logistics of stealing bases. This sounded illicit yet everyone took it for granted, rather like white-collar crime, with the most expert thieves held in high esteem like savvy Wall Street players. Then one evening—the turning point—I sat down, committing my body to the chair, my eyes to the screen, my soul to the national Oversoul.

I pretended an anthropological detachment. My quest was for the subtleties and symbolism—the tension of the 3–2 call, the heartbreak of men left stranded on base, the managers' farseeing calculations recalling the projections of chess players (if he does this, I'll do that), the baffling streaks and slumps, and above all the mystifying signs. For at critical junctures, advisors sprinkled on the field or in the dugout would pat their chests and thighs and affect physical tics in a cabalistic language. Soon it was clear I wasn't as detached as I pretended. The fortunes of the Mets, as well as the fluctuations of each individual Met, had come to matter. It was partly proximity, the *sine qua non* of most love, and partly aesthetics. When giraffe-like Darryl Strawberry lazily unfurled an arm to allow a fly ball to nestle in his glove, I felt the elation I used to feel watching André Eglevsky leap and stay aloft so long it seemed he had forgotten what he owed to gravity. Not unlike the elation I got from books.

I never watched an entire game, though. I hadn't the patience. I would enter late, around the fourth or fifth inning, when the atmosphere was already set—not that it couldn't change in an instant, that was part of the charm. I was like those drinkers who assure themselves they can stop any time they choose. I could start any time I chose. I was not compelled to scoot to my chair at the opening notes of the *Star-Spangled Banner* like a pitiful little iron filing within range of the magnet.

Night after astounding night became a season of protracted ecstasy. It was not just the winning but the beauty of the plays and the flowering of each distinct personality: modest Mookie Wilson's radiant amiability and knack of doing the right thing at the right moment, boyish Gary Carter's packaged public-relations grin, Howard Johnson's baffling lack of personality, absorbent like a potent black hole at the center of the team, Roger McDowell's inanity, Bob Ojeda's strong-jawed strength and the departures and returns of his mustache, Keith Hernandez's smoldering and handsome anger at the world, Len Dykstra's rooted insecurities packed together to form a dense and lethal weapon, Dwight Gooden's young inscrutability, reflecting the enigma of the team—arrogant or just ardent? All became crystallized.

Amidst the glory was an unease, a tingling of an inner layer of skin. I grudged the hours. I felt forced to watch against my will. Yet what was the trouble? Watching baseball is harmless, unless compulsion itself be considered blameworthy, but I am not that stern a moralist.

The games were depriving me of something. There it was. The instant I identified the uneasy feeling as "missing," all came clear. Reading. Reading was what I used to do through long evenings, the stable backdrop against which my life was played. Reading was what I got everything else (living) out of the way in order to do. The lack was taking its toll. I was having withdrawal symptoms.

I tried to give up baseball. I cut back, backslid, struggled the well-documented struggle. And then, abruptly, my efforts were needless. The burden fell from my shoulders as Zen masters say the load of snow falls from the bent bamboo branch at the moment of greatest tension, effortlessly. The Mets won the World Series and overnight, baseball was no more. I returned to reading, to my life. Or was it to a retreat from life, the void at the center, from which, the Zen masters also say, all being springs?

How are we to spend our lives, anyway? That is the real question. We read to seek the answer, and the search itself becomes the answer. Which brings Mr. Cha back to mind. He knows what to do with his life. He treasures his free mind, or that part of it which Shunryu

Suzuki, in *Zen Mind, Beginner's Mind*, calls "big mind," as opposed to the small mind concerned with particular daily events:

The mind which is always on your side is not just your mind, it is universal mind, always the same, not different from another's mind. It is Zen mind. It is big, big mind. This mind is whatever you see. Your true mind is always with whatever you see. Although you do not know your own mind, it is there—at the very moment you see something, it is there. . . . True mind is watching mind. You cannot say, "This is my self, my small mind, or my limited mind, and that is big mind." That is limiting yourself, restricting your true mind, objectifying your mind. Bodhidharma said, "In order to see a fish you must watch the water." Actually when you see water you see the true fish.

But some of us must see the fish in order to see the water. The water can be too transparent to grasp without varieties of fish to show its texture.

A poet friend of mine, after heart surgery, was advised by a nurse to take up meditation to reduce stress. "You must empty your mind," she said. "I've spent my life filling it," he replied. "How can you expect me to empty it?" The argument is verbal. In Buddhist paradoxes, empty can mean full, and full, empty, in relation to mind and universe. Either way, though, I keep worrying about those fish, flickering beautiful things of this world. A pity if they were to become only means to an end, to a serene mind.

In *The Ambassadors*, mild, restrained Strether is sent to Paris to rescue a young man from his passion, and instead falls prey to the same passion. In a whirlwind of exhilaration he exhorts everyone around him to live. "To live, to live!" Very heady. Was I living, I wondered when I first read it, or simply reading? Were books the world, or at least a world? How could I "live" when there was so much to be read that ten lives could not be enough? And what is it, anyway, this "living"? Have I ever done it? If it is merely a Jamesian euphemism for knowing passion, well, I pass. Reading is not a disabling affliction. I have done what people do, my life makes a reasonable showing. Can I go back to my books now? For if "living" means indulging the cravings, why then . . .

There was life before reading. Not until the sixteenth century were manuscripts even available, except to monks and royalty. What could it have been like? There was life before language, too—grunts and grimaces, tears and laughter (yet how much laughter, without language?), shrieks and groans and commiseration; all of that is easy to imagine. But to have language and no books? What to do after the corn is ground and the water hauled and the butter churned? Keep your mind free, as Mr. Cha suggests? Without stories to free the mind, emptiness might be true emptiness, like Freud's proverbial cigar. Well, there were storytellers, the old woman sitting at the fireside entrancing the family, or the troubador chanting verses near the fountain in the piazza while women walked from the village oven with warm breads on boards balanced on their shoulders. But that is a social experience. With books there are no fellow listeners, no fleshly storyteller, none of the exertions of fellowship. Historians contrast the unity and coherence of the Middle Ages with modern social fragmentation: among the hundreds of causes for the change might be numbered the privatization of stories—from a communal, binding activity to a voice whispering in your ear. Without that voice, my ghostly familiar, how could I have become myself?

I read at an early age, three and a half. The girl upstairs taught me. Late afternoons, we stood at the blackboard in her hallway and she drew signs that were the same, but in another sensory costume, as the words that came from our lips. Once I grasped the principle of conversion, that airy puffs of voice could have a visual counterpart, the rest, what teachers call "breaking the code," was routine.

The world existed to be read and I read it. Diamond Crystal Kosher Coarse Salt on the cylindrical container my mother shook over simmering pots, and Reg. U.S. Pat. Off. on every box and can, had the rhythms of the pounding verses the bigger girls chanted out on the street, twirling their jump ropes. Before I knew who I was or what I might be, I became the prodigy, the "reader." When friends visited, my father would summon me and hand me the *New York Times*, his finger aimed at the lead story. "Read that." I read, though those signs had no meaning. Sometimes the guests refused to be convinced, suspecting I had been coached like the big winners on radio quiz shows. So my father would invite them to test me with any article on any page. No four-year-old could have memorized the entire paper. And while they marveled at my freakish achievement, which seemed to exist apart from my physical being, I could return to my paper dolls.

If my usefulness and value to my parents lay in this power to amaze, then I had to keep doing it. Reading was the ticket that entitled me to my place in the world. But in school there were other bright children. Soon everyone could read. My ticket was fraying, sadly devalued, and I felt something like the panic Samson must have felt, shorn. What can we do once we are ordinary? The choice of hair for Samson's strength is not as arbitrary or peculiar as I once thought. If your identity rests in special powers, you shiver without them, naked to the wind whipping at the back of the neck.

It was too late to fashion another ticket and besides, I didn't have the means: irresistible charm or beauty or athletic prowess or saintliness. Could I just be here, of no special use at all, simply by having been born? I envied my blithe peers who didn't seem to be paying any stiff admission fee. I still do. When I stand on a platform and speak, I envy the audience who need only listen. My father's ghost is at my shoulder, his gaze not on me but on the guests. With a swift jerk of the head he chuckles and says, Just get a load of this.

Because I read when I could still believe in magic, reading was magical, not merely breaking a code or translating one set of symbols into another. The idea of translatability was itself magical, and so it remains. Semiotics, before it became a formal branch of study, was the sleight-of-hand way of the world: signs and things, things and signs, layered, sometimes jumbled, partners in a dance of allusion.

But living amidst so many words, I overestimated their power and breadth. The world does not turn on words alone; it only seems so if the eye and mind are saturated with them. I undervalued the other senses. I wrote of the disproportion in a story about my father, "The Two Portraits of Rembrandt," but it goes for me too.

He lived by the word. Pictures were a crude, provisional mode of representation and communication, happily supplanted by the advent of language. People who still looked at pictures for information were in a pre-verbal state, babies or Neanderthals. The *Daily News*, "New York's Picture Newspaper," was a publication designed for the illiterate. . . . Likewise *Life* magazine, which prided itself on its photography; he would not have it in the house. . . .

Maybe it was their limitation and finiteness that he disliked about pictures. He loved what was bountiful and boundless and hated anything mean and narrow. . . . Pictures were circumscribed by their frames. A house, a tree, a cloud, added up to a landscape, and that was the end of it. The space of pictures is inner space, but he didn't look into, he looked at. Words, though, could go on forever, linear, one opening the door to a dozen others, each new one nudging at another door, and so on to infinite mansions of meditation. Nor was there any limit to what you could say; words bred more words, spawned definition, comparison, analogy. A picture is worth a thousand words, I was told in school. Confucius. But to me, too, the value seemed quite the other way around. And why not ten thousand, a hundred thousand? Give me a picture and I could provide volumes. Meanings might be embedded in the picture, but only words could release them and at the same time, at the instant they were born and borne from the picture, seize them, give them shape and specific gravity. Nothing was really possessed or really real until it was incarnate in words. Show and Tell opened every school day, but I rarely cared to show anything. You could show forever, but how could you be sure the essence had been transmitted, without words? Words contained the knowledge, words *were* the knowledge, the logos, and words verified that the knowledge was there.

Incidentally, living by the word, by organized series of words, which is narrative, is a handicap when it comes to operating modern electronic devices like telephone answering machines or vcr's, not to mention computers. Such ineptness is not due, as laughing children suppose, to quaintness or premature senility. It is simply that readers are accustomed to receiving information in the narrative mode. A row of minimally labeled buttons means nothing if the nerve paths aren't trained for it. True, the machines come with instructions, but these hover near the borderline of language, closer to the pulsating fragments of rock and roll, a different semiotics entirely. The teen-agers laugh at their parents, while it is we who should be laughing at them, except that the loss of language is a somber joke. When my younger daughter translates the manuals into narrative form I too can make the machines work: "Instructions for a happy vcr: Turn tv switch on. Turn vcr switch on. Watch little red button light up. Keep vcr on while doing all the rest of this. Little red button should stay lit." I feel the familiar comfort of language performing its original task. If those of us who live by language become superfluous in years to come, it will not be because of the advance of technology, but the loss of coherent discourse.

It started—my reading, that is—innocently enough, and then it infiltrated. It didn't replace living; it infused it, till the two became inextricable, like molecules of hydrogen and oxygen in a bead of water. To part them could take violent and possibly lethal means, a spiritual electrolysis.

I read whatever I found in the house. It was an age of sets, and several were stored in the bedroom I inherited when I was ten and my sister left to get married. Dickens in brown leather with a black horizontal stripe was cozy-looking, but the Harvard Classics in black leather and gold trim were forbidding—especially Plutarch's *Lives* and Marcus Aurelius and the *Confessions* of Saint Augustine. I did manage to find one, though, number 17, containing all the Grimm and Andersen fairy tales, which I practically licked off the page. They tasted bitter and pungent, like curries. Best of all was the Little Leather Library, several dozen books the size of a cigarette case and bound in soft forest green, their crumbling pages the color of weak tea. Rudyard Kipling, Shakespeare's sonnets, Ibsen's *A Doll's House*, Conan Doyle side by side, strange bedfellows, sticking together damply, crackling when you pulled one volume out. Next to Oscar Wilde's "The Happy Prince," the saddest story I knew, was the almost equally sad but unpoetic story of *The Man Without a Country*, by Edward Everett Hale. Here too, the hero loves his country and ends unappreciated, in ignominy. Philip Nolan, no prince but a Navy officer, in a moment of rage denounces the United States, wishing never to hear of it again. His words are taken literally. His punishment is to live out his life aboard ship, never permitted to hear a word about home. It was a fairy tale horror—those thoughtless wishes!—in the Harvard Classics number 17 come true: a flaring impulse rashly given voice, a slip of the tongue really, becomes destiny. Words are indelible, said the story. Watch each one before it hits the air!

Alongside *The Man Without a Country* were *Hiawatha* and *Carmen* and *Alice in Wonderland*, "Pippa Passes" and *Sonnets from the Portuguese*, those last not so strange bedfellows, and strangest of all, *The Strange Case of Dr. Jekyll and Mr. Hyde*: " 'Is this Mr. Hyde a person of small stature?' he inquired. 'Particularly small and particularly wicked-looking, is what the maid calls him,' said the officer." I was small too. Was that a bad omen? *Tales from the Arabian Nights* flanked *Tales* by Poe and *The Rubáiyát of Omar Khayyám*. I had barely begun life when I was told how dispensable I was:

> And fear not lest Existence closing your
> Account, and mine, should know the like no more;
> The Eternal Saki from that Bowl has pour'd
> Millions of Bubbles like us, and will pour.

Another volume contained *A Message to Garcia*, which my mother spoke of with reverence. The author, Elbert Hubbard, a turn-of-the-century journalist for a periodical called *The Philistine*, rightly calls it a "literary trifle" and describes how it was written in an hour, printed in the March, 1899 issue, and to his creditable surprise sold in the millions. It was translated into "all written languages," with a copy given to every railroad employee and soldier in Russia and every government employee in Japan. Starting with the example of a dutiful messenger dispatched to Cuba by President McKinley during the Spanish–American war, the little homily extols the employee or underling who gets the job done, no questions asked. Who can fault diligence and efficiency in the performing of one's work? At eleven all I managed was a shrug for such unexciting virtues. But today the call for unquestioning obedience rings ominously. No accident that its context is military (were the Russian soldiers given Tolstoi too?). Had the great reading public, in 1899, possessed the imagination to see where slavishness could lead, they might well have preferred the "slipshod assistance, foolish inattention, dowdy indifference, and half-hearted work" which Hubbard finds so offensive. A precursor of Reaganomics as well, he sees too much sympathy wasted on the " 'downtrodden denizens of the sweatshop' " and the " 'homeless wanderer searching for honest employment' " (his skeptical quotation marks), and suggests it be redirected:

Let us drop a tear, too, for the men who are striving to carry on a great enterprise, whose working hours are not limited by the whistle, and whose hair is fast turning white through the struggle to hold in line . . . slipshod imbecility and the heartless ingratitude which, but for their enterprise, would be both hungry, and homeless.

With some streamlining of style and diction, these lines could be part of a current White House study. *Le plus ça change . . .*

No shrug of indifference, only of bafflement, for "La Belle Dame sans Merci." I couldn't imagine what ailed the knight-at-arms, "alone and palely loitering." So he went with the fair lady to her "elfin grot," and when he woke she was gone. Why this outing should leave him drained and doomed was a mystery. Children accept magic; intractable passion is asking too much.

Equally mysterious was "The Lady of Shalott." *Why* was she confined to her island and forced to see the world only in a mirror, to weave webs "with colours gay" depicting scenes she could never be in? *Why* would she be destroyed if just once she followed her desire and looked directly at Camelot? *Why* does she inspire fear, what horrid curse could she spread, so that no one comes to save her or cares about her plight? Tennyson feels no more need to explain the "fairy" woman's imprisonment than Keats to explain his knight's languishing. But the knight is a thrall to love. The lady? Thrall to what? Some unspeakable curse. The poet delights in the utter arbitrariness of it, and his perverse delight is the power of the poem. As I pondered these perversities—it was a Sunday afternoon, I was about ten, hunched on my bed in confusion—my parents kept calling me. It was time to go visiting, and then, for my uncle the dentist and his wife never gave us more than tunafish salad, we would drive out towards the ocean, Rockaway, and stop for hot dogs (fried clams for my father). I went downstairs to be carried off and forgot the Lady of Shalott, as the world forgot her.

It may have been from that moment that I contracted a phobia for which there is no name, the fear of being interrupted. Sometimes at the peak of intoxicating pleasures, I am visited by a panic: the phone or doorbell will ring, someone will need me or demand that I do something. Of course I needn't answer or oblige, but that is beside the point. The spell will have been broken. In fact the spell has already been broken. The panic itself is the interruption. I have interrupted myself. Oddly enough, very often the phone does ring, just as paranoiacs can have enemies. Life is designed to thwart ecstasy; whether we do it for ourselves or something does it for us is a minor issue.

I envied my older sister her uninterruptability. While I looked up immediately from my book when my name was called, she had the uncanny ability not to hear. I would test her as she read. It was like addressing a stone, except that with a stone, if we are imaginative enough, we can infer some kind of response, albeit in stone language. My sister appeared to be present, but she was in the book. This is a great and useful gift. The stunned petitioner retreats, daunted by an invisible power that can drown out the world.

When questioned, my sister said that she really did not hear when she was spoken to. Years later I observed the same power in my older daughter. Did she too fail to hear? No, she said, of course she heard, she just didn't answer. And clearly it was not the same, in her mind, as out-and-out rudeness. Feeling herself elsewhere, she acted accordingly. Perhaps I have never been that absorbed, but I doubt it. What I lack is pure negative self-assertion. These two are oldest children in the family, quite secure about what is their due. Younger children may be so glad to be called upon at all that they respond indiscriminately, ears cocked for any meager chance to be legitimized.

My younger daughter hears when she is spoken to, but has yet another reading peculiarity. She reads with music playing. Apparently she absorbs both book and music; she remembered that Billy Budd's blow killed Claggart, while I had read the story in total silence. I regard this tableau—so symmetrical, hands, ears and eyes plugged in—with no comment, since I know how it feels to have one's personal habits always scrutinized and challenged. It was the *modus vivendi* of my youth. But I am confused. For the words are a song entering the ear too, an intricate *recitative*, and how can anyone listen to two pieces of music at once?

The practice, by the way, of questioning or criticizing any aspect of a family member's behavior is not an undiluted evil. It shows attachment to each other's lives and the curiosity that marks a loving, engaged intelligence, though enemies of the nuclear family would claim it is the loving engagement that kills. I was impressed, at an impressionable age, by a friend's father who never made any direct personal comments (though as I came to know him I heard plenty of oblique ones). A remarkable freedom seemed to be proffered— nothing you said or did could raise his eyebrows. Of course he never praised anyone either. While such a leveling of affect may be useful in a Zen master with a student, I do not think in this case that it was part and parcel of a transcendent world-view. After a while I would feel homesick for the overheated ambiance of my own family, where little went unnoticed. You could never doubt you had made an impact.

Besides being preternaturally engaged, my parents were people of the book. Not people who kept up with literary trends but who revered and trusted the civilizing influence of the written word (though my father could be skeptical of its truth). Like me, they never threw away a book. There were books stored in both bedrooms I occupied, first the small one and then the larger one I inherited when my sister got married, my brother succeeding to the small one, all of us like children advancing through the grades.

The books in the first bedroom were etched into visual memory along with the design of the wallpaper and angles of the furniture, the shadow a chair cast on the rug and how it was reflected in the mirror: *Captain Horatio Hornblower* and *Hercules, My Shipmate* and *Down to the Sea in Ships* (why the pervasive nautical theme I shall never know), and *Stars Fell on Alabama*, which I later learned was a song too—Billie Holiday sings it. I never read these books, but staring for years at their luridly-colored jackets, I penetrated them in another way. My conjectures of them are as vivid as the books I read and forgot. And their titles, in my mind, are the opaque emblems of an era, while *A Message to Garcia* is transparently emblematic.

I would occasionally be invited into my sister's room to help her memorize poems. She was already in college while I was barely in grade school. She started young, at fifteen, a fact of which my parents were very proud. It was the custom, for a number of years, to skip bright children through the grades as quickly as possible. Those who took the regulation time and finished high school at eighteen were regarded in my household as dullards. My sister's record was among the speediest, and I would not be able to surpass or even equal it since there was less skipping in my day. The poems were for her college English class—another, more worthy custom was learning by heart. I was honored to drill her, in the bedroom that would someday be mine. This was before my brother was born and before I ever dared dream I would have a brother, for my mother would come up with a child at widely spaced intervals as if it had just occurred to her. Only later did I learn she had suffered frequent miscarriages— we three were the tenacious ones.

I sat on my sister's bed with a couple of fat anthologies on my lap as she flitted about the room tossing her long chestnut hair and reciting, "I must go down to the seas again, to the lonely sea and sky, And all I ask is a tall ship and a star to steer her by," or, in her excellent clear diction, "Ah, distinctly I remember, it was in the bleak December, And each separate dying ember wrought its ghost upon the floor." Then she would go out in cars with soldiers, leaving me with Louis Untermeyer and the others on my lap. As I pored over their selections, she, in my visions, danced in the romantic arms of men in uniform.

My favorite among my sister's poems was "Annabel Lee." There are many decorative things for a child to love in "Annabel Lee," but beyond all particulars, it possessed a quiddity, the "whatness" Stephen Daedalus defines as Aquinas's *claritas* or radiance. "This supreme quality," Stephen says, "is felt by the artist when the esthetic image is first conceived in his imagination." And that instant when "the clear radiance of the esthetic image is apprehended luminously by the mind," he calls "the enchantment of the heart." I felt enchantment of the heart on the receiving end, the reader's, when I first apprehended certain works, and I feel it, with some puzzlement, today.

"It was many and many a year ago, In a kingdom by the sea, That a maiden there lived whom you may know . . ." Whom I might know! How incredible! I never knew any of the people written about in books; I never knew anyone who wrote them. Yet the very suggestion was a gleam of hope. Also, despite being included in the fat gray book and taught in college, this poem was unmistakably written for children, with clippety-clop rhythms and alliteration and predictable rhymes. Other poems in the collection clearly proclaimed Adults Only, Children Keep Out, but this was *about* children. It said so plainly enough. "*I* was a child and *she* was a child." Children were being taken seriously, in a poem granting, at last, their love-life. "But our love it was stronger by far than the love Of those who were older than we—Of many far wiser than we—." The lines that enchanted me most were, "Can ever dissever my soul from the soul Of the beautiful Annabel Lee." It was those "s" sounds, hissing defiance, mourning, passion, threat. Especially "ever dissever"—a palindrome for the ear.

That children could love passionately was not a phenomenon adults took into account. But here the word "love" was repeated over and over—six times in the first two stanzas—as if the poet's mouth couldn't get its fill, insatiable for it. In my family we rarely used that word to each other or about each other, or about anyone else. When my mother spoke of couples who were "keeping company" or getting engaged, she would say, "Of course she likes him," or, "she seems to like him," never that they loved each other, far less that they could be "in love," a phrase that seemed to denote a silly, weak-minded condition, embarrassing to own up to, bordering on the irresponsible or disreputable, and certainly not to be bruited about. Romantic love, from what I could gather, was for far less decent and intelligent people than we, who should know better. At the same time I had the impression that we took love (serious, abiding love) so much for granted, dwelt so intimately with it, that it was beneath our dignity to mention it; it would be as superfluous and vulgar as people mentioning that they bathe daily or pay their bills. Love might even be too powerful or holy a word to use, just as we were not supposed to write the word "God" but "G–d" instead, which offended me aesthetically, a distraction in the flow of reading, besides calling attention to a figure already receiving more than adequate attention.

Later on I was surprised, in books and in life, to find love named explicitly: "But, Father, I love him," or indulgently, "What could the poor girl do? She loved him," or soberly, "Are you sure you really love him?", or fatefully, "He took one look at her and fell in love." In other families, evidently, love was neither too holy nor too foolish to name. But there in the poem, "love" was all over the place: my sister was enunciating it in her clear voice and mellifluous diction, in the bedroom with the casement windows that would be mine when she left to get married (having, tacitly, fallen in love).

There were a number of words in "Annabel Lee" that I didn't understand. I figured out from the context that "seraphs" were something like angels. "Coveted" soon became bitterly clear—I heard its echo farther on in "envying." "The angels, not half so happy in heaven, Went envying her and me." My sister explained "kinsmen." But, strangely, I didn't ask about the crucial word, "sepulchre," so oddly shaped and spelled. I couldn't acknowledge—didn't want to— that Annabel Lee's kinsmen put her in a tomb. A mere child with a slight chill? How could a draft kill anyone? Maybe she wasn't really dead, maybe her kinsmen just took her away because they didn't like the narrator—he wasn't highborn as they were. Besides, how could angels kill out of envy? Angels were supposed to be good. To chart the precise degree of my comprehension and where it crossed with my ignorance is impossible. I have lost the child's ability to know and not know simultaneously, which is the most savory part of aesthetic pain, like the salt in tears.

I loved the outrageous ending—the narrator says he sleeps every night next to Annabel Lee's tomb—yet it made me uneasy. I took everything literally. I had often seen the sea—Brooklyn too is a kingdom by the sea—and even at five I knew what would happen if you buried someone in the wet sand at the water's edge. But no matter. The narrator is mad with grief, and madness makes all things feasible. I imagine the stories told to five-year-olds today, in the therapeutic era, feature narrators who diligently "work through" their losses to reach some emotional stability. With all the rampant conformity of my early years, eccentricity was still tolerated as a mode of being in itself, not a stage on the way to cure.

Above all, the poem was about loss, my perennially favorite theme. I sensed I had lost something too, though what it was I have yet to discover. Maybe I lost it when I learned to read, or learned to speak, or first opened my eyes: that fullness of being of the infant—empty yet full, the Buddhists' and Mr. Cha's paradox—before it begins to detach self from surroundings.

On some shelf or other in the small bedroom I found Eugene Field's "Little Boy Blue," a masterpiece among tear-jerkers. If you don't cry at "Little Boy Blue" you have to laugh, and I am not quite ready to laugh. Along with "Annabel Lee," it gave enchantment of the heart and set a standard for all future reading. Or rather it wasn't the poems themselves that set the standard, but the strong emotions they aroused. *Lycidas* never wrenched me as "Little Boy Blue" did, which can hardly mean it is the lesser poem, but does mean something about the capacities of childhood and the powers of simplicity.

"Little Boy Blue" was satisfying to my ear, though it did not swarm and buzz with Poe's inner rhymes. It too had some fine new words: "stanch" and "moulds": "His musket moulds in his hands," an admirable line. And "trundle-bed," which sounded like something children in poems would sleep in. There were two odd, unfamiliar phrasings: "The soldier was passing fair," which I read as "passably" fair, fair enough; only years later did I realize "passing" meant, literally, "going beyond." And "Time was when the little toy dog was new," one of those locutions you seldom hear but grasp immediately (though hard to parse or justify to a non-native speaker). How compressed and forceful: "time was," irony laced into the syntax like threads of chocolate in a marble cake.

I must have been five or so when I read "Little Boy Blue," and I wondered, as did his bereft toys, what happened to him. Where did he go, why did he never wake? I thought the poem was a mystery (indeed there is an awful mystery at its heart), a sort of detective story that didn't give enough clues, or else I didn't get them. If I had suspected the truth, I would still have been put off by the "angel song" that "awakened" him, for "awaken" suggests life and action. The boy had awakened from life into death, meaning we are only sleeping before the eternal day. I could never have accepted that. So far as I could see, he vanished into his sleep. For as with "Annabel Lee," that children could die without warning was unthinkable.

I wasn't aware that two babies in our extended family, both boys, had died not long before. They would have been my first cousins, which was no inconsiderable bond: we were a large and close family, seven pairs of aunts and uncles on my father's side and five on my mother's, all of them constantly visited and visiting with their two or three or four children, a huge array of characters whose progress through life was an open book. With so many near destinies to keep track of, the critical intelligence my parents brought to bear on the ongoing vicissitudes of the families was positively literary. On Saturday afternoons my mother and her three sisters would gather around my grandmother's kitchen table to report and analyze the doings of their late adolescent daughters. Since I was a good deal younger than most of my cousins, I got to sit and listen while they were out providing us with material. Some went to college, some worked, a few were idle; some had boyfriends and some didn't. Where had they been and with whom and what had they said and worn? Here was the patient building up of character I was used to and enraptured by in novels, and so what I was really doing, as I sat silently drinking glasses of tea and cracking walnuts, was reading, without a book. The presiding spirit of the book, supplying context and narrative tone, was my small, august grandmother with smooth white-gold hair, wearing an apron, circling the table now and then to scrape the oilcloth clean of bits of walnut shells. She made swooping arcs with her knife; the sound of the dull blade against the oilcloth was portentous, like a Beethoven motif. Then she scraped the assembled crumbs and shells into her waiting palm at the edge, never dropping a crumb. On a cot in the corner of the spacious kitchen sat her half-brother, who rarely spoke but was a fairly benign presence, more than a plant but less than a full participant. The sisters could say anything they liked in front of him because he was deaf.

I don't know whether the babies died unaccountably, like Little Boy Blue, or caught a chill, like Annabel Lee. I didn't discover their brief passage until decades later, through words dropped here and there. Death was the untold story, grief not graced with words. No wonder I read. In books I found explicitly, flamboyantly, everything censored in life.

For I must have known, somewhere, about Little Boy Blue. Why else would I have wept at the image of the toys "stanchly" await-ing the child who will never come, their dignity a blend of loyalty and ignorance? My sympathy was all for them. The poem is skewed in that direction, making the boy a renegade and betrayer, and the toys abandoned victims. The skewing is what rescues it from being a maudlin set piece. To side with the toys, as we are led to do, is to avoid the danger of siding with the child. But our safety is a delusion; as the poem rights itself in the mind, we feel the aftershock. Even today it is startling that Little Boy Blue should vanish so suddenly. He didn't even have a chill. He fully expected to return the next morning from his dream voyage: "Now, don't you go till I come," he tells his toys, "And don't you make any noise!" But it is he who will never again make noise.

We realize we are mortal very early, as soon as we begin to put inkling and evidence together, and "Little Boy Blue" trades on that secret the way other works trade on sex or cruelty. Anything that nudges so temptingly at the forbidden, and offers the lures of sonority besides, can hold us hostage forever, just as the clever witches of fairy tales capture innocents by preying on their vulnerabilities.

The bookshelves were lined with real mysteries, not just meta-physical ones, and of these my favorites were Erle Stanley Gardner's. Perry Mason, Hamilton Burger, Paul Drake and Della Street, that all-suffering secretary who I knew even then was missing something, a self, were fleshed out in my imagination long before they be-came shadows on a television screen. I read racy, hard-boiled *Ellery Queen's Mystery Magazine*, which arrived every month, and I was astonished when my father casually mentioned that Uncle Dan, his brother, actually knew Ellery Queen. (So what "Annabel Lee" sug-gested was true: you *could* know the people in books, or behind them.) What is more, Ellery Queen was not one person but two, neither bearing that distinctive name. They were not detectives at all but partners in the writing business. I was shaken with wonder that this could be, and even more, that Uncle Dan could know them, speak to them, and visit them in, wonder of wonders, an apartment in Manhattan. But if anyone would know a writer (writers, in this

case), it would inevitably be Uncle Dan, a figure bathed in sophisti-
cation. He wore expensive clothes and drove flashy cars and ate in
fancy restaurants where he appeared to know the waiters and liked to
pay the check, and was not married. He had started out married but
his wife died of a mysterious illness, and so, though a middle-aged
man, he actually took women out on dates, women we occasionally
met in the fancy restaurants. Their style matched his, and while they
were sometimes mothers too, widowed or divorced, they were not
like the mothers I knew, plump and sage, who wore aprons and pre-
sided over the kitchen and prefigured what their daughters would
become. I did not have it in me to become one of these be-aproned
figures, or the other, sleeker kind, either. Meanwhile I read, maybe
hoping to find out if there was anything else to become.

The year I was ten or eleven years old I sat on my bed cross-legged,
churning my way through *A Tale of Two Cities*. My mother had rec-
ommended it. I often complained to her that I had nothing to do, and
she invariably suggested I sew something or read. I didn't like to sew,
I had no interest in any of the housewifely arts. I didn't like doing
anything much, really, perhaps because children were supposed to
like doing certain things—sports, excursions, arts and crafts—and
for me any pleasure was weakened once it was sanctioned, invested
with respectability and obligation. What I liked was sitting on my
bed and having a book happen to me. No one could manipulate or
interfere with that.

A Tale of Two Cities was difficult and boring, especially at the be-
ginning, but I was determined to read it because the name of Dickens
was synonymous with great writer. Scattered amidst the tedium were
magnificent passages like the reunion of Lucie and Dr. Manette,
or the trial scene, or the wicked Evremonde's driving his carriage
through the slums, which carried me through the boring stretches
as a week-end trip with a lover carries a lonesome person through
solitary months. I didn't hunt for the "good parts," though, as I
did later with books hotly passed from hand to hand—*The Amboy
Dukes, Never Love a Stranger*—whose plots were merely bridges to
the moments when fingers began surreptitiously inching up thighs. I
read every word of Dickens, in the belief that I could not properly
appreciate the good parts unless I read the boring parts. Maybe this
is true, and shows a precocious sense of the relation of figure and
ground, or maybe, despite my rebellious passivity, I was caught in

the overpowering moralism of the age: pleasure was a reward after suffering or "discipline," never *gratis*.

As it happened, I might have done well to sew when my mother suggested it, for I was about to be humbled for my disdain of the housewifely arts. When I entered sixth grade, still reading *A Tale of Two Cities*, the girls were required to sew aprons and caps in preparation for cooking class in junior high the following year. The apron quickly became my albatross, though what misdeed it symbolized I didn't know—a sin of omission, no doubt.

The white shapes were mercifully cut out for us by the teacher, her only act of mercy. We were to sew a strip of red binding around the apron's perimeter in a neat running stitch, approximately six stitches to the inch, then turn the binding over and hem it around the whole perimeter. In addition, there was an enigmatic little pocket over one hip, too small for kitchen utensils, and anyway, cooks do not carry their tools slung phallically from their hips like handymen or telephone repairmen. Nevertheless the pocket was required and it too got the red binding, twice around, and had to be stitched to the apron. The cap was a triangular piece of white cotton to be worn bandanna style, also with red binding. This endeavor, with its ripping and repairing, was the work of an entire school year, for I could not do the binding to the teacher's satisfaction. She was an aesthete: "Yet if it does not seem a moment's thought, Our stitching and unstitching has been naught." We would not graduate or embark on junior high school, she warned, unless the aprons and caps were finished, and well finished, no sloppy edges or crooked stitches. I cannot remember doing anything else in school that year except watching one girl's phenomenal breasts grow. At home I wept and stormed and finally got it done with my mother's help. She was not a much better seamstress than I but she was more patient and did not have the weight of resistance cramping her fingers.

I suspected we would never use the aprons, that they were only a refined instance of the sadism the schools excelled in. I was wrong. There was a cooking class in junior high, a large room with eight or ten units of sink, stove, cabinet and counter, and we did wear our aprons and caps as we cooked cocoa and grilled cheese sandwiches and spaghetti with a tomato and onion sauce. Whatever we cooked we had to eat, under the gaze of cheerful Miss Sklar, who laughed at our mishaps, and her colleague, Miss Sherry. She was old, with a pinched face and steel-rimmed spectacles and white hair and a stiff rubber collar around her neck which I later learned was a thera-peutic device, but since Miss Sherry had reportedly worn it from time immemorial I presumed it had symbolic import, maybe a form of self-discipline like a hair shirt. When Miss Sherry presided, the cooking class had the austerity of a convent.

Still wearing our aprons and caps, we were promoted in the spring to The Apartment, four fully-furnished rooms behind an ordinary classroom door, signalling the wonders that doors might conceal. Several times a week we cleaned The Apartment and cooked in its kitchen; again, under Miss Sherry's rigid stare, we ate what we cooked. The Apartment had virtually everything an apartment needed except bookshelves.

Meanwhile, at home, I was plodding through the two cities from the first word to the last, alternately hating and loving but ever will-ing myself to go on, while the light faded beyond the lovely black-bordered casement windows that looked out over a row of back-yards. Those were the two halves of my life that year, *A Tale of Two Cities* and the apron. They were hair shirt, neck brace, discipline.

My parents were people of the magazine as well as of the book: the daily mail—dropped through a slot in our front door—held treasures in brown wrappers. I liked the *Reader's Digest* best be-cause of the jokes and anecdotes. Indeed everything in it was short and pithy, numberless capsules of cheap optimism that lodged in my young brain and required painful dislodging later, like bits of shrapnel. I also read the *Saturday Evening Post, Esquire,* and sev-eral women's magazines, *Redbook, Cosmopolitan* (not today's sexy rag but a sedate guide to female behavior), *McCall's,* the *Ladies' Home Journal,* and *Good Housekeeping.* Each contained four or five stories, sometimes serialized, as well as a condensed novel. The stories were "women's fiction," that is, about family and love, and were an invaluable index to the world, or I should say to the pre-vailing middle-class fantasy of the world. I studied the monthly col-umns—"Can This Marriage Be Saved?" and "Tell Me, Doctor." The gray-haired doctor's kindly face (a photograph accompanied every column) bore an unearthly wisdom, and the tone of his readers' ques-tions was correspondingly pious. The war, which uprooted so many comforting assumptions, paradoxically reaped an age of belief and submission. Perhaps it was simply exhaustion that made people love advice, rules, anything to relieve the burden of living in the raw. The marriages, it seemed, could always be saved with a bit of patience and forbearance. I had little use for forbearance, I liked a good fight, and my judgments were at odds with those of tepid Dr. Popenoe. I wanted the harassed wife to throw her interfering mother-in-law out of the house, or get her snoring husband up from his armchair and over to the sink. I longed each month for a marriage that could not be saved, and I think this happened once or twice in the course of ten years. Probably the husband was an alcoholic or a compulsive gambler, or had even kissed another woman.

The *Reader's Digest* ran a condensed book each month, the prize at the end. I had no violent feelings, then, about condensation, so I enjoyed these without worrying over what was left out or in what relation the author now stood to her mangled work. For a while my favorite condensed book was Thor Heyerdahl's *Kon-Tiki*, about a perilous trip across the Pacific in a raft, but *Kon-Tiki* was soon outranked by a book even more charged with suspense, which to this day evokes the tenuousness of every mortal moment: *Miracle at Carville*, by Betty Martin, a true story set in a then-contemporary lepers' colony in Kentucky or thereabouts. I have forgotten a good deal about the book but am loath to go back and check it out. I might laugh. Bad enough to laugh at lepers in Kentucky; worse to laugh at what was indiscriminately receptive in my young self.

The story, in my probably distorted memories, is narrated by a young woman—a wife and mother—found to have leprosy and sent to Carville, which has the feel of an adult boarding school or camp, a less lofty magic mountain where struggle and aspiration are distilled into purer form. Carville's guiding motif—religion, almost—is illness; salvation is measured by degrees of health.

The heroine enters the insular society of doctors, nurses, fellow patients and routines, all described in exhaustive and, to me, fascinating detail. Life at Carville is structured around the monthly blood tests. Positive means despair, negative means hope until the following month. A patient needs twelve consecutive negative tests to be declared cured and return to the world outside. The book, too, is structured around the test results, with the tension of a poker game or a tied ball game, where each moment promises a new future or prolongs the agonizing present. Time and again our heroine has four or five or six negatives, dares to dream, then draws a positive and must start all over. I read with every cell alert, curled up tight on my bed, choking with anticipation, hoping, despairing, marshalling new hope out of despair: the leper, *c'est moi*. Would we ever achieve the impossible twelve negatives and leave Carville? The constant temperature takings of *The Magic Mountain* are bland compared to Carville's ups and downs.

Then there is the love interest. The heroine's husband visits at intervals, but inevitably some estrangement creeps in. She inhabits an alien world with new premises and uncertain prospects. The very word "leprosy" is, to say the least, a turn-off. Who could love a leper, if not another leper? Yes, a man leper waits in the wings. They fall in love . . . Should they stay with their spouses who understand nothing of the critical experience of their lives, or start anew together? Even I, with all my experience of "Can This Marriage Be Saved?," hadn't the usual prompt solution. I think that after much agonizing the leprous pair decides to stay together. And then the beauty of the structure is made manifest. Just as you expect the easing of a dénouement, the tension thickens. The twelve tests balk the lovers, as in a fairy tale or myth. He's almost made it, and she fails and has to begin again. She is practically cured, and his next test is positive. Relentless frustration. Years go by, maybe longer than Jacob labored for Rachel. (Are they sleeping together? I hope so. It didn't occur to me to ask; I was barely eleven.)

I can't vouch for the outcome, but given the title I suppose they eventually passed the tests and lived happily ever after. Such was *Miracle at Carville*, a seminal book of my youth. Does the long reach of its influence lead me to invent torturous plots, suffering and redemption in maddening alternation? Not at all. Next to *Miracle at Carville* my own novels are uneventful. I wish this were otherwise, but it does not seem within my control. I was surprised to hear a writer once say she wrote the sort of books she wanted to read, since no one else was writing them. Many people, most of them dead, have written the sorts of books I want to read. But not me. What we love to read is not necessarily what we write. The great Italian writer Natalia Ginzburg, who in her early years translated Proust, has described her longing to write lush, allusive prose entwining the complexities of soul and universe into every helical sentence. When she set pen to paper, what appeared was terse and straight as a bone.

But the tests, those twelve tests. They were what gripped me so tight, because my childhood was fenced at every turn with tests—from performing the *New York Times* to attending school, where understanding was quantified by tests, a world of measurements light years from the way things felt inside. I tangled my insides trying to shape them to the world of quantification, quite like the leper who, however well she felt, however much in love she was, got tied in knots every month, her inner truth twisted by numbers popping out of a test tube and labeled, unaccountably, with her name.

My parents were people of the book: my mother read family sagas, historical romances, popular fiction by the current household names—Anya Seton, Faith Baldwin, Rumer Godden, Taylor Caldwell. My father read mysteries and, like many men, was in thrall to the *New York Times*. The relation between those pale loiterers and their *belle dame sans merci* is visceral, more potent than any mere sexual or emotional connection, and would require a Keats to do it justice. Some can loiter for fifteen minutes or more on a single page. An observant woman once informed me, "Don't you know? They're not really reading. It's their way of daydreaming, but they have to have the paper in front of them to justify it."

After the *Times* and the mysteries, my father liked books on political and historical topics: biographies of the presidents, Theodore White on the campaigns, William Shirer on the Third Reich. He was always interested in a new book on Roosevelt. He read as I do, slowly, absorbedly, the book at arm's length from his eyes, but as I cannot do, he read lying down, stretched diagonally on the bed, stockinged feet crossed. His right hand, which held a cigar, was behind his head, the right elbow sticking out at a sharp angle, while his left arm was extended, the hand supporting the book from the bottom and turning its pages at the lower spine with a right-to-left flick of the thumb. He was still in his business clothes, white shirt unbuttoned at the neck and tie either hanging askew or removed, for he did not change into casual clothes when he came home from work. He had very few casual clothes, shorts for the summer and a few sports shirts he paraded around in on rare occasions, looking jauntily pleased with himself but slightly awkward too, seeking approval. He dressed in the morning and undressed when he went to bed and that was it, and he hated our walking around in pyjamas or bathrobe once the day had officially begun. Or rather it was the dressing that made the day official—without our wearing the proper clothes, the day could not take hold, was tentative, amorphous, unpredictable, and he needed to have the day official and under control as soon as possible. When I lounged around in a robe on week ends, his look of distaste conveyed that my dishevelment was morally inadequate. To this day I have trouble walking around in a bathrobe past eleven in the morning, even though I am in my own house and he is dead. I feel unprepared for what life might require of me.

He could stay in that position for a couple of hours so I guess he found it comfortable enough, and then he would fall asleep, his glasses slipping awry, the book coming to rest on his leg, the other hand still behind his head with the dead cigar between two fingers. I fall asleep reading too, and the last sentences filter into my dreams, where I continue writing the book. Just recently I spent several late evenings reading Ved Mehta's biographies of his parents, *Daddyji* and *Mamaji*, and in dreams I invented long passages about Indian marriage rituals and domestic life, spinning off from the facts. I picture my father in his habitual pose whenever I see new books he would have taken pleasure in, about Entebbe or Watergate or the assassination of Kennedy, biographies of Johnson or Truman, books about General Westmoreland's case against *Time* magazine, and PAC's and oil conglomerates and the misdeeds of Congressmen. Sometimes I feel a funny urge to read them for him.

As much as my father approved of reading, he objected to my habit of reading at the table. He wanted civilized dinners with the family gathered round in conversation. Reading at the table is uncivil, yet few acts are so completely satisfying. The two infusions, food and words, intermingle. The rhythms of chewing and swallowing join with the rhythms of sentences in a fantastic duet where the ear can barely separate the melodic strands. Parallel lines meet: food and story converge in mouthfuls of narrative, and the misleading duality of flesh and spirit is overcome. I will never be able to dissociate *Heidi*, a book I read again and again, from the accompaniment of lambchops and mashed potatoes—a far cry from the fresh goat's milk her grandfather was forever pressing on her—just as some people cannot dissociate sex from marijuana or baseball games from hot dogs.

I would get to the last page and flip back to the first, unwilling to let it go, have it end. It didn't matter that I knew what was going to happen. I never read for the story, only for the taste. I can't say how many times I read *Heidi* before I moved on to *Heidi Grows Up* and *Heidi and Peter*, each one more attenuated, like succeeding cups of tea from the same tea bag (and indeed, I recently learned that the sequels to *Heidi* were written by the French translator, Charles Tritten). For some reason, maybe the alien sound of the name, I assumed the author of *Heidi*, Johanna Spyri, was a man, even though I knew women wrote books: there was Louisa May Alcott, whose entire sunny *oeuvre* I had read (only lately, with serious studies of women's writing, have her darker works been reissued). When I had had my fill of Heidi I found a new book by this remarkable "man": *Cornelli*, addressed directly to me. How could "he" have known?

Cornelli is another displaced Swiss girl. Her mother has died, and to ease, or, more accurately, correct her inconsolable grief, her father sends her to live with a wholesome happy mountain family, where her gloom makes a sharp contrast. The mother of the family tells Cornelli that if she persists in frowning she will grow two little horns between her eyes, like the ubiquitous goats. Cornelli was as literal-minded as I. We didn't realize that the horns were the bumps between the eyes of a perpetually furrowed brow. Since she cannot stop frowning, Cornelli takes to wearing her hair hanging over her eyes to mask the horns. Everyone in the happy family mocks her messy hair and tries to get her to comb it back, but she is horrified that the horns, sign of her grief, will show, that suffering will have deformed her into an animal. Meanwhile her pain has been forcibly shifted from the loss of her mother to her dehumanized state. She is made ashamed of feeling as she does, being what she is. Naturally I didn't see all this when I read it. I worried endlessly and indignantly over Cornelli. She was entitled to her horns, I felt, entitled to sulk and shield herself with her hair, just as I felt entitled to the sulks I had to fight for.

At last someone, probably the kindly mother, breaks through the veils of error to the source of Cornelli's trouble and explains that she will not grow horns, it was only a figure of speech. Relieved, reached, Cornelli allows her hair to be combed back. The furrows in her brow smooth out, her mourning recedes and she can regard the

39

world without a protective mask. If I could uncover why I cherished this book so deeply, what exactly I was grieving for and why I clung to the grief, it would be a great unmasking.

There were some books I wanted to possess even more intimately than by reading. I would clutch them to my heart and long to break through the chest wall, making them part of me, or else press my body into them, to burrow between the pages. When I was eight I felt this passion—androgynous, seeking both to penetrate and encompass—for *Little Women*, which I had read several times. Frustrated, I began copying it into a notebook. With the first few pages I felt delirious, but the project quickly palled. It was just words, the same words I had read over and over; writing them down did not bring me into closer possession. Only later did I understand that I wanted to have written *Little Women*, conceived and gestated it and felt its words delivered from my own pen. But that could never be, unless I did as Borges's Pierre Menard, who undertakes to rewrite *Don Quixote*, but in order to do so must reinvent in himself the sensibility of a seventeenth-century Spaniard. I did not want to feel and think like Louisa May Alcott, however, or even to know more about her. I wanted to write my version of *Little Women*, what Louisa May Alcott would write were she in my place, or if I were she, yet living my life. But the notion of "if I were she" or "if she were I" boggles the mind, an absurdity even grammatically. (If I were she I would no longer be I.) When we yearn to be someone else, what part of the "I" do we imagine detached and transplanted? The self has no discrete movable parts.

Since then, from time to time I have felt the urge to copy certain books: *The Death of Ivan Ilyich*, and *Middlemarch*, and Margaret Drabble's early novel, *The Millstone*; stories by William Maxwell and Pavese and Natalia Ginzburg (I have translated some of hers, a more useful way of possessing); and Calvino's *If On a Winter's Night a Traveler*, a paean to the act of reading in all its richness, infused with tenderness to readers, a novel whose narrative thread is drawn by the needle of reading.

I don't copy them. I do recognize them as books I want to have written, which, given enough talent and ingenuity and time, I might have written. I was groping towards them and might have reached them in a few centuries, but others reached them first. And it appears that the critical thing these others were able to do was identify and localize a subject which for me remained undefined and elusive—until I read their books and saw it clear and pristine. In that light, writing seems less a craft than a quality of mind and discernment, a rarefied focusing. Or sometimes the other writers have lit on the perfect form, which obviates any struggling for subject—Proust's ruminating novel, or Herbert Morris's meditative poems like an intimate conversation, both unabashed about their length. Then I think, Had I only known you could do it that way . . . and writing seems a function of inventiveness and nerve. In any case, the books I have wanted to write brood about what I brood about, and they move in uncannily familiar rhythms. Reading them, I feel caught out. Some stranger, like the author of *Cornelli*, has pre-empted my secrets. I am disarmed, but less alone.

There are equally fine books that, much as I admire them, I would not have wanted to write, indeed have been relieved I didn't need to write: *Madame Bovary, The Idiot, Mrs. Dalloway, Dubliners.* Too difficult, too impossible to sustain such crushing moods and temperaments. But I am judging by my own powers of endurance. Again, were I those writers, I could and would be they; the issue evaporates into tautology.

Ticklish questions of identity inform another treasured book, which few people seem to know: *Martin Pippin in the Daisy Field*, by the prolific British writer of children's books, Eleanor Farjeon. The French surrealists would have approved of it—arbitrary, dreamy, mystifying, leaning heavily on the *non sequitur* and the extravagant. Martin Pippin, part rural Prospero, part Puck, is in the daisy field with six little girls—Sally, Sophie, Selina, Sue, Sylvia and Stella—who insist he tell them each a bedtime story, which he does. Meanwhile, in interludes, a riddle of identity is worked out. Martin Pippin must guess who the girls' parents are, with nothing to go on but six pairs of names and a handful of character traits. The girls tease and confound him by mixing up names and clues, cavorting with the mysteries of identity; the narrative often sounds like Virginia Woolf rewriting *The Waves* for young readers. In the end the girls, their fathers and mothers, are figments of Martin's bucolic dreams, projections of the child he may someday have—for he has gotten married that afternoon, it turns out.

Martin Pippin embodies a name game of the highest order, playing with the protean nature of names, which can empty or swell like a bellows according to what we know or imagine of the thing behind the name. It is the sort of game Proust plays with the names of towns in Normandy and Brittany, or with Florence and Venice, whose syllables, he finds, not only evoke but contain, in tiny quanta of impressions, the light, the smells, the flavors and texture of the place.

Our sense of a name and the people who bear it may depend on someone we knew in childhood, a Katharine, perhaps, prim and chirping and knock-kneed, so that we expect every Katharine thereafter to wear Peter Pan collars and be a soprano. If we find a variant, Katharine Hepburn, for instance, we must laboriously detach the original qualities from the name and graft on new ones. And still the name is never entirely free. No matter how many variants, it keeps vestigial traits of its original. So, with primitive attachments, parents name their children Richard (the Lion-Hearted) or Arthur or Helen, but rarely Cassandra—few want a truth-teller. Many such names are chosen for their singular destinies—kingly Davids and wise Samuels—while others are shunned: who names a child Cain or Goliath or Judas? And naming boys after their fathers is not only a bid for literal immortality but a wish that the boy carry on the virtues of his father, be his father. Among Jews that particular *hubris* does not operate. Children are named after the dead, so that the dead won't be lonesome but will, as my mother used to say, "have someone." In the end it is the names, not the people, that are immortal, absorbing the history of everyone who has borne them. The delicate infant, innocent of the density of her name, unwittingly adds her bit of character and fate.

Besides the intrigue of names, Martin Pippin's game hinted at the enigmas of heredity, which children love to ponder. They dazzle themselves with fantasies of being adopted, and the adopted ones dream of finding their "real" parents and grasping the ineffable. Why are we who we are? I would ask, sitting on my bed under the casement windows. I imagined springing from different, idealized parents, but then I would not be myself. Had I been conceived on another day or in another room, even, I might have been someone else.

How energetically we resist becoming updated versions of our parents. Of course we cannot create new genes, but with effort, we believe, we can grow new traits and modes of life: self-generated mutations. Yet when we do manage to create ourselves anew, isn't there always a suspicion that the new identity fits over the old like a second skin, at times itchy or uncomfortably tight, not quite covering the most vulnerable patches? Caught unawares—awakened from sleep or weakened by illness or stress—we find ourselves behaving exactly as our parents did, the genes asserting themselves through the flimsy new skins, their power unabated.

My favorite of Martin Pippin's stories was "Elsie Piddock Skips in Her Sleep," set in the village of Glynde, under Caburn Hill, where the children "lived mostly on bread and butter, because their mothers were too poor to buy cake." When she is three years old Elsie Piddock hears the bigger girls outside skipping rope to the rhyme,

> *An*dy
> *Span*dy
> *Sugar*dy
> *Can*dy
> French
> Almond
> ROCK!
> Breadandbutterforyoursupper'sallyourmother'sGOT!

She starts skipping at that early age—just the age I learned to read—and her fame spreads throughout the county, for she is a born skipper. The fairies soon hear of her, and she becomes the protégé of their skipping master, Andy-Spandy. Every month at the new moon, fast asleep, she joins their midnight skipfests on Caburn Hill, where Andy-Spandy teaches her the magic skips. She can skip high and low, fast and slow, she can skip over the moon or to the earth's core; she can skip through a keyhole and land on a blade of grass as lightly as a drop of dew.

Andy-Spandy is the source of art, imagination given shape; as his apprentice, Elsie Piddock follows all he says without question. When her training is done he licks the wooden handles of her rope and they become Sugar Candy and French Almond Rock. "You shall therefore suck sweet all your life," he tells her, and though I was too young to know the links between Art and Eros, I must have known somewhere, as I knew about death, that they were holographic, sliding into each other depending on the slant of light and the tilt of the mind contemplating them. Elsie Piddock can return any time to the tool of her craft, touched by the lips of imagination, to find solace and nourishment. After a lifetime of skipping, "when times were hard, and they often were, she sat by the hearth with her dry crust and no butter, and sucked the Sugar Candy that Andy-Spandy had given her for life."

Years later, when Elsie Piddock has become a legend, a great Lord, a prototypical industrial magnate, decides to fence off the skipping ground at Caburn Hill and build smoky factories. The village girls, their mothers and grandmothers who grew up skipping there, are heartbroken. But what good are feeling and tradition against the march of industry? Suddenly an old woman appears, tiny as a child, and bargains with the Lord for one last moonlight skip. Only when everyone from lithe girl to achy crone has skipped till she stumbles, the Lord agrees, will he start building his fence. He waits impatiently. Just as it seems over, the tiny old woman reappears: Elsie Piddock, one hundred and nine years old. "When I skip my last skip," she announces, "you shall lay your first brick." But she never does skip her last skip. She goes on forever. She is skipping even now. Thanks to her moonlight dreaming sojourns among the fairies, she has become immortal. Her art will outlast the greed of entrepreneurs and the machinations of city councils and the carelessness of Parliamentary decrees. It will last as long as the hill she skips on and the moonlight she skips under.

Here was a story for me to lean on, and live on. It said that the things I loved were not foolish or frivolous. Elsie Piddock may have been dreaming when she apprenticed herself to Andy-Spandy, but in the end art is not only dreaming but action.

My parents were people of the book but I did not appreciate this, and as I started college and acquired a dim sense of literary history, I indulged the adolescent's need to reshape them, to make them fit my ideal. I tried to redirect their reading. No life could be complete, I thought, without studying the great works of Western literature. I burned with the zeal of a born-again reader; my bumper sticker would have proclaimed, Lit Saves.

I pressed books on them, cajoling or commanding, according to the mood of the hour. Thought they didn't often read what I urged, they took the suggestions docilely, never challenging my campaign to educate them. In households where everyone criticizes everyone else, privileges accrue even to the youngest, if they can wait.

I had my greatest success with *The Trial*. It was not hard to get my father interested because it fit marginally into his preferred category of political books; also, he was a lawyer and the title promised legal proceedings. I was spending the July Fourth week end blissfully alone at home while my parents were in the country. I received a long-distance call.

"That book you recommended," my father began with his customary abruptness. "By that Kafka. *The Trial.*" "Yes?" I said eagerly. "Did you read it?" "Well, that's what I'm calling you about. Your mother and I both read it and we have very different opinions on what it means. I say it's about the injustices of the legal system and the modern state, how you can get lost in the bureaucracy and red tape and so on. And she says it's just about life itself, how you're always guilty about something or other and you feel you deserve to be punished simply for being alive." He paused. My heart leaped. This was exactly what I wanted. We should theorize this way every waking hour.

"So," he said, "what do you think?" My years of reading had brought forth fruit. I was an acknowledged expert on what things meant.

"Well, actually," I said in the cool, patronizing manner I had picked up from my professors, "you're both right. Those interpretations aren't mutually exclusive. The beauty of the book is that it can encompass so many points of view simultaneously."

My father was disappointed. He liked to have things one way or the other, and he liked to be right. He had probably been counting on me, for I usually supported his tough-minded as opposed to my mother's more humane, though no less sturdy, formulations. He argued his case for a while, then my mother got on the phone and pleaded hers, but I steadfastly refused to choose one over the other. They must have hung up vexed, but I was delighted, envisioning a future transformed. I would lead them through all of Western Lit, as I was being led, only a few steps ahead.

This never came to pass. In the fall I rented a room near school and began growing up. My life was no longer centered on home. What my parents read or didn't read stopped mattering. I had to learn to cook for myself. I asked my mother how come she had never taught me to cook (all I knew were the grilled cheese sandwiches and cocoa and spaghetti in tomato and onion sauce from junior high), had never trained me in the various housewifely arts for which I had

had such scorn. She replied that I was always reading and she hadn't wanted to interrupt me.

I often ate alone and read uninterrupted, and I would feel myself once again—since only when you move on can you truly get anything back—sitting at the kitchen table reading *Heidi*, the book propped up on the flowered tablecloth and the old silver fork weighty in my hand. Whenever I eat alone and read, I retrieve the whole emotional apparatus that was mine before education and independence and all the experiences that make us unable to respond to books as children do.

On a long car trip some years ago, the kids in the back seat were restless—they were seven and four—and we had run through all our car-trip games. I found my mother's solution leaping to mind—the genes, in moments of weakness, reasserting themselves. But there was nothing in the car to sew and my daughters didn't know how to sew anyway; they would never make aprons and caps but would take woodworking and metal shop and bring home funny-shaped boxes of indeterminate use. "Why don't you teach her to read?" I burst out to the older one, hardly thinking of the implications, only that this would be a long project, longer than the car trip, surely. A few minutes later, having supplied pad and pencil, I heard her explaining the "at" family—cat and rat and fat and hat. (Why does it always start with the "ats"? Because cats and rats and hats figure prominently in nursery rhymes?) Some miles later it was the "an" family, and by the time we arrived, the "its" and "ots" and "ets" had been traversed. And so the younger one was launched on the perilous journey, crossing the bridge that can never be recrossed. I could only watch as mothers do when children leave home to seek their fortune, knowing that from now on her adventures would be beyond my ken, I could neither protect nor accompany her. The written word was about to carry her off like the tornado that took Dorothy.

Children generally read what they please, but addictive adults (writers especially) can get tangled in the toils of choice. There may be as many kinds of reading as there are books, each one demanding its own form and degree of active participation; our choices can depend on whether we relish the exertions of volleyball, as it were, or prefer a meandering round of croquet. A writer like Henry Green, for example, sets down the merest hints on the page, leaving us, practically, to write the book ourselves, the way archaeologists reconstruct a tomb from three chunks of stone and a dip in the ground. Others, George Eliot, say, make us feel a trifle superfluous. We come ready to do our share, only to find that the author, like a solicitous mother, has anticipated our every need and errant fancy. I'll choose the coddling every time, yet more spartan types rave of the beauties of Henry Green, about whom I feel as I do about marathon running: I'd like to do it, but I just haven't the constitution.

At times the ramifications of choice verge on the metaphysical, the moral, even the absurd. To read the dead or the living, the famous or the ignored, the kindred spirits or the bracingly unfamiliar? And how to go about it—systematically or at random?

At bottom, of course, the issue in choosing what to read (and what to do and how to live) is the old conflict, dating from the garden, of pleasure versus duty: what we want to read versus what we think we ought to read, or think we ought to want to read. Set out this way, it seems a simple distinction. And the extremes are indeed simple— books I am paid to review, as opposed to unheralded, unfashionable books I gravitate to like a respectable businessman shuffling into a porn movie house. In between lie acres of ambiguity, the many books (the many acts) I cannot in all decency leave unread (undone)—or can I?

An unusually clear case some years ago was Katherine Anne Porter's *Ship of Fools*. Reviews proliferated like cells splitting in an embryo; literary pages were monopolized for weeks. (Pity any less celebrated author whose book appeared at the same time.) Yet something put me off. Beyond the reported twenty-year gestation period and the arrogance of its metaphor (such relentless meaning), it was the awe which greeted it, an awe more fit for hugenesses like the Grand Canyon, and which made it obligatory reading. How to escape? In conversation, I lay low. Lying, as I mentioned earlier, was out of the question. But you can always say you haven't read something "yet." "Yet" extended longer and longer, like string from a spool. I still haven't read it but the "yet" is gone—I let go the string. I waited it out.

Much of the time, though, the distinction is not simple at all—at least I am not among the happy few who can promptly distinguish want from ought. We are taught from the first breath to want what others think we should want. They dress up "ought" in the insidious garb of want, a wolf in sheep's clothing, so that life's great task becomes the unmasking of false desire to reveal the bleak bare-toothed ought, and the unearthing of true desire.

Aside from the magazine pieces, the authors I read as a child were dead, and I still fancy the dead, a taste nowadays almost dowdy. To read current books, in our age detached from history, is to be forever young, forward-looking, partaking of the relentless energy of daybreak joggers and successful deal makers, rubbing shoulders with celebrity-writers. (Could Villon or Baudelaire have dreamed writers would join the ranks of the beautiful people?) Current books are modishly sleek, inside and out, low-fat, low-cholesterol, sort of like Lite beer—not bad on a hot day yet hardly the thing for a seasoned bourbon drinker. Meanwhile the books of the dead stay heavy and dun-colored, their pages not quite white, their type face stolid and ingenuous (except for those fortunate few treated to brand-new paperback attire, like a face lift or hair implant). Reading the dead is being a meat-eater in a vegetable age, mired in superseded values. When someone at a dinner party asks, Read any good books lately? *Jane Eyre* or *Pamela* is not a fertile answer. These are closed issues, closed books.

The pressure to read the living is moral as well as social. We must know our own times, understand what is happening around us. But I know my own times. I am in them. I have only to walk down Broadway or Main Street to see what is happening. It is the times of the dead I do not know. The dead are exciting precisely because they are not us. They are what we will never know except through their books. Their trivia are our exotica. As writers, transmitters, the dead can be more alive than some of the living.

I can hear the protests: I am romanticizing, not even granting the dead their proper context but allowing distance to contour and laminate them. Today's living will someday acquire that fine airbrushed otherness. Why not be daring and appreciate them now? Besides, the dead writers have been pre-selected; no discrimination is necessary. I needn't sift through five dozen nineteenth-century Russian novelists and decide, okay, this arrogant, tormented count, this loony gambler with the dubious past, this dapper smooth fellow, that sweet country doctor. I am forfeiting the opportunity to judge, to rank, to shape the tradition.

The question of judgment, of who is worth reading and what constitutes the tradition, has grown difficult and complex. Until lately it was assumed simplistically that the writers whose work endured were the most significant. With the spur of feminist criticism, with the freeing of vision to include literatures other than Western and attitudes other than white and male, the idea of the "canon" has come under cross-examination—not only its contents but the notion of an exclusive body of "the enduring" or "the best." Who has chosen the revered works and by what standards? What has escaped their vision? How do such decisions and rankings encourage some voices and discourage others? Above all, how does a biased literary tradition cramp the present and future of what we write and read?

These are not new issues by any means, but they need to be re-examined with each shift in social circumstances. For very possibly the canon of great works does not emerge naturally from history, but our view of history from a fairly arbitrary canon, in which case the way to a truer history is through a more inclusive tradition. The familiar dead have brought us to where we are. But supposing we wish to take ourselves to a different place? What if our forms of political action and discourse had been determined not by reading Machiavelli, but, say, Confucius or Lao-tzu?

Being truly current (not merely low-fat) demands that we resurrect or re-emphasize works—by the dead and the living—overlooked through faulty vision, which is presently being done by scholars and editors. It does not mean, though, that the canonized dead must be crowded out because others join them. In art there is no problem of space. The road is broad and forever under construction, as Eliot has pointed out, forever being refurbished and widened. With the advent of each new writer who will someday be "dead" in my romantic sense—a Garcia Marquez or Gordimer or Coetzee or Calvino—it undergoes major alteration. Every writer's work is changed. Not that we are influenced in any specific or noticeable way, simply that we work with an awareness of new lanes, new curves and new road signs.

On a small island off the coast of Spain I met an American writer, an expatriate, if the term still applies—he had not been stateside in many years. He had never heard of Raymond Carver. A good or a bad thing? I wondered. It definitely mattered one way or the other, as it might not have mattered centuries ago. Whatever Carver's work means decades from now, today it signifies a development, a provocative shift. If the man I met was a genius, I decided, a Shakespeare or Sophocles, the gaps in his knowledge would matter very little: he would go his own way, creating his context out of genius, not temporal conditions. (Though what would Shakespeare have been like without his Italian forbears?) But if he was simply a good and serious writer, he ought to know.

The more purposeful a writer is, the more her work defines a particular connection to her time and surroundings. Or, if "defines" sounds a bit deadly, let's say "shows," for no writer consciously sets out to do it (or does so at her peril). The connection is evident in the writing to the degree that it is strong in the writer. If she does not feel context—time, place, spirit—pressing in on her like humidity, the work will be ephemeral and self-referential, brittle as a fallen leaf. Part of context is what other writers are doing with the same context.

So despite my necrophilia, I read the living to know in what terms the connections are being illustrated. Then I can use, abuse or neglect these terms in full consciousness. For inevitably, every living writer is a part of every other, all of us bumping up against each other like passengers in a loaded bus. Some feel and smell better than others, and we may wish certain ones would just disembark, but for the moment they must be taken account of. When there is a pothole in the road we are all jolted.

I can vacillate lengthily, and foolishly, over whether to read at random (as I did on my bed in the fading light) or in some programmed way (as we all did in school). I like to cling to the John Cage-ish principle that if randomness determines the universe it might as well determine my reading, too; to impose order is to strain against the nature of things. Randomness continuing for long enough will yield its own pattern or allow a pattern to emerge organically, inscrutably, from within—at least I hope so. On the other hand, how comforting to have a plan. It harks back to the satisfaction of pleasing authority and earning a gold star. With a few months' effort, anyone can become an expert on Balzac or medieval epics or Roman comedies, and how reassuringly American, too, are expertise, thoroughness, inclusiveness—offshoots of manifest destiny, no doubt, the need to control the entire territory.

The case of random vs. order is an old duality among the many that Western thought likes to ease into, safe harbors after the tossings of ambiguity, just as nineteenth-century symphonies, after fretful harmonic uncertainty, resolve into their tonic chords, somewhat begging the question, it seems. Isaiah Berlin, in *The Hedgehog and the Fox*, quotes the Greek poet Archilocus: "The fox knows many things, but the hedgehog knows one big thing," meaning that hedgehogs connect everything to one all-embracing principle, while foxes "entertain ideas that are centrifugal rather than centripetal, . . . seizing upon a vast variety of experiences and objects for what they are in themselves." The quote may be read more literally and mundanely too. The hedgehog knows one thing—physics or ballet or the movements of the tides—and therefore knows the world, for nature works the same patterns everywhere, with surface variations; while the fox is a quite respectable dilettante, knowing the huge range of variations, with a smattering of methodology.

Swift divided writers into spiders and bees, the one buzzing from flower to flower gathering their diverse sweetnesses to transform into uniform honey, the other gazing inward, spinning elaborate, sticky webs out of the dirty stuff of the self. And yet true contemplatives are not self-absorbed in Swift's scorned and narrow sense. The Zen master, sitting and breathing, sees, or will see eventually, the whole world via the emptiness (readiness) of the self, the world compellingly real and multiform, flashing into the receptive eye.

I tend to think writers—and readers too—may be spiders *and* bees, foxes *and* hedgehogs, depending on mood and timing and need. I spent a hedgehog winter years ago reading the Greek tragedies. There are many good reasons to read them. Mine was that I had ordered a set from a discount catalogue. Anything acquired in such a carefree way—sitting at the desk, a mere matter of pen and paper— must be used, to justify the indulgence. All the frosty season I lived with royalty, amidst high tragedy. Clearly, life was not the endless trivia it sometimes appears to be, but a struggle of principle and impulse, passion and duty bearing down on primal family bonds. Yet for all we know, even Sophocles had his eye on the clock while gouging out Oedipus's, for the moment when he had to go to the fishmonger or write a recommendation for a promising student or drive his mother-in-law to the dentist. Without biography, which cannot help but take its subjects down a peg or two, we are free to imagine him dwelling nobly in the realms of tragedy. So reading ennobles life, or at least makes noble illusions possible.

Without any calculated plan, though, I read every novel by Jean Rhys and Barbara Pym as soon as I could get my hands on them. It was like eating candy—the chocolate-covered nuts of the cinema or the celebrated potato chips of which you can't eat just one. The variations in their novels were in fact no more than the slightly different planes and convolutions in each potato chip, and each one predictably tasty. I became an expert in self-indulgence.

When, every so often, I have a spasm of needing to get organized, I make lists of books to read. In between reading the books on the list I am sidetracked by the books pressed on me by friends, or the shelved books suddenly demanding loudly, after much postponement, to be read right away, or the piles of books arriving in the mail with notes from editors beseeching that I read them. If they only knew the convoluted agonies of choice!

Except for a few that capture my fancy, these last can be skimmed or shelved or passed on to the needy. But the urgings of dear friends— "You must read this, I loved it"—present a graver problem. They represent more than books; they are an index of the friendship's value and durability. Although sharing a love of the same books is affirmation of a friendship, not sharing it may be an even stronger testimony. "You wouldn't like it, it's not your kind of thing," is a happy sign that the friend understands, as well as a reprieve. But when she raves about a book, what else to say but, yes, thank you? For us conscientious types, the words become a pledge of the same order as, "I'll be there to hold your hand before the surgery," or "Sure I'll take the kids so you can meet him"—i.o.u.'s we must be ready to have called in. Luckily, our friend often forgets the book or gets excited about a new one. We may escape with reading one in four, we may well love them. What I love for certain, though, is listening to the friend talk about the book, sometimes the best part.

Months, even years, go by. I return to my list to find I've read perhaps a third of the books on it, not bad, under the circumstances. But by then I am a new person, with a new list under way. The unread books get carried over, and over, until eventually I cross them out. They are no longer necessary. I can hardly recall what allure they held for the person I used to be. Still, drawing a line through a title feels like inflicting a flesh wound—that much of me remains the same.

I am glad, at heart, of the inefficiency of my reading lists. Who wants to be an efficient reader? For a short time I was one, or was expected to be. Besides cooking and The Apartment, in the junior high smorgasbord we called "departmental" was another new course: Library. Twice a week we repaired to an unusually pleasant room for a public school at that time—big windows, lots of light, thriving plants, walls lined with books, blond wood tables comfortably seating six. Maybe memory embroiders—it sounds too lovely.

Speech Is Silver But Silence Is Golden, said the sign on the library wall. What bizarre alloy did this make of reading, a form of silent speech? On the first day, the librarian, a gentle grey-haired woman with no special subject to impart and thus no anxious fervor, told us to choose a book from the shelves, any book, and sit and read it. This was familiar, I did it all the time at home. But I had never done it in a room with thirty other people. In fact, reading was about the last activity I would have associated with school. For those forty-five minutes, school took on a homey feeling. I got absorbed, as I did curled on my bed, and almost forgot the surroundings. But not entirely. Any private pleasure appropriated by an institution is in danger of losing its savor, and alas, reading took on an official tinge.

The librarian taught us how to keep a chart of our reading. A narrow column for the date, a wide one for the title of the book, one for the author, and finally, one to note the pages read. It had not occurred to me that the number of pages, the rate, mattered. What could quantity have to do with reading? Yet from that moment there it was, sour and inescapable. In college we groaned ritually over long reading lists—how to get it all done? We calculated our speeds in different subjects (fifty pages an hour for a novel, thirty for history, twenty for philosophy) and parceled out our time. It is a blasphemous way to read, like a Black Mass, mocking the act by denaturing it. What a mercy it was to finish with school and be able to read again.

When I can't remember what I read last week or mean to read tomorrow, I think of keeping better lists, and keeping to them. Then

I recall that sour old library chart recording prowess. Better to forget than to chart. Anything I really need will spring to mind sooner or later: chance is provident.

That is to say, reading at random—letting desire lead—feels like the most faithful kind. In a bookstore, I leaf through the book next to the one I came to buy, and a sentence sets me quivering. I buy that one instead, or as well. A book comes in the mail and I begin it out of mild curiosity, to finish spellbound. A remark overheard on a bus reminds me of a book I meant to read last month. I hunt it up in the library and glance in passing at the old paperbacks on sale for twenty-five cents. There is the book so talked about in college—it was to have prepared me for life and here I have blundered through decades without it. Snatch it up quickly before it's too late. And so what we read is as wayward and serendipitous as any taste or desire. Or perhaps randomness is not so random after all. Perhaps at every stage what we read is what we are, or what we are becoming, or desire.

To recognize desire is itself a reading of the body. Every twinge and throb, every quickening of the pulse and melting of the muscles is a message to be deciphered. As infants we read these messages instinctively, then quickly forget how. Learning to read words on the blackboard echoes that early, crucial reading of ourselves. It feels familiar, *déjà vu*. But because it starts with figuring out signs and giving proper answers, we mistake its nature for cerebral. True reading is sensuous: words, with their freight of connotation, speed through us unrestrained, suggesting unimagined possibilities, a future cut loose from settled expectations. And once the mind is freed that way, recognizing desire—unmasking the false and unearthing the true—can become instantaneous again, like not having to move your lips or sound out the words. The whole body, radiating from the heart, waves us on or warns us off like a semaphore. We cannot always follow, but at least we are not deluded, at least there is clarity. We know how to read anew, to distinguish our own signs and meanings.

Quite the opposite is reading to confirm what we already know, who we have resolved or consented to be. Yes, we nod, settling the brain into a stiff smugness, that's pretty much what I thought I'd find. Naturally. We would find it anywhere, because we bring it with us.

Readers with a particular agenda to support or advance—Marxists, Freudians, feminists, to name the strongest—are most susceptible, for reading this way clarifies and reinforces ideology. But everyone does it to some extent. My parents did it when reading *The Trial*, as I did when I urged it on them, for with my agenda at the time, value was conferred by being listed in a college catalogue. In this seductive mode we are not so much reading as rewriting. The book is not happening to us; we are happening to it. It is to a book's greatest credit that it can withstand such repeated onslaughts and remain serenely intact, ready for the next assailant or, with luck, the next reader.

That brand of reading has nurtured the thriving critical distinction between text and subtext. When I hear books called texts I feel a pang, as if family treasures were being relegated to the distant airless safe deposit box. Who ever curled up happily to spend the evening with a text? For that matter, what writer ever set out to write one? The critics would reply that the work becomes a text once it leaves the writer's hands, but isn't that a form of sophistry? Even the Supreme Court has acknowledged that the fate of a work of art and the uses to which it may be put belong in the control of the artist.

No, the businesslike use of "texts" for stories or poems is undeniably punitive, dismissive. We address people more formally than usual when we feel disapproval or distaste; we take an aloof tone with irksome children. Just so coolly does Prince Hal cut Falstaff, and the audience winces.

What is wrong with being unashamedly a novel or a poem? What offense could they have committed to so alienate the critics? Clearly the poor work of imagination has sunk to demimondaine status, someone we might relish visiting in private, like Swann with Odette, but cannot publicly acknowledge—although Swann, man of the heart as he is, not only acknowledges Odette eventually but marries her, which in critical circles would be the equivalent of Jacques Derrida's confessing he simply adored a certain novel, he couldn't quite justify it but it touched his heart. This would be a little foolish and impractical, it could cause talk and snickers, yet it would open the door of a stifling room to some fresh air.

I first heard the companion word, "subtext," used around writing workshops. I was puzzled, but briefly; it is not an opaque word, not one you need to look up in the O.E.D. If there is a text, naturally there can be a subtext. A peculiar tendency of Western thought is that everything sooner or later is perceived in terms of surface and subsurface; we rarely trust that what we see is the real or the entire thing. Like paranoiacs, behind an innocuous surface we infer a threatening intent (seldom the other way around). We love tales of disrobing (Salome), of unmasking, of mistaken identity. Of course many things are obscure and require penetration. I am not suggesting we stop at immediate impressions, simply that positing a hierarchy of surface and subsurface can complicate perception. What is hidden does not arise from a built-in perversity or coyness in the nature of things (or books). The veil may be in our eyes. In Eastern thought both the apparent and the obscure are immanent. Nothing is "wrong" or tricky with the way things present themselves. If we look keenly enough for long enough, it is all there.

The paradigm of text and subtext suggests that while a book seems to be about such and such—how Pip encounters the great world and learns the vanity of ambition, how Emma Bovary is ruined by illusion, how Macbeth descends, act by act, from human to brute—beneath the story line is something else, probably undercutting the surface. But what else? All fully realized works are about exactly what they are about.

"Text" and "subtext" are more fitting for analyzing dreams than writing. We accept that the dream images and events are not "really" what the dream is about, but the available detritus of the day, cunningly adapted to shield the dream's actual "meaning." Writing is not dreaming. True, we must write about *something*. There must be events and images and furniture to occupy reader and writer while the elusive other thing—the idea, the book's *raison d'etre*—snakes its way along. But the beauty of a story, unlike a dream, is that the screen of events and furniture becomes primary. The original, embryonic idea, if there is one, adapts to fit their shape, rather than the reverse. So a novel is finally about the things of this world, a world of things. The screen is infused and penetrated by the depths; there is only surface. Or if that sounds too frivolous, there is only wholeness, immanence.

For purposeful, dutiful reading, the reading of "texts," we apply a special sort of concentration, special because it is applied. Willed. Such reading may be pleasant, but it is pleasant work. It goes fast because we are looking for something rather than allowing something to happen. When waiting for something to happen we never move fast, hardly move at all. Between the turning of the pages, eons pass. We drift suspended in the words, all stillness and expectancy. Concentration is effortless yielding, as I yielded while sitting on my bed under the casement windows that opened on the rows of tiny back yards, not noticing the fading of the light until the words got fuzzy on the page.

I am still a slow reader, but when I read to be informed, the pages fly by. There is no need to adapt to the style (there often is no style to speak of), no need to wrap myself in it, to tune my ear to the timbre of another voice. For here is the essence of true reading: learning to live in another's voice, to speak another's language. Reading is escape—why not admit it?—but not from job or troubles. It is escape from the boundaries of our own voices and idioms.

The good writer offers a new language, the silent language of the inner voice, the silver and the gold. He tries on lingoes and accents as we all do in private, and invites us to the startling intimacy of hearing him talk to himself with abandon, camping it up, doing all the voices. For all its originality, *Finnegan's Wake* makes flagrantly explicit what has always been a tacit strategy of fiction. It is not the use of a private language *per se* that distinguishes Joyce, but its rare lexicon and his refusal to translate.

Imagine Whitman's contemporaries first coming upon his poems. Surely the biggest shock would have been how he handled the first person pronoun, giving it the place of honor as well as a magnetism that draws every other word into its orbit. It is a syntactical shock, jolting the sense of order and placement. In Proust the shape of a sentence—tenses and clauses intricately braided—prefigures the entire structure of past and present interpenetrating, supporting each other. From Hemingway to Gertrude Stein to Virginia Woolf, the writers who claim our attention do so by voice and idiom, which are the audible manifestation of the mind. This is how it sounds inside, they declare. Listen, hear the shape with me. There is good reason for the addictive cravings of readers: the only new thing under the sun is the sound of another voice. Hearing it truly, we know what Shun-ryu Suzuki, in *Zen Mind, Beginner's Mind*, calls "not just ordinary language, but language in its wider sense." This language is hardly interference but—to return to the much put-upon Mr. Cha—a way of keeping the mind free.

By the same token, it is the abdication of voice that makes some authors irredeemably dull, regardless of clever plots or exotic settings. Dull writers use a generalized undistinguished language, not an inner language in the making. Some have lost faith in language altogether and use as little as they can get away with. (Why are they writing? To illustrate the failure of language?) Ben Jonson said, "Speak, that I may know thee." But dull writers refuse to speak. Someone or something is speaking through them, maybe a newspaper or television voice, or maybe our very own voices, as the writers infer us to be. They hope to give us to ourselves, to mirror their times—but mimicking is not mirroring.

Speak, that I may know thee, we implore those who address us publicly, from television anchormen to political candidates. But none will oblige. Do they find it unseemly or scary or inconvenient, or what? Do they use pre-fab phrases to their children, their friends, their lovers? Have any of them, lately, spoken a sentence bearing the shape of the thought inspiring it? Or do they no longer think? This is Orwell territory, and in fact the prophesy of "Politics and the English Language" was once again grotesquely enacted in the 1988 Presidential elections. Neither candidate revealed a genuine voice, though the irrepressible nastiness of George Bush may have been more genuine than the lacklustre tones of Michael Dukakis. In trying to be what he believed others wanted him to be, Dukakis managed a staggering feat of self-erasure. He is a warning to writers whose ambition is to mirror their times. They may end by becoming invisible; the mirror they hold up will be blank.

When I began, I thought reading would transform my life, or at least teach me how to live it. It does teach something, many things, but not what I naively expected. In the thick of experience, snatches of bookish wisdom do not serve. If no girl was ever ruined by a book, none was ever saved by one, either. (Even less useful is looking to fictional characters. The best of them travel in confusion and come to a bad end: this is what makes their lives worth inventing. It is we, the readers, who have the counseling role. Do this, do that, we tell them. Don't forget to mail that letter, don't get on that plane. Divorce him, marry her, look over your shoulder for heaven's sake. But to no avail.)

So what has been the point? Not to amass knowledge, since I forget the contents of books. Certainly not to pass the time, or "kill" it, as some say. For killing is jumping the gun, so to speak. We "kill" time to leap over its body to a future event, if only dinner. But after dinner we find, like Macbeth, that we must kill some more, till the next event. Plainly the events are just a more dramatic means of killing. What we are waiting for, killing time to arrive at, is death, the only event that can release us from the burden of living time. Killing time is to living what Evelyn Wood's speed reading is to reading, sprinting as opposed to leisurely walking, where you can appreciate the scenery. The goal is to get it over with, to no longer have to do it. (Speed reading is not actually reading at all but eye exercises.)

The underside of killing time is rushing about, going and doing in order to feel that each moment is actively, assertively "lived"—simply another bout with mortality. Reading is an activity of the moment too; having read is no more palpable than yesterday's feast. But unlike classic activities of the moment, dance or sports or sex—movement through phases—in reading, the body is still. Indeed what reading teaches, first and foremost, is how to sit still for long periods and confront time head-on. The dynamism is all inside. It is the mind that pirouettes, leaps for the ball, embraces and trembles. Outwardly we are languid. We have made the preparations Calvino advises in the opening pages of *If On a Winter's Night a Traveler*:

Find the most comfortable position: seated, stretched out, curled up, or lying flat. . . . Stretch your legs, go ahead and put your feet on a cushion, on two cushions, on the arms of the sofa, on the wings of the chair, on the coffee table, on the desk, on the piano, on the globe. Take your shoes off first. . . . Adjust the light so you won't strain your eyes. Do it now, because once you're absorbed in reading there will be no budging you. . . . Try to foresee now everything that might make you interrupt your reading. Cigarettes within reach, if you smoke, and the ashtray. Anything else? Do you have to pee? All right, you know best.

We gaze at marks on a page, put there by a machine, recognizable as words. Each one denotes something discrete but we do not, cannot, read them as such, except in the first days of learning how. They offer themselves in groups with wholes greater than the sum of the parts. As in human groups, the individual members behave in relation to their companions: each word presents aspects of itself suited to the ambiance, amplifying some connotations and muting others. Their respective rankings must change too. A word will be key here, play a supporting role there, and in each successive appearance will be weightier and more richly nuanced. All this we register faster than the speed of the light illuminating our page, hardly aware of noting the valence, assessing the role and position, of each word as it flies by, granting it its place in the assemblage.

Still more remarkable, these inky marks generate emotion, even give the illusion of containing emotion, while it is we who contribute the emotion. Yet it was there in advance too, in the writer. What a feat of transmission: the emotive powers of the book, with no local habitation, pass safely from writer to reader, unmangled by printing and binding and shipping, renewed and available whenever we open it.

Semioticists have unraveled these miracles in detail; even to call them miracles sounds ingenuous. After all, most aesthetic experience rests on transference through an inanimate medium. What is painting but oils smeared on canvas, or chamber music but bows drawn across strings? Reading is not the same, though. There is no sense organ words fit like a glove, as pictures fit the eye or music the ear. Intricate neural transactions take place before words find their elusive target, before the wraith we call the "writer" finds the reader.

For dwelling in the book, however remote in time and space, is this imaginary being, this missing link whom no reader has ever glimpsed. Readers flock to see writers, to meet the person who has given them pleasure; perhaps the consumers of telephone sex also yearn to meet the purveyors. But they are sure to be disappointed. The writer "in person" is no more the voice behind the book than the employee who murmurs salacious tidbits is inclined to stir us in actual life. Like the owner of the telephone voice, the writer is born of our fantasies. Reading her book, we fashion her image, which has a sort of existence, but never in the flesh of the person bearing her name.

Since the book, too, doesn't possess an independent or sensory existence but must be opened and fathomed, we enjoy the heady power of being necessary to its life. The real book is the prince hidden inside the frog. We open it, and our eyes give the kiss of regeneration. This power is what intoxicates. The thinking of others does not interfere with our own free thinking, but meshes with it in a splendid rite of recovery.

If we make books happen, they make us happen as well. Reading teaches receptivity, Keats's negative capability. It teaches us to receive, in stillness and attentiveness, a voice possessed temporarily, on loan. The speaker lends herself and we do the same, a mutual and ephemeral exchange, like love. Yet unlike love, reading is a pure activity. It will gain us nothing but enchantment of the heart. And as we grow accustomed to receiving books in stillness and attentiveness, so we can grow to receive the world, also possessed temporarily, also enchanting the heart.

Reading gives a context for experience, a myriad of contexts. Not that we will know any better what to do when the time comes, but we will not be taken unawares or in a void. When we are old and have everything stripped away, and grasp the vanity of having had it and of grieving for its loss, yet remain bound in both vanity and grief, hugging the whole rotten package to our hearts in an antic, fierce embrace, we may think, King Lear: this has happened before, I am not in uncharted territory, now is my turn in the great procession.

So much of a child's life is lived for others. We learn what they want us to learn, and show our learning for their gratification. All the reading I did as a child, behind closed doors, sitting on the bed while the darkness fell around me, was an act of reclamation. This and only this I did for myself. This was the way to make my life my own.

Help

M Y E D G Y feelings about maids go way back. As a child I lived next door to the only family on our all-white block to employ a black maid. Not a "colored girl" appearing once a week, which was not quite so uncommon, but a "live-in" maid. Roselle, who was about twenty, cleaned, cooked, and generally catered to the family's every domestic need, and they in turn made a point of telling the neighbors she was "just like one of the family," a piece of unexamined hypocrisy which irked me even before I could say why. I knew in some way that her work in the house and her color, both of which made her distinctly not like one of the family, were connected. The lady of the house boasted of how they had "gotten" her from the South when she was still in her teens, while I also knew that was not how any other family member had been gotten. Moreover, though Roselle did sit on the small brick porch on warm evenings, chatting with neighbors taking the air, she came out later, once she had cleared up the remains of the dinner she had prepared and served.

Above all, claiming her as part of the family seemed to obliterate any family Roselle might possess on her own, a family evidenced by a grandmother who occasionally traveled north to visit her and sat out on the porch chatting and gossiping too, yet for all I knew helped with the housework in exchange for hospitality. I suspected that had Roselle or her grandmother or any black person bought a house on our block, my neighbors would have been among the first to flee.

As I grew up and perceived the way things were, I was certain I could never be so insensitive, patronizing, and disrespectful as to boast of friendship with an employee, especially one so intimately placed. It would be a point of honor not to mistake the civility of common interests for true friendship, not to appropriate someone's private life along with her labor. Certain relationships existed, I reasoned, because of deplorable inequities; every connection based on economic necessity was shaped and warped by it; to pretend otherwise was to exploit still further, adding personal insult to social injury.

I was young. I thought in terms of abstract principle. I hadn't learned there are times, crucial times, when you find yourself doing in good faith something you have scorned in others on principle. The act sneaks into your life like an infiltrator, confounding, unnerving you: how did it manage to get past the border guards? Not very effective guards, after all; no sooner do simple instincts present themselves than principles are bared as straw men, scarecrows that scare no winged impulse.

In any case, it seemed I needn't worry about being tempted or tainted, since I would never be in a position to have a maid or cleaning woman. During the early years of marriage, while I held various jobs and went to graduate school, my husband and I did the minimal housework together, with the feeling of playing House. No doubt we ate real food, not the airy food consumed in childhood games of House, but though I remember marathon shopping trips and bulging bags of groceries, what those groceries turned into and by what means has sunk into oblivion. Then as soon as our first daughter was born we slipped unthinkingly into the ready-to-wear habits of working husband and stay-at-home wife, for lack of imagination and with no other visible model. It was the early 1960s. We instituted some enlightened variations—I worked part-time doing writing and public relations for a civil rights agency in neighboring Harlem, with my mother filling in at home—but not so as to make a significant difference in the standard pattern. Three and a half years later our second daughter was born.

I did not take easily to the grown-up version of House—quite the contrary. One day I announced that either we found someone to take care of the children so I could get out and work, or I went to Kings County. Kings County was the Brooklyn hospital now called Downstate, but for those who grew up in its shadow, the label was generic: as Kafka's castle has come to signify state bureaucracy and, more broadly, the hopeless intransigence of the human condition, Kings County meant the psycho ward, the terminus.

My husband replied earnestly, without irony, as if, like the wife on the TV commercial, I had proposed a choice between stuffing or potatoes: "In that case we'd better find someone to take care of the children." Strictly speaking, this meant I must find someone, since besides my mental health, the children too were apparently my responsibility. Naturally whatever money I earned would go to pay for the maid, who represented my sanity. With luck I would break even. Sanity, in any event, is beyond measuring in dollars and cents.

Nothing had been stopping me from making this move on my own, but one didn't then. At least I didn't. Besides—or as a result of—my distaste for the maid situation I had observed as a child, I didn't believe in having servants altogether. I believed, and still do, that people should clean up after themselves. My rudimentary social philosophy went as follows: if people tended to their own needs, pernicious hierarchies of class and race would be abolished (I was not yet keenly aware of those of sex), the artificial ranking of different kinds of work would fall away, the power-hungry would be kept from making trouble. Everyone would stay close to the primitive, necessary tasks of maintenance and child care, which would engender respect and reverence for the essentials—family bonds, children, useful work, a salutary life on earth: all sorts of unquestionably fine goals would be accomplished. I still believe this, though I have not found or created a setting in which I can live by it.

Now suddenly, with my quaint beliefs lost in eddies of boredom and despair, what stood between me and collapse was a maid. She, this person I didn't even know yet, was my lifeline, my life. With my husband's official sanction, I called the New York State Employment Agency and they sent Mattie Lou Colton to be interviewed. The children and I liked her and she appeared to like us. I telephoned her previous employer, one Mrs. Zimmerman, who sounded a bit highhanded but gave an excellent reference. As we came to an agreement, Mattie noted that I needed to pay social security and unemployment benefits, something the maids of my childhood had either not demanded or not known about, nor had their employers enlightened them. The bargain was struck and she was hired.

I had a cleaning woman. That was the term I used in my mind, where it was fraught with the discomfort and unease soon to be diagnosed as liberal guilt, a widespread affliction in the sixties, for the civil rights movement, over and above its specific accomplishments, was forcing whites for the first time to take the existence of black people seriously. In my childhood, women who were paid to do housework and who were invariably black—as was Mattie—were called "girls," which had struck me as absurd even then and was now scandalously incorrect. (As a matter of fact Mrs. Zimmerman had sounded like the sort of woman who might call her cleaning woman a girl.) "Maid" felt upper-crust and demeaning, while "Nanny," with its Anglo and aristocratic associations, was out of the question. "Babysitter" overlooked the household chores and had girlish overtones. "Housekeeper" seemed pretentious—the employer of a housekeeper should be a more grown-up and established member of society than I felt myself to be. In the end, cleaning woman seemed the most straightforward and dignified, though it omitted the crucial task of child care. As time went on, Mattie, in referring to her position, used the term "maid."

Mattie was about thirty-three, a couple of years older than I, and was tall and heavy, with straight glossy black hair, huge liquidy dark eyes, dark skin, full cheeks and lips. She would arrive at work dressed as if for a casual lunch date or a shopping expedition, usually in a pants suit or slacks and a sweater, and then change into a white uniform—a short-sleeved polyester dress that suggested a nurse's costume. The uniform made me uncomfortable, advertising that I was undeniably the employer of a maid, but I felt it hardly my business to dictate what she wore.

She lived in the Bronx with her husband, Charles, who worked downtown in the garment center. They had been childhood sweethearts in rural Alabama, where her family had farmed, and Mattie kept a strong Southern accent—a true drawl—which I had to strain to understand, the first few weeks. Her body language was a drawl as well: large, soft and bulky, she moved with a sense of consciously transporting her weight, yet at the same time managed to appear calmly dextrous; her movements had a luxuriance which I came to see concealed an inner turbulence very familiar to me, very much like my own.

Mattie had diabetes, childhood diabetes, the more serious kind—this she told me when she began work. She said I needed to have orange juice around the house in case she ever started slipping into a diabetic coma. Only a couple of times in the four years she worked for me did she ever need the orange juice. I was ignorant, then, of how serious diabetes could be, and thought her something of a hypochondriac for dwelling on it as she did. She was meticulously careful about her diet. In the course of time, as we sat around talking I once or twice offered her a drink, but she said she couldn't touch it; it would kill her. This categorical refusal set off ironic reverberations, for in the local lore of my childhood, black or "colored" "girls" were reputed to rifle the liquor cabinets when the lady of the house was out. "See, she doesn't!" I wanted to hurl out to the ladies on my old block, now mostly dispersed to the outer boroughs in the wake of black neighbors. "They don't all do it!" Then my own voice retorted indignantly, "What do you mean, *they*? Who are 'they?'" You sound just like *them*," "them" in this case being the ladies. I hated my own smugness: caught between fixed, abstract "theys" on either side, I alone seemed to occupy the mediating ground of reality, made unsteady by bad faith.

The plan was that I would work temporarily in my husband's office, editing and writing reports, and use the phones and typewriter there to find a teaching job: at home I could hardly make a business call or type a resumé without interruption. I postponed starting until I was certain Mattie had learned the routine and the children were used to her. For several days I stayed at home along with her and the girls, who were one-and-a-half and five, doing the usual chores— lunches, diapers, shopping, trips to the park. There was an awkward excess of authority, two grown women tending two small girls, but I needed to feel sure. Maybe I was reluctant to take up my new independence, such as it was. Mattie evidently thought so. After the third day she turned monumentally to face me in the kitchen, hands on her hips, a Maillol in nurse's garb, and asked in an ironic tone I would come to know intimately, "Well, are you going to keep hanging around here forever?" I was mortified. The children seemed to be getting along fine, possibly even better than with me. I left.

During those first few months, Mattie alluded often to Mrs. Zimmerman, her East Side apartment, her personal habits. Though I knew it was foolish, I felt jealous. It seemed Mattie's loyalty and engagement remained over on the East Side with Mrs. Zimmerman while I, as the new employer, could never claim such attachment. I didn't know if there was a Mr. Zimmerman and was too proud to ask; clearly there were no little Zimmermans. From Mattie's allusions, Mrs. Zimmerman appeared to lead a leisurely, privileged life, staying in bed late into the morning, then going out to shop or play cards. I imagined Mattie was very fond of the indolent Mrs. Zimmerman and missed her, and that I could never hold an equal place in her affections. It seemed inconceivable that she would ever reminisce about me to a future employer with the same zeal. Of course I didn't want that blighted attachment, I reminded myself, but the reminders did little to change my feelings.

After a few months I found a teaching job for the fall, which meant that on two nights a week I wouldn't get home until seven o'clock. I wondered if I might ask Mattie to cook dinner. So newly and unexpectedly an employer, I didn't know the rules of the ruling class, wasn't even sure what I was permitted to ask Mattie to do. Besides, she was moody, sometimes unperturbed in the face of domestic chaos, other times irritated by trifles. Her moodiness made me uneasy because it was so like mine. Knowing the vagaries of moods, I also knew that Mattie's might have nothing to do with me or my household, but they intimidated me nonetheless, and then irritated me, for I knew at the very least that a member of the ruling class shouldn't be subject to timidity in the face of an employee. I could tell when she walked in the door what kind of mood she was in, depending on whether she said a brief hello and went off to change into the distressing white uniform, or started talking right away about some curious scene she had observed on the bus, or what was in store for the day, or what she had cooked for Charles's dinner the night before. Cooking Charles's dinner, or "fixing his plate," as she called it, seemed the key event in her day, a ritual of near-sacred proportions in which she was the high, the only, priestess and he the boy-god. After I got to know her better she would say, in the bad moods, what was on her mind: something to do with her health or Charles or her family, some real or imagined slight from a friend or a stranger—for she saw slights everywhere. Whatever it was, it was a relief to know. I wondered if people had to pussyfoot around me in the same way.

With trepidation, I raised the question of her cooking on the nights I taught. Mattie took my humble request in her imperturbable mood. She said she was a good cook, which was soon borne out by Southern-style dinners of hush puppies, greens, fried chicken. My older daughter, just past six then, commented that Mattie's chicken was better than mine. Crisper. Or "crispier," she probably said. I felt a faint pang, but mostly I was glad, secure in my new dignity as a college teacher. Here was one more thing I didn't have to do.

The same thing happened with laundry. Gradually I realized Mattie would do most reasonable household tasks, and I thought how silly I had been to hesitate with the cooking and laundry. I got bolder: one night when friends stayed very late, I left the dirty dinner dishes. When Mattie found them heaped in the sink the next morning she was angry, and when she was angry she not only sulked but also spoke her mind, which seemed oddly redundant: in my case, one usually precluded the other.

"How you expect me to do all this and get them out to the park and everything else?" She had never bargained for dirty dishes from the night before, she said. I said I didn't see, under the circumstances, how dirty dishes were different from other chores. But I never left them again. Thinking it over now, I suppose dishes from the previous night's dinner party are different from the ordinary demands of daily life—they are the leavings of a sort of indulgence, and Mattie defined her work as dealing with necessities. The issue was not dishes, really, but who was doing the defining.

Insofar as Mattie or I had any formal ideas about raising children, on the other hand, they were identical, except mine were edged with anxiety mounting to a kind of panic over whether I could do it properly. While Mattie was anxious about a number of things—primarily health and money—she was serene with the children. She would stop any kind of housework to play games or read books or listen to them read to her; this was as I would have wished, but never thought to say. After she began cooking twice a week, I would come home from work to find her at the stove, the children dancing around her and chattering as they did with me; unlike me, she could both cook and be thoroughly engaged in their whimsy. Other days she would be sitting on the floor playing Chinese checkers or coloring pictures or building fantastical structures with blocks, nor did she look abashed to be found at these pursuits, as I might have done in her place. She simply glanced up, said hello, and continued playing. I envied her certainty that whatever she was doing at the moment was the right thing to be doing. She never jumped up to rush home either, even though there was Charles's plate to fix and, more important, Charles himself.

For she talked about Charles all the time, never saying what he was like exactly, just weaving his name in and out of conversation, making him an abiding, immanent presence. He was good, she said.

"Charles is *good*," she would say emphatically. "He's *good*!" which might have meant all sorts of things but meant, I think, the simplest. I nursed an enormous curiosity to see this good man.

Just as I was prepared—or so I thought—to show Mattie the respect of not claiming or expecting to be her friend, I was prepared for her to regard my children as no more than a job, to be handled with care and sympathy, but a job nonetheless. Still, every mother secretly hopes the person watching over her children will love them. Mattie did. She came to regard them as hers to such a degree that had I been a different sort of person, I would have been jealous. But while I was jealous of her presumed affection for Mrs. Zimmerman, I was not jealous of her possessive love for my children, nor of theirs for her. On the contrary, it was a kind of relief. I didn't have to be a mother all alone any more. My children knew quite well that I was their mother; meanwhile I was glad they had someone they could love as another mother in my absence, the capacity for love not being finite, like energy or patience. And since Mattie was so like me in the way she treated them, I felt it was not very different for them, whether they had her or me around. In a sense she was more like me than I was, for often I became too anxious to act on my enlightened attitudes and generous feelings, and reverted to old jittery ways.

It may seem unconvincing, and very likely politically incorrect, to say she loved them almost as a mother—as dubious as my old neighbors' "just like one of the family" line. Nevertheless, she recognized exactly who they were, and recognition is the yeast of love. Each day she would report in detail on their doings and the fluctuations of their spirits in the same proud, sagacious tone my husband and I or their grandmothers used, thoroughly aware of and intrigued by every illustration of character and habit, every like, dislike, and inclination, every virtue and flaw. And miraculously, she found all of this as noteworthy as I did. I had an ally of the most intimate sort, someone to share not merely the work but the secret, succulent pleasures of motherhood, and this alliance was my private and delectable comfort, very like my older daughter's blanket or the younger one's thumb.

As I came to know Mattie, I found our likeness uncanny. I was hardly a drawler, but I too moved calmly and gave off an aura of ease, I had been told: only I knew the turbulence beneath. Yet in both of us, beneath the turbulence lay another, deeper calm, a sanity dependable as bread, which helped hold it in check. (I wouldn't have gone to Kings County, only suffered and fretted and grown embittered.) The turbulence was sandwiched between the surface and the more sustaining calm; it swelled or lay dormant depending on our moods or situations, but the bread remained.

Since the children were not one of Mattie's anxieties, her turbulence never invaded her feelings for them. When I was exasperated at my younger daughter's stubbornness and burst out, "What are we going to do with her?" Mattie said, "I guess we just going to have to let her be." This jolted me, not because the words were wise but because they were self-evident. I should have known that. I did know it, but my painful and tortuous anxiety about being a mother screened it from view.

Perhaps Mattie saw so clearly about letting things be because she had borne a child once, a boy named John, who died at birth as a result of complications from diabetes. She talked about John often, almost as if she had seen him grow and develop, gotten to know him. In her visions she did know him—he lived as a complete person, arrested forever at a few hours old. She noted his birthday and referred to him from time to time, dating events by his birth—before John was born, after John was born. I found this odd at first, even a little eerie, but once I got to know her it didn't seem odd at all, and there was nothing eerie or mystical about it. John was important, that was the point; he was not to be dismissed or forgotten because he had not lived as long as other children. It came to seem natural to refer to him and I did too, asking whether certain events in her life had happened before or after John was born. And as my family got to know Charles, first in legend and then in the flesh, as we grew a connection as two families, John was part of the connection.

She often talked about the rest of her family too: her older sister Thelma, serious and steady, who worked in an office and lived in Mattie's apartment building, and younger sister Lila Jean, barely twenty, who had recently come up from the South to live with Thelma. Mattie considered Lila Jean potentially wild and, now that she had hit the big city, in need of constant supervision. Lila Jean took the Broadway bus to her job downtown, and according to Mattie, indulged a regrettable tendency to make friends with bus drivers. Every few days Mattie would report ruefully, yet with a kind of pride, on Lila Jean's escapades. Not far from my house was a diner where the Broadway bus terminated and the drivers congregated, and one day while we were taking a walk, Mattie pointed out this diner. "That's where Lila Jean found out about life," she said. Her younger brother, George, whom she described as handsome and irresistible, got married, and when the couple had a baby a year later, Mattie paid doting visits to Boston and brought home Polaroid snapshots to show me.

Over the years I met the family one by one, always with that curious stirring of anticipation you feel when people have been described in such detail that you know them already—their physical presence will merely touch up the picture. Thelma was indeed a homebody, huge and phlegmatic, Lila Jean was attractive in a snappy sort of way, George was smooth and charming. There was another brother down South whom I never met. Mattie's sisters and brothers called her Sister, and they called their mother Miss Lucy. They portrayed Miss Lucy, still living in Alabama, as difficult, egotistical, and exacting, though when I met her years later she seemed a mild, harmless old lady. Mattie told me that was her public manner, I shouldn't be fooled.

Mrs. Zimmerman's name hardly ever came up now, which was highly gratifying; on the rare occasions when it did, I realized Mattie had not liked Mrs. Zimmerman at all. The zeal expressed in her reminiscences was the zeal of disapproval. She had found Mrs. Zimmerman lazy, demanding, inconsiderate and generally disagreeable. I was very pleased. Since we felt the same about many people we knew in common—neighbors, children in the nursery school and their parents—I felt sure I would have shared her feelings about Mrs. Zimmerman.

By this time, Mattie always tacitly defined her own role, which beyond the routine housework included dealing firmly with repairmen as well as with the social life at nursery school. Rather than being "like part of the family," she wished to take us as part of her family. She kept urging me to bring the children over so she could "keep" them for the weekend and have Charles meet them, so we finally arranged this—I wanted to meet the famous Charles the Good myself. I was curious, too, to see where Mattie lived, and how. She spoke pridefully of her apartment and furniture, and I suspected everything would be alarmingly neat and orderly.

We brought the kids up there on a Saturday morning: not the

notoriously ruined South Bronx as, with a native Brooklynite's geographical ignorance of the Bronx, I had imagined, but the East Bronx, a poor, slightly shabby but not slummy neighborhood. The three-room carpeted apartment, filled with puffy furniture, knick-knacks, and framed, glassed-in family photos, was even more orderly than I had anticipated: it made me wonder what her secret judgments about our household must be, for she had firm judgments about everything and everyone she encountered. No doubt she would have been as skeptical as I am about the current injunction to be "non-judgmental." She would have considered it a sacrifice of her best qualities of discernment.

Mattie's furniture was more like real furniture—heavy, solid, and enduring—and more carefully chosen than our haphazard graduate school items. The bedroom was dominated by an enormous king-sized bed piled with soft fluffy pastel-colored quilts matching the floral window drapes. I was startled to see her living room furniture covered in plastic, just as the furniture in my parents' house had been shielded through most of my childhood. That felt familiar, to me if not to the children.

There, at last, was Charles, the well-fed and much beloved: a tall, athletic-looking, mustached man, a soft-spoken man of few words, who smiled a lot. We all felt we knew him already, and I imagined he felt the same. He greeted the children by name and immediately began talking to them, more, in fact, than he talked to my husband and me. Perhaps he was shy, or perhaps he knew us so well by proxy that there was no need for small talk. Whenever we met him afterwards he was quiet, not a chilly but a placid, benign quiet. Perhaps he let Mattie do the talking for him, as she did so many other things.

We returned Sunday evening, having relished our rare solitude, to find the children in no hurry to be reclaimed, but hovering around Mattie in the kitchen as they did at home, while Charles watched a ball game on television. Besides Charles, they had made the acquaintance of Mattie's sister Thelma, and of Cora, a friend, as well as several neighbors. Mattie showed us Polaroid snapshots of the girls posed with Charles, with her, with both of them, in the living room, the bedroom, the kitchen. Some of these eventually got hung up alongside photos of a niece down South and the baby in Boston.

That outing emboldened us: we decided to go to London for a real vacation alone, something we hadn't had in recent memory. Mattie and Charles came to stay in our apartment for the week so the children could keep going to school, and we flew away. From across the ocean, I reveled in images of Mattie and Charles sleeping in our bed, eating in our kitchen—Charles's plate being fixed right at our table—hearing the creakings of the floorboards and the hum of the refrigerator, watching "our" sunsets from the front window, grumbling over the slowness of our elevator—in short, being us, taking over our children and our domestic lives. It made me feel I could be in two places at once.

There were times when I did need to be in two places at once, such as the long day I spent in a hospital lounge, waiting for the outcome of my father's operation for cancer. It had begun at noon and six hours later was still not over, with no word of its progress. I had lurid fantasies of the doctors and nurses going out for a snack and forgetting my father, his innards bared on the table—nothing in their manner indicated this was impossible. Mattie had gotten to know my parents and was fond of them; still, I knew she would be wanting to go home and fix Charles's plate. When I called and explained, she said, sure, she'd stay another hour. An hour later—no report yet—I called again, to find that my in-laws were in town and had dropped in. How fortunate, I thought. "Mattie has to leave," I told my mother-in-law on the phone. "Could you stay with the kids at least until I know whether my father is dead or alive?" "Oh, I don't think so," she said. "We're supposed to go visit Aunt Rose."

Mattie had of course overheard half this exchange. Back on the phone, before I could speak, she said with a steely indignation that exceeded even my own, "Don't worry, I'm going to stay." When I got home—my father survived and was to live another seven years—she announced with a sniff and a toss of the head, "I told them they could leave and they did."

I can't remember whether she accepted money for those extra hours. Perhaps my memory has tossed out the fact because it is unimportant; perhaps the transfer of money is not as decisive a factor in human relations as I once thought. Surely that day was one of the many instances when the unlovely categories of employer and employee—always tenuous in our case—fell away to leave a fluid connection responsive to simple need. For more and more I see that far beyond running the household, our shared endeavor, our half unwitting and only half successful struggle, was to have our relations shaped spontaneously by nature and circumstance rather than by predetermined roles, to leap past the chafing strictures of class and race into a free state.

Later that year my father-in-law died suddenly. We had, in our shock, less than a day to organize a funeral and prepare food for a large group at our house afterwards. Mattie said not to worry, she would take care of everything. When we returned from the funeral, the table was laden with the foods Jewish families like to eat after funerals and on less momentous occasions as well: bialys, cream cheese, lox, whitefish, baked salmon, sable, radishes, tomatoes, cucumbers, tea, coffee. . . . Perhaps she had learned all this from Mrs. Zimmerman, who was finally serving some purpose in my life.

Generosity of spirit was not in Mattie's job definition as it might have been formulated by either of us. No, I thought, this was done out of friendship. For friends we were, at least it is the closest word for what we were. In fact, my musings at this very moment arise because there is no satisfactory or ingenuous word to label what we were, just as it was not a satisfactory or ingenuous condition. Because even as I was overwhelmed at how a burden could so easily be lifted, in a more callous part of my mind informed by the very strictures I chafed against, I was finally appreciating the age-old allure of having servants, something my high-minded social theories had not let me imagine. So this is how the rich must feel! So this is what money can buy!

Bought or not, it was friendship as I felt it. And it wasn't Mattie's competence or generosity that made us friends; she was generous *because* we were friends. Nor was it the gratitude on either side, mine for having someone to be a mother with, hers for having children to mother. No, what made us friends was what makes any two people friends—emotional affinity or some great passion shared. Our great shared passion, clearly, was the children. As for the emotional affinity—we felt the same way about many things. We told each other, as friends do, about our parents, our past, our present, our plans. We trusted; we knew what the other was likely to say or do or feel, and we knew what irritated each other—often the same things, dirty dishes, lateness, incompetence, injustice, too many simultaneous demands. We liked peace, but we also liked speaking our minds, being righteously indignant about people who didn't meet our standards, who didn't try hard, didn't almost wear themselves out with effort for the things they cared about, as we did and as we recognized and esteemed in each other.

Would she so readily have called us friends? I sometimes wonder. Yes, of course: she was no casuist, she would not have indulged in finicky analyses to define the obvious. But at other times I think, of course not: she knew better than I, knew in her bones, the palpable boundaries drawn by class and race and money, cutting mercilessly across the landscape of delicate feelings. Maybe as Mattie saw it, she had simply landed a good job in a household where she could feel genuine affection for her employer and her charges. Or maybe she would have comfortably felt yes and no—she was clear-eyed and worldly enough for that. People in her situation learn to be, of necessity.

We did not, as ordinary friends do, go to the movies or arrange to meet on the week ends, but we did do what was ritualistic among friends in those days, which was to get high together, though we did it inadvertently: on a patent medicine aptly named Cope, advertised to relieve what was euphemistically called premenstrual tension—the periodic inability to Cope. I was home that afternoon, wandering around fretfully, and announced I would give Cope a try. "Let me have some too, would you," said Mattie. "I have the same thing." We popped a couple of Copes, sat around in the kitchen, and within twenty minutes were buoyant with hilarity, floating above our chairs, light and loose and dreamy. No one cooked dinner that day, or did any dirty dishes, only laughed and floated, the neglected children watching in wonder. "This stuff sure does work," Mattie remarked with a throaty laugh, as we sat at the table giggling and telling raunchy anecdotes and sipping tea. When it began wearing off we were a bit flustered at its power. Maybe we should take it one at a time, at least when the kids were around.

Besides the fact that she was my paid employee with all the attendant uneasy nuances, there was something more bothersome, almost shameful, about our friendship, and this was that she persisted in calling me Ms. Schwartz while I called her Mattie. We had started off this way, unthinking, and though I quickly asked her to call me Lynne once I had an inkling of how things would be between us, she never did. (I partly blame Mrs. Zimmerman for this.) I asked her several times, but she would only nod and look uncomfortable and end up calling me nothing at all, so I gave up.

To make matters worse, Mattie had begun working a couple of mornings a week, while the kids were in school, for a friend of mine downstairs, who also had two young children. Since our kids played together, Mattie had often had to deal with Dale, and since the kids and I called her Dale, Mattie did too. Now that Dale had begun employing Mattie, it galled me that they were on a first-name basis, especially as they were not friends, which I well knew from Mattie's detailed reports. It seemed inconsistent at the very least, even unjust. I mentioned it to Dale, a rather imperious person with a strong will, who said, "Yes, well, when she started working she suddenly switched to Ms. Lambert. But every time she said it I stopped short, stared at her, and repeated loudly, '*Dale!*' until I got it through her head."

"Mattie," I confronted her. "You call Dale Dale. So . . . ?" "Uh-huh," she grunted, and got busy with something. I had a pretty powerful will too, but I could not force Mattie to call me something she didn't want to call me. I couldn't stop and stare every time she said Ms. Schwartz, and say firmly, Lynne, until she succumbed. It would feel like appropriating her as part of the family; it would be worse than her calling me Ms. Schwartz.

Much as she loved and depended on Charles, whom she spoke of and cared for as though he were a large child, buying his clothes, speaking for him, whipping up delicacies and fixing his plate, Mattie fell into frequent conversation and soon flirtation with a cop pounding the beat in our neighborhood. She would run into him coming to and from work, going to the park, taking the kids to school. At first they merely passed the time of day, and then it became clear he was keeping an eye out for her. As their talk gradually slipped into a kind of teasing banter, she gave me periodic progress reports: it soon reached the point where the cop was urging her to meet him somewhere, indoors.

"Well, are you going to do it?" I asked. "I don't know, maybe." But nothing much happened. "Did you see him today?" I'd ask when I got home. Yes, in the park, or near the bus stop, and she would recount their conversation. Things moved at such an imperceptible pace that I was convinced the affair was going nowhere and stopped asking. One day when I returned from work she sat me down at the dining-room table while the kids were in another room. From her gravity I assumed she was about to relate some troubling incident—maybe the girls had quarreled and she had had to adjudicate, or one of the mothers in the cooperative nursery school had looked at her sideways, for she was sensitive to every shade of behavior and there were several mothers whom she judged were "not stitched together too tight."

Instead she said, "Well, I went to the hotel with him." "You did? So what happened?" She wouldn't say right away but kept up the suspense with her hemming and hawing, had me itching with anticipation. "So we got undressed and laid down." She paused. "So?" "So that was it." "What do you mean, that was it?" "There was nothing there," she said. "It was like a pencil." "A pencil?" "A pencil, I'm telling you." It was like a re-enactment of the Cope episode, but without Cope this time. "You mean small," I said. "I'm not talking 'bout small. Small's not the issue here," she said with haughty indignation. "I said a pencil." It seemed the cop had not developed properly, had had some illness or injury that left him physically like a young boy. "So what did you do?" "I said to him, You drag me all the way up here for *this*! I swear, what some mens won't do."

This was her foray into infidelity, and I suspected she was glad it turned out as it did. For weeks after, all she had to do was mutter, "Like a pencil," to set us tittering like adolescents. All the same, here was another bad-faith trap, like a little patch of quicksand in a cheerful stretch of meadow: I knew that had anything similar happened in my own life I would not have told Mattie. I could not have given her that power over me, while her information, in my hands, was no power at all.

One day Mattie came to work limping in pain: a woman on the crowded bus had stepped on her little toe, crushing it. She went to the doctor and continued to complain about the toe for a long time—excessively, it seemed to me, for a toe and a little one, at that. I didn't know then what she knew all too well—the many and dire ramifications of diabetes: a common one is the danger of gangrene. In the end, Mattie had to go to the hospital to have the toe amputated. Though she wasn't as naively incredulous as I, she couldn't quite get over the nonchalant malice of fate: that some stranger's misstep could have such a grotesque result. We went to visit her in the hospital, which happened to be in Brooklyn and quite near where I had

77

grown up, next door to the people with a maid just like one of the family.

Soon she returned to work. Knowing Mattie, I figured she would want to show me her toe, or the place her toe had been, and I dreaded it. When she did, I held my breath as she slowly removed her shoe, prolonging the action, I was sure, for dramatic suspense. But it wasn't so bad—the little toe wasn't there, that was all. The foot didn't look deformed; it merely had a longer arc ending at the fourth toe. From then on she wore closed shoes—for safety, not vanity. I could not foresee, as perhaps Mattie did, that the lost toe would be the first of a series of side effects of diabetes, coming to plague her.

When the children were about five and eight Mattie mentioned now and then that Charles was talking vaguely of moving to Los Angeles, where he had family and thought he might find a better job. She was determined not to go and swore she'd refuse if it came to an actual decision, but I saw she was worried. She loved New York—as Charles did not—and liked her apartment, liked being near her sisters and her friends, liked her job, and loved the children. She couldn't possibly leave them, she said. But I knew she could; of course she'd go with Charles if it came to that. Still, to myself I tried to dismiss it as idle talk—who, in the course of a bleak New York winter, has not had fantasies of moving to California?

She talked more often of the possible move—first it was maybe, then someday, then some time next year. The talk became specific: Charles's mother and stepfather were there, as well as a married sister. They had a job lined up for him in a Ford assembly plant.

Much as I tried to ignore the inevitable, it was upon us in no time at all. Mattie was very depressed over the move. She didn't like California, she said, and it did no good to point out she had never been there. I have completely forgotten her last few days. Repressed them, I suppose. One morning, despite all her vows to the contrary, she was gone. Ten o'clock came—her hour—and I was alone. It was almost four years that she had been helping me raise the children. I have no memory of how they responded, whether they were deeply upset or only mildly so. I have no memory of any good-byes. We promised to keep in touch, that I remember.

The girls were about five and a half and nine now. I was teaching and writing a novel. Reluctantly, I looked around for another housekeeper and found a Haitian woman who seemed able and good-natured. The children liked her well enough; she was not Mattie, needless to say, but they no longer required a mother around constantly—they were in school all day, had their friends, the beginnings of independent lives. The new woman did her job but was hardly enthusiastic about it. I reminded myself that I wouldn't be enthusiastic about taking care of someone else's household either—Mattie was an exception.

For several days in a row I came home to find the new woman sitting at the kitchen table with her head in her hands. I asked what was the matter and she said, Oh, nothing. The children, when I asked, said she habitually sat that way when the housework was done. I felt sorry for her, but apart from being sympathetic, I couldn't help her—we were not friends—and I equally couldn't bear thinking of the children home alone with a despairing stranger sitting at the kitchen table with her head in her hands. Probably it hinted at what I might have become had I not found Mattie. I asked her to leave.

I never hired another cleaning woman. At that point I could manage on my own, with my husband's "help," a bitter word for working women. Over the years that followed, it would have made life considerably easier to have someone take over a goodly portion of the household tasks, but I could never get around to hiring anyone. I said it was my old principles about having servants, but that was a pretty transparent excuse.

We kept in touch. Mattie and Charles settled in one of the towns clustered around Los Angeles, and though she kept saying, over the phone, that she didn't like California, things seemed to be working out all right. Charles had his new job, they had a small house with a yard, and Mattie found work as a chambermaid in a hotel, where very soon she was promoted to head chambermaid. Still she complained, vigorously at first, weakly later. Like me, she had a complaining streak, and it showed most strongly in new situations and in adversity. To begin with, she wasn't crazy about Charles's family; back in the Bronx they had been surrounded by her family, whom she much preferred. And the house was in an all-black area—she liked New York, where there was a great mix of people, she said, and you didn't feel so insulated or segregated. She had come up from Alabama partly to get away from that sense of separateness. Her job was all right but she missed the children painfully. I would call them to the phone for long conversations about school and games and friends and whatnot. She wrote them a few brief letters—correspondence was clearly not her medium, physical presence was—and they wrote back.

One thing I accomplished through her absence was persuading her to call me Lynne and not Ms. Schwartz. "You're not working for me any more, okay? Will you do it, do me a favor, once and for all?" So she did, over the phone. She'd call and say, "Hello, Lynne?" But she never sounded happy saying it, and I felt some remorse for, perhaps, forcing her.

Little by little things began to be not all right for Mattie. Charles had frequent lay-offs at the plant and finally lost his job and spent a long period out of work. There were petty quarrels with his family. Worst of all, the diabetes began to torment her—minor symptoms at the beginning, and then she had to go to the hospital several times for kidney problems. Her eyes began to get bad, until soon she had to give up her job at the hotel. A year or two went by. The girls had to write their letters in large block print. Mattie wanted a job working with children but was afraid she couldn't manage it—her eyes were so bad she could hardly see.

Charles found another job, eventually. Though Mattie still managed to take care of the house, she said, she didn't feel well at all. They got a dog so she could have company, alone at home all day. She didn't like the neighbors. She still didn't like California. Then there were money problems—the ever more frequent hospital bills were ruining them. It took me longer than it should have to realize what I must do. Because of my old notion of respect, of not patronizing her precisely because she was an employee—though she wasn't my employee any more—I hadn't thought immediately of money. Had she been an ordinary friend, a friend in the untrammeled sense of the word, I would have thought of it sooner. I asked if I should send some. She said, "Yes, that would surely be very good," in her faintly ironic way, as if to say, why didn't I think of that earlier.

One day Mattie announced over the phone that she was coming East for a visit, at long last. We were both very excited and arranged to meet at Thelma's apartment, where she would be staying. She couldn't wait to see the children. Even though they were too old by now to be brought for display—about nine and twelve—I was determined to do so anyway. But it wasn't necessary to drag them. They hadn't seen Mattie in four years and were eager to go. They knew she was sick and blind, and I took pains to explain that she might look different, so they wouldn't be shocked.

In Thelma's apartment, also neatly furnished and carpeted, we found Mattie sitting in an armchair like someone who didn't move about very much. She had never been one to move breezily, but now she seemed attached to the chair. Beside her sat her mother, Miss Lucy, visiting from Alabama, a slight, docile-seeming old lady who said very little. She was dressed in a narrow, prim flowered dress, and it seemed incredible that she should have borne such large, luxuriant daughters. We were not shocked at Mattie's appearance. Apart from her stillness, she looked almost the same, though heavier. I was relieved. I had tried to prepare the children, but no one could prepare me. She couldn't see, but she ran her hands over the girls and talked to them. It was tearful and awkward. They still loved her, but hadn't seen her in so long that they didn't know exactly what to say—their conversation had been rooted in dailiness, not generalities and certainly not pleasantries. They told her about school, brought her up to date on friends she'd known. Mostly Mattie sensed what they had become. Thelma called Mattie Sister, as she had always done; even Miss Lucy called her Sister. It was not a satisfying visit for me, maybe because there were so many people in the small room and we couldn't swap stories or gossip and laugh as we used to.

Back in Los Angeles, she spent long periods in the hospital; I wouldn't hear from her for months at a stretch, and no one answered when I phoned. During those silences I would call Thelma for information, to learn invariably that Mattie was in the hospital again. When she got out she would call, her voice sounding thinner and more subdued each time. Her mother, Miss Lucy, died, and besides the sense of loss, she had all the mixed feelings that go with losing someone you have loved and resented for decades, who has loved and resented you as well. She told me her niece, a daughter of the brother down South, who had just finished training as a nurse, was coming out to stay and take care of her. She couldn't be left alone all day. I was glad Mattie would have the niece for company, but alarmed that she needed her. She was also getting upsetting crank phone calls and suspected various acquaintances. There were troubles between her and Charles because of her illness. He was still *good* and looked after her, but it was hard on him, she said; he couldn't help feeling frustrated sometimes. She couldn't cook for him any more, or fix his plate, the greatest indignity.

Feeling frustrated myself, I sent more money. The unfairness of things brought me down. That was one of Mattie's expressions— things would "bring her down," and now I knew how she meant it. When my life had been crumbling around me, she had appeared so I could put myself back together, but there was nothing I could do against diabetes, no more than against the army of inequities which sent us to lead our lives in such different, distant territories.

I didn't hear from her for a long time and got no answer when I called. I tried every couple of weeks, knowing it would be useless— only the formality of dialing. I put my thoughts of her to one side in an attitude of half-acknowledged waiting, almost glad to have no news. When many silent months went by, I even tried to imagine it might all miraculously be coming right: she was thriving, as in our younger days, and hadn't a spare moment to call.

One afternoon the phone rang and the voice announced, "It's Thelma." She had never called me before. I was surprised just for an infinitely small instant. I didn't need to hear the words.

"Sister died," she said.

Sister died.

It seems strange to me now that I didn't tell anyone for quite a while, not the children, or my husband, or Dale downstairs. But at the time, I think I wanted to cling to the loss all alone, to embrace it in private and give it full weight before it became a public fact. All the more so as there was nothing I could do, not even a funeral I could attend, where grief becomes the great cathartic leveler, for tears are all alike, untinged by class or race or social role. I did write a brief note to Charles, which helped neither me nor, probably, him.

The great majority of losses can be weighed fairly accurately; you can locate the gap in your life, probe and measure its depth and breadth. I could never even locate her properly when she was alive. She haunts me because I cannot place her still; she falls in no easy category, or has a shifting place in several—family, friend, person defined by function or need. Her memory will not be pinned down, will not rest, is pervasive. She was more important than she was supposed to be, more than I bargained for when first we struck our bargain. What was clumsy between us crystallizes, now, all that is wrong with our human arrangements in this place, in this time, and what was good mirrors the strivings of the heart, pushing against the meanness of barriers to rise into a pure clarity.

Rags and Tags and Velvet Gowns

Hark, hark, the dogs do bark,
The beggars are coming to town

A F A M I L Y legend: the Bowery, early 1950s. A man comes up to my father and asks for money for something to eat. What most Bowery beggars really want is a drink, my father knows. But food is healthier. "Okay, come on with me. You're hungry, I'll buy you lunch." They go into a restaurant and have lunch together.

For a long time I found the story touching, as I was intended to do: how generous my father was with time, money, wisdom. I could hear his spontaneous, snappy voice—for his voice could be like the snapping of a finger, cheery or threatening depending on the circumstances—"Come on, then, I'll buy you lunch"—and picture the swift, peremptory jerk of his head in the direction of the nearest restaurant, a simple but decent place. How gallantly he led the beggar to a table, appropriating the two enormous illustrated menus coated in plastic and handing him one: "Anything you like," rather grandly. Did the beggar order a substantial meal, steaming pot roast nestled in long-simmered carrots and onions, or something more austere, like an egg salad sandwich? The legend didn't say whether it was summer or winter, which might have made a difference.

Knowing my father, I assumed they did not eat in silence. Was the beggar gregarious, eager to tell his tale of adversity, or taciturn? The tone of the legend allowed only for his being humbly grateful, but perhaps he was choked with resentment, so choked he could barely swallow and nudged the food around on his plate as the bile rose in his gut. Did my father use the opportunity to expound on his political views as he liked to do, making provocative statements, raising his voice and blood pressure, which he also liked to do? And did the beggar offer counter-assertions or simply listen, paying for the meal with his only abundant possession, his endurance? Finally, did my father dab nattily at his mustache and, rising from the table, toss his napkin onto the plate and declare, "No offense meant. All for the sake of argument," somewhat puzzled at why the beggar seemed less than delighted to be harangued? Was there a handshake, as between gentlemen, or did the beggar grunt his thanks and turn away with sullen relief? Most important, did they like each other, or was liking beside the point? Could that ever be beside the point, even among grown men? Alas, the story was never told as I would have liked to hear it, with each nuance of gesture and dialogue, setting and timing, the shifting underpinnings of emotion and small stirrings of heart and mind as revealed in the face and voice, all of which, to me, *were* the story, as opposed to bare events. Still it was a good story.

Until many years later, that is, when I told it to my friend A. as we reminisced about families. She was aghast. The story exhibited the worst kind of political condescension, she informed me heatedly. Giving was my father's free choice, but how to spend the money was the beggar's choice. Otherwise giving is an abuse of power. An ego trip.

A. had ruined my moment of nostalgia, and I was stunned. For she was right, of course. Yet wasn't my father right too, in the context of his life and times? His own scramble for success had demonstrated that he knew what was best; doing good, by his lights, was scattering abroad his earned knowledge. How could I scorn him when I myself would not have volunteered to spend an hour with a probably un-appealing stranger? True, A. might have done that. She would have taken him to a bar, I thought bitterly.

Long after my father's episode I happened to see, from a third-floor window, another lunch given away on the Bowery. A be-draggled grizzled man shuffled northward across steamy Delancey Street as a young black woman wearing shorts and a halter and bit-ing into a frankfurter crossed in the opposite direction. When they met in the middle he held out his hand, palm up. Barely breaking stride, for the light was changing and four lanes of impatient traffic would instantly engulf them, she handed him the half-eaten frank-furter. Between the north and south corners of Delancey Street the frankfurter passed from one pair of lips to another, as the milk from Rose of Sharon's breast passed to the lips of the dying man in *The Grapes of Wrath*.

Nowadays the city streets are thick with beggars, and people of my father's virtuous persuasion could take a beggar to lunch every day, ten times a day, incensing the politically correct. Or, in keeping with current "lite" aesthetics, they might follow B.'s strategy: weary of beggars asking for money for food, she has taken to fixing daily packets of sandwiches before leaving the house—whatever she herself is having for lunch—and hands out her neatly wrapped tinfoil squares to whoever asks. "What's in it today?" one of her regulars inquired. "Peanut butter and jelly." He scowled, hesitated, but in the end accepted it indulgently, as if she were the beggar, asking to be relieved of the burden of good fortune.

With roles so much more fluid than in the 1950s, askers and givers do change places with the swiftness of partners in a square dance. As the numbers of beggars increased, C., like B., came to loathe the discomfort and impotence of his assigned role. No more awkward doling out useless quarters and half-dollars, he decided. He would give a significant sum every couple of weeks, rather like paying a bill, a sum that might make a real, if temporary, difference in a beggar's life. No classbound judgments, either: he wouldn't choose the apparently deserving or speculate on how the money might be used. A gratuitous act, a declaration of freedom from the powers above and below that make for beggardom. The first time he tried it, the beggar looked at the bill handed to him, then up at C. "But this is twenty dollars." "Yes, I know," said C. "Hey, this is terrific! Come on, I'll take you to lunch."

Some hold that begging is a job, not one which anyone would aspire to, but one which a share of the population regularly does, through family tradition, lack of drive or opportunity, possibly even natural talent. George Orwell takes this approach in *Down and Out in Paris and London*:

There is no *essential* difference between a beggar's livelihood and that of numberless respectable people. Beggars do not work, it is said; but then, what is *work*? A navvy works by swinging a pick. An accountant works by adding up figures. A beggar works by standing out of doors in all weathers and getting varicose veins, chronic bronchitis, etc. It is a trade like any other; quite useless of course—but, then, many reputable trades are quite useless. . . . A beggar . . . has not, more than most modern people, sold his honour; he has merely made the mistake of choosing a trade at which it is impossible to grow rich.

Here in these United States, for historical reasons, begging will never be a career track, nor am I suggesting it should. For one thing, the pursuit of happiness works as an injunction as well as a right, and part of the pursuit is ambition, labor, and sweat. Also, there is the famous liberal guilt at being privileged in a supposedly classless society. Above all, our horror is attached to a certain pride: we are enlightened enough to be horrified at beggary, if not enough to do anything significant about it.

My mother told sentimental stories of the old days before the first World War, when hoboes turning up on her parents' doorstep in Brooklyn were given lunch in exchange for sweeping the yard or hauling the garbage. A fairly clear and guilt-free transaction, compared to begging and giving. Today few city people are at home to offer lunch—they are out doing what Orwell so disparagingly calls "work"—and those who are would hardly open their doors to a stranger.

Today's beggars baffle us. The working poor are familiar. We have been told they are always with us, a state of affairs many find comforting, a reminder of what they are not. Also a reminder of certain virtues once quaintly associated with the poor—resignation, diligence, humility—as if along with the burden of poverty, the poor could cheerfully keep those difficult virtues alive for us. (Of course the actual poor, not the apocryphal, would prefer money to the odor of sanctity.) The beggars, though, are something else—have-nothings as opposed to have-nots—and they haven't always been with us, not lining the streets, at any rate, in such a vast and variegated array: from bedraggled to shabbily genteel to casually hip; sick or drugged-out to robust; pathetic to genial to arrogant. Why they are with us is no mystery: jobs are scarce, drugs rampant, education poor; when low-cost housing was eliminated from the Federal budget under Richard Nixon, it was predictable that a couple of decades would generate thousands of homeless people. (Though their numbers overlap, not all beggars are homeless nor all homeless people beggars.)

To confuse matters further, not all beggars view their situations in an Orwellian light, as my friend D.'s experience illustrates. D. is the opposite of shy. She can say virtually anything to anybody with impunity. She marches up to the regular on her street corner, with whom she has friendly relations, and asks in her warm, brusque manner, "Look here, why can't a healthy strapping young man like you get a job?" He tells her about the sad state of the job market and how demoralizing it is to be turned away. "Look here," says D., undaunted, very like my father in her certainty of what is right and her eagerness to disseminate the knowledge, "Everyone and his brother has had bad luck with jobs. You win some, you lose some. You've got to get back in there and keep trying." And so the conversation goes. Enduring it is how the beggar earns his keep. When he feels he has put in enough time for the money, he says to D., "Look here, I'll decide when the vacation is over."

Like any new social phenomenon, the beggars become an index by which we read our state of affairs. Through them, or rather through reading the spectrum of our response, we locate who we are. We range from open-handed A., who sets staunchly forth each day with a pocketful of change and gives democratically to all—"If they're desperate enough to ask, why then . . ."—to otherwise kindly Z., who never gives because she suspects every beggar is making a fool of her. To give, she feels, is to be taken.

In themselves, A. and Z. do not represent extremes of generosity and meanness, or of wealth and poverty. A. may have more money, but Z. is far from destitute. Nor is she stingy and insensitive; a therapist working in a social agency, she gives at the office, as it were. What can be read from their actions is something beyond degrees of generosity or attitudes towards private property; it is their degree of suspiciousness of the world and safety in it, their reflexive response to the unexpected and unwelcome. Maybe their whole psychic structure, had we enough data.

Coming out of my building, I recognized a familiar beggar approaching, a tall slender woebegone man with watery eyes, graying hair and neat gray clothes, who worked a four-block area slightly to the south. Immediately came the usual and tedious chain of thoughts. Do I have any change? Where is it? Do I feel like it today? How am I today anyway, that is, how firm is my place in the world? The unsettling thing about beggars is that unless we have a very thick skin or, like A. and Z., a strict policy, their presence compels these questions dozens of times a day. Like public clocks that force compulsives to check their watches, beggars make us mechanically, half-consciously check the inner dials of plenitude or neediness, well-being or instability. The readings determine whether and what we give.

In the midst of my reckonings, the man passed me by without even an acknowledgement. Imagine! Like one of those gnawing slights from a person met at a party—I remember him but he doesn't re-member me. I was just another client, one of hundreds a day. He didn't solicit because he wasn't yet at work. Why assume begging is a twenty-four-hour-a-day job any more than plumbing or typing? Any more an identity than grocer or engineer? Maybe I assume it because quite a few beggars in mufti—spiffy, sprightly—stroll past and say good morning so graciously that I'm moved to answer in kind even though this is New York City. At which point, my atten-tion snagged, comes the touch—a mutual joke at my expense: ha, ha, and you thought I was only being friendly.

> *Some in rags and some in tags*
> *And some in velvet gowns.*

In New York City, our attitudes towards the beggars have fol-lowed an unsurprising trajectory. It didn't begin, this age of beggary, on an appointed day, the way Errol Flynn in an old movie announced with a flourish of his sword the opening thrust of the Thirty Years War, but sneaked up in the early 1980s, around the time when the cult of money became highly respectable and the eating of designer food in pretentious restaurants was elevated to an aesthetic experi-ence. At first everyone was appalled. Not here; this wasn't Calcutta, after all. There was sympathy, naturally, of the innocent, slightly shrinking variety. And curiosity. New street phenomena always in-trigue city-dwellers—jugglers, break dancers, used-book peddlers, Hare Krishnas with their bald pates and tambourines. We stared un-easily, clucked somberly, catalogued: young, old, black, white, male, female. Sickly and strong. Addicts? Hard to tell. In rags and tags and velvet gowns.

Well-meaning people opened conversations with, "I had this strange [substitute absurd, weird, hilarious, upsetting] encounter with a beggar on my way over." The talk was that particular form of gossip about people one doesn't know, like gossip about celebri-ties, where from dubious shreds of data we envision their impossible, fantastic lives through the mild prism of our own.

The subways became our theatres—not off- but sub-Broadway. We compared performances, whipped up impromptu reviews. Have you seen the one in overalls who says he's not really a beggar but an unemployed carpenter with five hungry children? The one with no shirt who's a Vietnam vet waiting for his disability claim to be settled? The woman with orange hair who says she has a baby dying of AIDS: she looks about forty-five but anything is possible. The one who needs money for infant formula that the hospital down the block won't give him? The one who asks the entire car to pardon how he smells because he has no place to take a shower?

Performance art. Like stand-up comics, the beggars must display uniqueness of personality in a few swift, arresting strokes, for here in the city, claims on our attention are many and dazzling. We have seen plenty and have high standards; their stories require a certain narrative expertise. Verisimilitude aside, we treasure sheer inventiveness. As with any new art form, early samples ranged from the banal—"Lost in New York," for instance, was an overworked theme: where is Grand Central Station, and by the way a ticket back to Scarsdale is $5.45 and I've lost my wallet—to the memorable.

A justly renowned beggar works the festive nocturnal subway cars returning from Shea Stadium during the baseball season. He enters the car ominously bearing a tarnished trumpet blotched with ragged holes. He brings it to his lips; the sound that emerges is a Dantean assault. The passengers, fresh from their joy in the Mets, wince in pain, nonplussed. At last he mercifully lowers the trumpet and announces in a jovial, we're-all-in-this-together tone, "I'm not going to stop until you folks give me some money." A tense moment? Not at all. At once the crowd laughs, and gives. A good-humored crowd; they've paid for their baseball tickets and beer and hot dogs and subway ride; they'll shell out for peace too, and for a laugh. It's part of the price of the sportive outing, a kind of surtax. Everyone accepts it. By some mad urban alchemy it is acceptable to be assailed by this grotesque noise and have to pay to make it stop. He plays a few more measures, goading the recalcitrant, then moves on to the next car to repeat the performance, becoming part of the legend of the city, oh splendiferous city full of assaults and of relief, where you pay for both.

As the initial surprise wore off along with the entertainment value, as we got used to seeing beggars everywhere (but not for long, surely—whatever political glitch brought them out would soon be repaired), our interest became more defined. Refined. We found we have tastes in beggars as in everything else. E. will not give to those who look young and healthy, for why are they not out hustling for a living as he is? F. always gives to women because they seem more vulnerable, their lot harder to bear than men's. G. gives only outside his immediate neighborhood so as not to encourage beggars to congregate there, while H. will give no more than three times a day—after that it becomes a nuisance, and, fearful for her spiritual integrity, she does not wish to give out of irritation, only genuine sympathy. J. will not give to anyone who comes too close: she has strong feelings about her personal "space" being invaded. K. doesn't give because she is afraid to stop and take out her purse on the street: she views beggars and all passersby as potential thieves.

L. gives exclusively to those who ask humbly and politely: if he must be solicited and possibly "taken" (shades of Z.), he feels the beggars should at the very least make a pretense of a civil business transaction, to save face on both sides. Anyone loud or rude or claiming his contribution as if by right is out of luck. And if he is not thanked, he will not give the next time. M., on the contrary, prefers not to be thanked. It makes her feel guilty. "There, but for the grace of God . . . ," she murmurs. She will gladly engage in nongrateful repartee, though, while N., who also shuns gratitude, wants the briefest possible verbal exchange: he gives willingly but cannot stomach long-winded explanations or autobiography.

Quite unlike O., whose sense of the humane is offended by a bare financial transaction. He always says a few words with his donation and wants a few in return; he needs to act out an ordinary exchange between ordinary people, one of whom happens to be in straitened circumstances. P., an outlander who lived in New York for two years, went still further in the direction of the ordinary: he made friends with a local beggar, learned his story, chatted on the street, occasionally met him for coffee and introduced him around. Back home now, P. inquires after him and sends news through friends.

Q. refuses to give when pressured or manipulated, for instance when beggars obsequiously take on the role of doormen at the threshold of banks, a symbolic reminder: You have reason to enter a bank while I do not, and what is a bank but the stony emblem of what distinguishes us; or when beggars hover at subway token booths: You're riding, why shouldn't I? So much easier to hand over the change than put it back in your purse, isn't it? Hard to resist, and because the beggars make it hard, Q. resists.

R. can coolly resist dozens of dull pleas for change, but yields to the beggar who with grinning aplomb requests ten dollars for a steak dinner or five hundred for a trip to Hawaii. An epicure, he waits for a beggar worthy of his attentions, a beggar of kindred, subtle sensibility, an accomplice; then he can forget the mutual mortification.

With the passing of time, sympathy and selective appreciation edged off into frustration. We had given, we were giving, yet the beggars remained rooted to their posts, holding out the everlasting styrofoam cups. (S., in an expansive mood, dropped a quarter into the styrofoam cup of a ragged man on 34th Street and coffee splashed forth.) When we spoke of them, our tone was a bit distraught: apparently they weren't going to fade away gradually.

Just around that time, towards the close of the reign of real estate-friendly mayor Edward Koch, the heads of various city agencies cautioned the citizenry, through the offices of the *New York Times*, not to give to beggars: many of them used the money to buy crack, not broccoli or oat bran. (Fancy that.) Our handouts encouraged the drug trade, crime, and personal degeneration. Since we could not tell which beggars were addicts (they refused to help by wearing distinguishing labels such as a yellow star or a pink triangle), the better part of valor was restraint. Upright beggars should not beg but avail themselves of social services through official channels (a Brechtian suggestion, under the circumstances). This brand of morality emanating from City Hall went far beyond my father's ingenuous take-a-beggar-to-lunch policy. Liberal guilt was allayed. Hearts hardened with righteousness.

Meanwhile the beggars grew intemperate, which didn't help. No more meek charm and witty eccentricities. Their banter took on a hard edge. A nagging beggar trailed T. out of the 79th Street subway station for a block, until firm and direct, as is her manner, she announced, "Look, I'm having a really bad day. I'm not well, would you please leave me alone?" "Oh, I'm sorry," he replied. "Is there anything I can do?" "No, thanks. I'll be all right. Just let me alone." "Well, in that case can you give me a dollar sixty-five for a hamburger?" Caving in, T. fished around in her pockets and came up with sixty cents. "Here." He looked at it and said evenly, "But it's not enough."

Irritation set in. We had given and given, surely enough to expiate our comforts. Now could we have our streets back? As if we needed to give only to a certain point, as we need to give taxes or suffer unto the death. The beggars got aggressive—after all, they had been asking for as long as we had been giving. They implored, nagged, downright demanded. They hounded and pursued, sometimes menacing. They accepted small change grudgingly, muttering or even shouting their contempt, a form of blackmail, embarrassing us publicly as if we—we!—were the untouchables.

A sickly young beggar wrapped in a blanket in the Christopher Street subway station moaned his appeal. I had only a dime in change and no bills less than five dollars, but after stopping in front of him to rummage through my purse I couldn't simply walk away. Or so it seemed. I needed the five; a dime was better than nothing, wasn't it? A curious lapse for a one-time street kid. "You can keep your dime, lady," he shouted over the heads of the other passengers. Maybe he threw it back at me—I didn't turn to look. It would have cost me less to give the five.

In the end, the beggars became tiresome, like TV sitcoms. Their plots were always the same, leaning heavily on flashback and ending with the extended styrofoam cup. We got bored. We are bored. Soon came boredom's handmaiden: we are indifferent. A good deal of the time, at any rate. A few, like A., still give with a kind of moral fervor. Some try to renovate housing, others work in soup kitchens or give out used clothing. What no one can do is make the beggars disappear. They line the crazed streets, an unending funhouse mirror, confounding us, giving back our images *in extremis*, distorting our best instincts and bringing out our worst.

At startling moments they reflect us all too well. My friend U.'s strip of Broadway is a gathering place for beggars, among them a relentless badgerer. One day, in a vindictive mood, she walked along giving a pittance every few feet but bypassing this least favorite. He chased after her, yelling, "Hey, what about me? I'm a person too!" A cry from the soul. A universal truth that brought U. to a repentant halt. She turned, her hand already burrowing in the grit of her pocket, but the imploring face, the timbre of his plea resounding in her ears, sent a shudder of revulsion through her. That endless self-assertion, that merciless need: why, he was a replica of the inexhaustibly demanding husband she was on the point of leaving. She wheeled around and walked on.

Always a sucker for surface charm, I noticed I would give readily when I liked the beggar's looks and voice, male or female. A sucker for self-improvement as well, I now give equally when I am repelled. I give to the hollow-cheeked, prematurely gray man with a complexion the hue of old cheese; in front of a drugstore on upper Broadway, he chants an endless nasal litany: "Can you spare some change so I can get something to eat?," the opening words very clear, the last run together as if the eating part were an embarrassment, the "r" of "spare" razor-sharp—he must be from California, a long way from home. I hear him a block in advance and get the coins out so I don't have to linger; the sound twangs on like a harp string for a block after. I do not like to think of how he came to adopt this particular ritual or what it feels like to his throat muscles. I give the money fast, mechanically, without looking.

As I lugged my crammed shopping cart home over the cracked sidewalk, I was stopped by the woebegone man who had earlier failed to recognize me. My first thought was atavistic; it must have been my mother's stories about hoboes sweeping the porch in exchange for a hot lunch: If only he would offer to pull my cart home. Yes, by rights he *should*. Why not earn it with dignity for a change? But this is not 1910: the social contract has altered, as well as the connotations of "rights" and "earn" and "dignity." Whatever tasks I might need done were not his concern. If he noticed at all, chances are he resented my cornucopia on wheels. Or perhaps he prized his freedom from the banality of shopping carts, like the hoboes of legend. I gave him some coins and he drifted past—to the bar, the crack dealer, McDonald's, or his hungry family?—while I dragged the cart onward. We were farther apart than my grandmother and her pre-War vagrants, the distance becoming greater with each step: no common life, no basis for business, between us.

I think all the modes of giving, all the elaborate rationales, come down to two modes, the way art can be crudely divided into classic and romantic. We give from a feeling that the beggars are different from us, or that they are the same. The social critic Philip Slater has written that love of others is what we have left over when self-love has been satisfied. To give from a feeling of plenitude adds to our self-satisfaction. To give out of kinship is the more accurate feeling, though, as well as more raw and painful. I tend to give when feeling least in need, when the world has provided me with my share and maybe more. When I feel neglected, abused, invisible, unloved, and surly—rather like a beggar myself—I resist. What makes you think I'm any different from you? I want to say to the hand that holds the cup. That I have anything to spare, that I don't need help myself? I'm aware that my feelings are irrelevant to beggars—though theirs are not irrelevant to me, which makes for a deeper inequity and unease. They are not asking for my existential well-being but for my spare change, and while my well-being may vary from day to day, I always have change in my pocket. I can afford subtle distinctions. To the beggars, money is not metaphor.

Just as slavery imprisons masters as well as slaves, beggars beggar us. We are solicited and we solicit in turn, asking that their performance represent the world as we wish it to be, so that our place in it holds firm. We beg them not to jostle too noticeably the abstractions we have constituted in our heads and imprint on the physical matter around us. What we would most like to ask is the impossible, that they not be there, as perhaps they would like to ask for five hundred dollars for a trip to Hawaii (or that we not be there?).

Far more than in 1910, we can pick and choose our stimuli: sealed cars and sealed windows, suburbs, shopping malls, and retirement communities shut out the natural inevitabilities of weather, noise, dirt, chaos, and the technology of exclusion is hard at work on pain and death. But the beggars will simply not do as we wish; they will colonize even the central mall of Park Avenue, they will be truculent and flamboyant. And when they defy and deny our wishes, we sullenly withhold our aid. In turn, when we deny the full measure of their requests, they withhold their gratitude.

Our finely wrought distinctions shape a peculiar aesthetics of giving, fittingly traced on the urban mural of blank or battered faces. The pattern becomes a moral fever chart, as morality always underlies aesthetics. To read it is to know how tightly we need to clutch what we have and how much we can afford to loosen our grip without feeling destitute; what we ourselves feel entitled to, and how much we feel the entitlement of others falls on us to fulfill. It is to comprehend the nature of the distance between having and giving—how far apart those words that sound and look so alike, as if meant to be closely linked.

What is revealed most harshly are our pretenses about our work as the justification for our lives. Small wonder that we look at beggars with resentment: they appear to have opted out, gotten away with something, while we earn our bread by the sweat of our brow. And yet they certainly sweat, and also shiver, which confuses us. A paradox. Often we would like not to work either—there is more than a dash of envy in our tangled response—but we surely don't want to sweat quite so much. They outdo us in their ability to sweat and endure. We look again and imagine what kinds of beggars we would make, as we have idly imagined what kinds of politicians or pitchers or violinists we would make, and shudder at how grossly we would fall short. What a relief, then, how glad we are of our lives. The next instant brings a faint needling, as the beggars look back: But are we living right? Do our lives make sense? Any more than theirs? What do their lives say about our own? The worst suspicion, the one we must not look at too closely, is that our lives and theirs amount to more or less the same thing—breathing, sweating, waiting to die, only some far more comfortably than others. For then we would have to wonder, in more than a glancing way, why as a people we see no need to remedy this.

Either we are our brothers' keepers or we are not; the issue is simple. The government's answer has the virtue of being cruelly clear: it is no one's keeper but its own. Our individual answers are not exactly cruel, only ambiguous. Like aesthetics.

The Tapes as Theatre
(A Drama of Watergate, 1974)

The following piece is a response to the transcript of Richard Nixon's famed Watergate tapes (published in the *New York Times* in the spring of 1974), in which he and his closest aides discuss ways to handle the growing scandal. At the time, the "characters" referred to below were household names, recognizable even by initials. Readers unfamiliar with the cast need only know that they were all the President's (or P.'s) men, except of course for John Sirica, the Federal judge presiding over the case.

W I T H   O N L Y a ravaged script of the original performance at our disposal, it is premature to offer any sound literary assessment of the new and immensely popular drama of Watergate, *Tapes*. It is safe to say, however, that the work, treating a theme of political intrigue in modified Elizabethan fashion, and brilliantly improvised by an all-male cast, is extraordinary in scope, power, and originality. We can only hope that when the "inaudible" and "unintelligible" passages are restored by electronic equipment, the full beauty and coherence of the play—its *quidditas* or "whatness," as Joyce would say—will be revealed.

Drawing on a variety of rich sources, the drama is admittedly eclectic. Pirandello, naturally, comes first to mind. But *Tapes* goes daringly beyond Pirandello's innovations. Here are no mere six characters in domestic anguish seeking an author, but nearly a dozen powerful figures together creating a "scenario" in which each will play himself. Indeed each is simultaneously author and actor; each struggles with the painful knowledge that his script and performance will be limited by those of his fellow actors. We have, thus, a rare opportunity to observe the creative act in progress; the play within a play, so crucial in *Hamlet*, is no less effective in *Tapes*.

"I would like a scenario with regard to the presidential role," the character called the President, or P., states early on. Another, Dean, is no less assertive about his role: "I am a conduit." P. is concerned with staging:

> P: Now we got a plan
> On how we stage this damn thing in the first
> Stages. Ron's got it all worked out.

And W., a minor character, advises, somewhat belatedly, "This thing, Mr. President, in my judgment has to be played in steps."

The audience is spared none of the indecision so often endemic to the early phases of artistic conception. It seems that the team once projected the play within a play as a musical comedy. "P: And, he's [Dean's] going to give me some song and dance." Later P. says, "Let me ask you this, fellas, you want me on the television?" Questions of genre abound: "P: What is his [Wilson's] reaction to the whole damned thing? Comic tragedy of errors? H: He didn't characterize it." Uncertainty even over the cast of characters is expressed:

> P: I'm going to see him in the E.O.B.
> He said he had been up most of the night
> With Titus. Who is Titus?
> E: U.S. Attorney
> In the District.
> P: And what's the other fellow's name.
> E: Silbert.
> P: No, not Silbert.
> E: Glanzer.
> P: Petersen.

Mutual esthetic judgments are readily voiced. "E: He [Dean] brought in a lot of silly garbage." But Dean claims:

> I don't think
> I have lost my objectivity
> At all in this. Do you know why?
> (Unintelligible)

Ideas are developed cooperatively in antiphonal manner, reminiscent of operatic *recitativo*:

> P: Yeah. He says (unintelligible) take
> care of your kids.
> E: And I think Chuck's natural proclivities will
> P: Do everything
> E: Do anything we can possibly do.

An economy of style is apparent, often in stark words of one syllable:

> P: Magruder just caved, but it had to come.

It had to come, Bob. It was going to come.
H: Yes, I think so. I think it had to and should.

And over the entire scenario looms the enigmatic figure of one Sirica who, like Godot, never appears but against whose judgment all acts are measured. Even the powerful P. shows awe and despair at the prospect of confronting Sirica:

> Now Sirica's
> Got to see the point of this. My goodness,
> Because the point is Sirica's got
> To realize he's getting bigger fish.

Imagery, as always, is the vital key to the panic that, just as in Pinter's works, shivers below the drab surface of the action. The images of suppression have been widely noted—"putting your fingers in the leaks," "button it up as well as you can"—but one audacious reference has been overlooked. A protagonist's warning, "we have to keep the cap on the bottle," is an echo from the "Story of the Fisherman" in the *Arabian Nights*. When the fisherman pried open the cap of the yellow jug that came up in his net,

such thick smoke came out that he had to step back a pace or two. . . . When all the smoke was out of the jar it gathered itself together, and became a thick mass . . . a terrible-looking monster.

Images of food recall Shakespeare and the gourmand Elizabethans: Dean is the "hors d'oeuvre," Mitchell "the big enchilada," H. and E. "the big fish." H. comments, "We're in the soup," and E. refers to one character's coming up "with egg on his face." If P. fired everyone tainted by ugly Rumor, "the place would look like a piece of Swiss cheese." The "big enchilada," in a dubious metaphorical ragout, will be "thrown to the wolves," with far less ceremony than Brutus served up Caesar: "Let's carve him as a dish fit for the gods."

P. is far more concerned about his close colleagues, H. and E.: "the problem of you and John sort of being nibbled to death over a period of time," and he often expresses his gratitude to these noble men without whose aid the scenario would lose its savor. One thinks of Claudius and Gertrude:

> Thanks, Haldeman and gentle Ehrlichman.
> Thanks, Ehrlichman and gentle Haldeman.

But beyond bottles, "cans of worms," and food, the metaphor of water predominates, taking on Jungian breadth and drawing upon the unconscious shared heritage of the race. There are "undercurrents"; presidential aides will "get splashed with this"; "*E*: We are at kind of an ebb tide right now," but, P. observes, "Yeah, they'll get a full tide when they get to the Grand Jury." Nevertheless the original bug was "a dry hole," recalling Eliot's "Here is no water but only rock. . . . If there were the sound of water only." At last with a relief of tension comparable to Kurtz's "The horror! The horror!" P. brings out in all their *claritas* the fatal words: "Yelling. Watergate. Watergate. Tell us about Watergate." Later in a calmer mood P. restores the ironic tone of the play in a stunning deflation of this tempest in a teapot: "What was Watergate? A little bugging!"

A minor point that need only be mentioned in passing is the enhancement of the modern idiom by new and evocative verbs. A drama that extends the imaginative horizon, as *Tapes* does, is hardly required to do linguistic pioneering as well, but one must applaud the happy concurrence of thematic and technical novelty. "Deep six" and "stonewall" are verbs for which we had no previous equivalent. "It'll knock true," P. observes. And, "Now Ron, brainstorm that for us—" An illustration of "brainstorming" follows: "*Ziegler*: First of all, the way to do this, and I think we should do this, but the way to do this—the feeling that something is happening in town and you (inaudible)."

In last summer's justly hailed courtroom drama on the Watergate theme, Senator Sam Ervin, the principal actor, brought about illumination and catharsis by apt quotes from the Bible and folk legend, thus yoking the tale into the humanist tradition. This season's play, this "comic tragedy of errors," does the same, though to a lesser degree and, one might add, in a far less morally pretentious idiom.

E. I thought you were going to go with the Biblical conclusion that the guy who serves two masters but a—P. Yeah. E. He will hate one and love the other, but a (laughter). P. Yeah. (unintelligible) turn around and (unintelligible).

Allusion is made as well to the legend of Sherman Adams, with its Old Testament overtones. "P: . . . The poor guy—he sort of got— W: And he served him well. P: For seven years and that damned vicuna coat. Unfortunate thing."

All groundbreaking works receive their share of scorn from literary hatchet-men, and *Tapes* is no exception. The point especially chosen for vicious criticism in this case is an alleged lack of moral sense, a grossness of judgment by the actors in the meticulous preparation of their scenario. This line of reasoning ignores the very subtlety of the Pirandellian structure. The conscientious reader will surely discover those places where an unchallengeable morality erupts from the teasing ambiguities:

> *P*: So believe me, don't ever lie.
> *D*: The truth always emerges. It always does.
> *P*: Whether it is right and whether it is
> Wrong. Perhaps there are some gray areas.
> But you are right to get it out now.

Moreover, P.'s loyalty to his aides, almost to the point of self-sacrifice, is stressed:

> *S[trickler]*: But they are wonderful
> fellows.
> *P*: They are. They're great, fine Americans. And
> They tell the truth, too.
> *W*: Yes.
> *P*: I
> Can tell you one thing about your clients.
> They'll tell you the truth. They don't lie.
> *W*: Yes.

Tapes is a drama, then, rich in innuendo, fully partaking in those qualities which, after Henry James, Joyce, Eliot, and Beckett, we have come to recognize as distinctively modern. The Jamesian legacy, in particular, is one which the production cadre of *Tapes* has studied well. Witness the pregnant dialogue:

> *P*: A motive was
> Involved there huh?
> *K*: About the money?
> *P*: Yeah.
> *K*: You know
> *P*: If the money was raised
> *K*: If you plead guilty and he's guilty there's
> No crime committed.
> *P*: What's that?
> *K*: That's—I
> Don't know.

Occasionally the mask of sublety slips and a more poignant note is heard, hinting at the *angst* of the creative act: "*P*: I—I'm so sick of this thing—I want to get it done with and over, and I don't want to hear about it again."

For all their sometimes frivolous obscurity, however, their playful use of cliché, their bold deleted expletives, the authorial team of *Tapes* is keenly aware of political reality. Like Orwell before them, they have grasped the salient tone of political discourse, a "mixture of vagueness and sheer incompetence. . . . In our time," Orwell goes on, "political speech and writing are largely the defense of the indefensible."

Yet just as *Tapes* outdid Pirandello in structural ingenuity, it surpasses Orwell in moral vision. A new mode of personal relationships is depicted, in which the dominant motif is intentional deceit—self-concealment rather than self-revelation. The discovery of identity, for both the characters and the reader, is frustrated at every turn, until finally the protagonists are distinguishable only by their modes of lying. This is a development all serious future dramatists will have to grapple with.

In the end *Tapes* evolves into a drama not of "people whose zeal exceeded their judgment," but whose corruption exceeded their awareness. Eliot's prophetic lines come to mind: "We are the hollow men/ We are the stuffed men/ Leaning together/ Headpiece filled with straw. Alas! . . . Paralyzed force, gesture without motion." The multiple ironies of this uncommon work are best expressed in P.'s own words, uttered as he slyly forecasts public reaction: " 'Ho, ho, ho, here is something pretty bad.' "

On Being Taken by Tom Victor

Y O U   C O U L D   usually find Tom Victor, camera in hand or slung on his shoulder, darting about at a literary event, a reading or awards ceremony or publishing milestone. He would pause midflight to say an exuberant hello in his swift, smiling fashion, and then, as he slipped away—"Talk to you later!"—his face would change, and the sober, hermetic face of the man at work would show.

The secretive face intrigues me, the face of the man taking the measure of things. To see it again, I sometimes look at my pictures, the dozens of photographs he took, for they invoke him as much as they represent me. In every good artist's work the sensibility is immanent; in Tom's it is practically tangible, in the way the light sculpts the face.

I don't like having my picture taken. I am not one of those people who is "photogenic"; I don't even come out looking like anyone I care to acknowledge as myself. So I did not go to Tom Victor with enthusiasm. I was sent, for a book jacket, and apparently it was something of an honor, for he was one of the semi-official chroniclers of the brazen yet soulful world of books. Consciously or not, American readers know his work well; it is through his eyes that they see their writers.

You'll like him, I was told, everyone likes him—which made me immediately suspicious. (I didn't dare admit I was a trifle excited. And curious: I might even get a good picture out of the ordeal.) I called him first and suggested he come to my apartment—to get it over with quickly, for I imagined it would take fifteen or twenty minutes: set the stuff up, size me up, press the buttons. But I lived pretty far uptown, and Tom didn't want to haul his expensive equipment around the city. He urged me to come to his studio, which at that time was just south of Lincoln Center.

Very well, but how long would the session take? I had somewhere to go afterwards. That was hard to say, he replied, a couple of hours, maybe. The idea of being scrutinized so closely for so long filled me with dread, yet goaded that keen, obscure, semi-erotic anticipation. Since he sounded friendly and forthcoming, I risked a nervous question: what should I wear? Anything, he said, anything you like. Getting bolder and sillier, I said I had several possible get-ups, each showing me in a different way. Bring your costumes along, said Tom. Bring whatever you like, jewelry, things to fix your hair . . . Here was a man who knew about women, I thought, and who knew about vanity and anxiety, and accepted them with good cheer.

I went with my little bag of props, all set to impersonate my various selves. I found him to be small and dark and full of motion. He had a quick smile, an ingratiating voice and a midwestern accent, and I liked the way he lingered on the liquid consonants of my name. He moved like those great blue translucent flies we used to call darning needles, that skim along the water's surface speedily and unobtrusively. Tom was a slender shape skimming in total ease amidst large black mystifying paraphernalia with which he would do something to me. My part was to yield. I felt as you do when abandoning yourself to a dentist or hair stylist or make-up artist or psychiatrist, someone for whom you are raw material, who readies you for presentation to the world—a genre of experience I avoided as far as possible. But I was here for my work. I had to do it.

I barely remember the studio—my memories of it have been erased by or merged with memories of his later, better studio, farther downtown—but I know it was spacious and white and fairly empty except for the lights and cameras and photos of familiar faces on the walls. It seemed to take him forever to set things up, and as he did, he talked. Talked and talked. Funny, I thought, that he wasn't trying to "draw me out," which I'd expected. On a desk piled with books sat a telephone, which intruded frequently. Tom would dash over and, pacing about in small arcs, hastily say a few friendly, firm words of the No, I can't or Yes, I will variety, then resume where he had left off.

He talked about his family and his childhood in a small town in Michigan. No matter how many celebrated people he met, he said, or how often he saw his work in newspapers and magazines, he still felt like a small-town kid making his way in the big city. (Yet his telephone manner was distinctly urbane.) He mentioned a number of writers and poets he had photographed and told what they had been like; so many seemed to have become his friends that I was skeptical, for name-droppers can use the word "friend" rather loosely. But they had indeed become his friends, I found out later. And I found out why, when I saw how he had rendered their faces in the extraordinary collection, *Preferences: 51 American poets choose poems from their own work and from the past*, on which he collaborated with the poet and critic Richard Howard.

He talked about his various apprenticeships: years spent writing poetry, editing a literary magazine, and training as an actor at the Yale Drama School—though he later found acting too confining a discipline for his temperament. He also studied stage movement with the dancer and choreographer Pearl Lang, which led him to photograph dancers, a subtle task. A dance critic friend of mine saw in Tom's dance photos a curious quality of stillness.

I imagine he came to prize that stillness. It was perfect, in any event, for showing writers, maybe an even more subtle task. Unlike dancing, their act is undramatic, impossible to locate visually; the drama is within, a dilemma which suited Tom's gifts beautifully. He cared less for the outward act than the sensibility behind it, and its transformations: he knew all about that, about the way art happens, since it was his way too.

Meanwhile he kept on talking: about his work and the photographers he had learned from. August Sander, who had undertaken to document the faces of twentieth-century Germans, was one he revered; he showed me some of his photos. About books—poetry and fiction, particularly Katherine Anne Porter, the work and the woman herself, whom he had known and loved. He was a reader, which was rare in itself, many artists having little time for arts other than their own, and he made it a point to read the books of the writers he photographed. To my surprise, he had read mine, and since it was my first I was especially delighted.

By this time he had gotten to work—clicking, that is—though I know now he had been at work from the instant he opened the door. Soon I was talking quite a bit too, and more intimately than I generally do with strangers. How was he getting these anecdotes and memories out of me, these very private observations, attitudes, tastes? But I was having such a good time, moving about in the large space as he casually suggested, that I didn't draw back. Now and then I would change clothes or play with my hair, put it up, put it down, make it wild or austere. Very silly, no doubt, but he didn't seem to think so, which made it just fine. He understood the nature of every small change; he took me in all my guises.

And kept talking. His travels: Paris, where he had lived for a few years, and Greece, and Italy, where I had lived too. Health foods: he joked that if we ever had lunch he'd drag me to his favorite health food restaurant (which later on he did, full of half-serious apologies, recommending the soba noodles, "not so bad").

We must have talked for several hours, that first meeting, just as if he weren't clicking away all the while, a steady background of clicks, just as if we were making friends and finding all sorts of affinities, saying, Yes, yes, and Me too, every few moments. At some point he told me about an old girlfriend and showed me pictures he'd taken of her. "She's beautiful, isn't she? Women never think they're beautiful. They don't know how beautiful they are." Typical seducer's lines, aren't they? Couldn't be more calculated if they were a parody. Indeed, thinking it over later I grasped, as you always do later, that he must talk this way to everyone, fickle fellow.

Well, he had to. How else could he get it all out of us, men and women both, it didn't matter, sex, age, nothing mattered but the face and its play of spirit. Somehow, he had to find the means to induce the recalcitrant, impalpable thing out of hiding and at play in the lineaments of the face, to coax forth the mysteries of flesh and spirit and make them visible, incarnate. He was very good at it, a genius. He knew what the best seducers know: the trick is to talk. The trick is to give something. Not to coax or to wheedle, but to extend.

To link art and the erotic, in thinking of Tom's work, is inevitable. The process was, for him, a kind of love, both spiritual and exploitive in the highest sense: he could turn the love on, for his work. He didn't love his subjects, he loved the process, or rather, each subject as it took part in the process, which couldn't exist on its own. Of course he had to seduce, to fit himself so cleverly and naturally to our contours that we would stop guarding the borders. What he was asking of us was everything, yet in a sense nothing: none of the trappings of self, only what Borges has called "that kernel—. . . the central heart that deals not in words, traffics not with dreams and is untouched by time, by joy, by adversities."

Like so many other writers, I came away from an anticipated chore having had a lark instead, a kind of fantastic voyage behind the surface face. He led people to become, in his presence, the people they are in their best solitudes. No wonder everyone liked him. It happens he was indeed both good and charming, but that is not the point. If he hadn't been amiable by nature he would have learned to be, I am quite sure, as an obligation of his craft.

In the end, you didn't know how far you had gone till it was too late and you had shown him everything, given him exactly what he needed, the kernel. The pictures tell: I look at them and realize, my God, anyone would think we had spent the day in bed or something, they are that naked, I am that free, that present.

He died on February 7, 1989, still young, long before his work was completed. At the memorial service a few weeks later, many who got up to speak recalled his eyes. It is difficult, when describing eyes, not to fall into clichés—only a limited number of adjectives apply. His eyes were unusally black and velvety, as everyone said; glittering and warm and animated and intense were other words his friends used. But they were hard, too, almost metallic. The best thing about them was not what they gave but what they withheld. What was behind the velvet: a quality of vision that had nothing to do with amiability.

His eyes held his craft, and they were crafty eyes. When I caught him off guard (seldom), when the concentration outwitted the charm, I glimpsed their hardness—a cold formidable focusing, as if he were peering through me, which was unsettling. But I think he wasn't peering through me or any of us; he was not a portrait painter who spends hours, days, probing. He made his search quickly, like a raid, looking for the pictures we could become, imagining us as photographs—eventually, as part of his gallery, his life's work.

The hard thing screened by the eyes, the thing withheld, was the art. The scrutiny, the penetration, the sizing up, the shaping. The skill of the Zen archer so thoroughly at one with his craft that he can hit the target with eyes closed, taking inward aim, and at the spiritual peak of his skill hits not only the target but himself.

All of this, the unique part, he had to keep back. He was a truth-seeker, a truth-giver: the art was not warm or friendly but had truth's utter indifference. Even, in a way, love's utter indifference—he was indiscriminately loving to dozens of captured faces. But in the end, unlike habitual seducers, he kept nothing for himself except what was rightfully his, the work. He gave, in the end, the greatest gift, and the rarest. I look at his pictures—at my own faces—and find there what I know best in the world but never imagined I could see or hold in my hand.

STORIES

The Melting Pot

R I T A S U F F E R S from nightmares. This morning's: she is summoned from San Francisco to New York for her grandfather's funeral, where she causes a catastrophe. She enters the chapel with her Russian-born grandmother, Sonia, on her arm, she sees the sea of men and women segregated by a carpeted aisle—solid people, bearers of durable wisdom—and her legs become immovable weights. Everything in her hardens, refusing to move towards the women's side, where she belongs. Even her teeth harden. Sonia, a scrawny, vinegary woman in perpetual haste, tries to drag her along, but Rita cannot be moved. Suddenly from the closed coffin comes a choked, rising moan almost like a tune, the voice trying to break out in protest. Rita's grandmother gasps in horror, clutches her chest, and collapses. All the mourners look at Rita and gasp in unison, like the string section opening a great symphony. One by one, they topple over in shock, both sexes heaped together, mingling. Rita's teeth clench in the dream, biting the hands that fed her.

She wakes up and holds on to Sanjay, who grunts in his sleep. The nightmares dissipate more quickly when he is there. He is a very large, smooth man and she clings to him like a rock climber. In the limbo of waking she cannot even remember which house they are in, his or hers—for they are next-door neighbors, only a wall between them for six years. They live in similar narrow row houses with luscious little flower beds in front, on a sunny San Francisco street lined with eucalyptus trees.

Sanjay, a seeker of practical solutions, thinks the ideal solution to Rita's nightmares would be for them to marry. Why should they live on opposite sides of the wall, like those silly lovers of legend? They are not children, there are no watchful parents hindering them.

"One day soon it will strike you," he says now and then in a half-humorous, half-cajoling way, a man of many charms, "that it is the right thing to do. It won't happen when we are making love, but at a more trustworthy moment. Maybe after you have asked me for the fifth time to fix your dishwasher, or after I have consulted you for the ninth time on how some fourth cousin can satisfy the immigration authorities. Some very banal moment between us, and you'll suddenly know. You will want to belong to me forever."

Rita usually laughs. "You've seen too many Fred Astaire movies." But she is afraid. She doesn't want to belong to anyone forever. She has grown up watching that. And she is afraid she won't know how to fit herself in, fit with another life. She looks at their bodies, which do fit sleekly together. Parts of them are the very same color, side by side. The palms of his hands are the color of her thighs, his cheeks the color of her nipples. "What would our children be like?" she says lightly. "What would they call themselves?"

She is not really worried about possible children or what they would call themselves. She mentions it only to deflect his yearnings, because Sanjay has three children already, grown and married. The oldest, who has gone back to India to study his roots, is Rita's age, twenty-eight. It is only natural that Sanjay's fatherliness should appeal to her, a fatherless child—that and his size and bulk, his desire to possess and protect, his willingness to fix her dishwasher and to accept the silences during which she tries to extricate herself from her history. His willingness to accept her history itself. But marrying him seems so definitive.

Now she sits up, leaning on her elbows. The room is suffused with a pre-dawn tinge of lavender. It is Sanjay's house. Of course. There are the faint smells of cumin, coriander, anise—bitter and lush. They are strongest in the kitchen but waft through the other rooms as well. Sanjay's daughter comes two afternoons a week to cook for him. She was born right here on Russian Hill, but she cooks the way her mother did. She doesn't know that her father and Rita eat her food in bed. Sanjay cannot bring himself to tell his children he sleeps with the young woman next door, although he is ready to present her as his wife.

"Why do you let her do that?" Rita asked at the beginning, three years ago. "Doesn't she have enough to do, with the baby and all?"

"I don't ask her to. She insists, ever since her mother died. She's very old-fashioned." A soulful pause. "And she's such a good cook."

"What do you cook when you're alone?"

He made a wry face. "Hamburgers. Tuna fish."

Besides the lush smell, she sees it is Sanjay's house by the shadowy bulk of the large chest of drawers, the darkened sheen of the gilded mirror above it, the glint of the framed photograph of his wife on the chest. When Rita first came to his bedroom Sanjay used to turn the photograph to the wall. As a courtesy, she assumed, for he is a man of delicate feelings, of consummate discretion; but she wasn't sure if the courtesy was directed to her or to his late wife. Now, grown familiar and cozy, he sometimes forgets. Rita has always imagined that she reminds him of his wife, that he wants her because of a resemblance. With the picture facing front, perhaps they two are communing through her body.

Well, all right. Rita is used to being a link, endlessly malleable. She is used to reminding people of someone, and to being loved as a link to the true loved one. Even at work, she helps people locate their relatives, and at times she is present at the reunion and watches them embrace. When they finish embracing each other they often embrace her too, as the link. She helps them find ways to stay here. If they succeed in becoming citizens, then Rita is the bridge they pass over to their new identity.

"Immigration law!" Her grandfather, Sol, expected the worst when she started. "You'll see," he grumbled over the phone, wheezing long-distance. "You'll be always with those refugees, you'll wind up marrying one, you with your bleeding heart. And who knows where they come from, what they—"

"Enough already, Sol!" Sonia's rough voice in the background. "Enough!"

"Sometimes these people have to marry someone just to stay in this country," he explains to his granddaughter, the immigration lawyer. "They see a pretty young girl with a profession, what could be better?"

True enough. In three years Rita has had several tentative suggestions of marriage. But she tries to find those desperate souls a better way. She reminds them that they came here to be free, free, and that marriage to a stranger is no freedom. Besides, there is Sanjay.

Sanjay works all day in a laboratory, or la*bor*atory, as he calls it; he wants to cure hemophiliacs, bleeders. (Contrary to popular notion, hemophiliacs do not bleed more intensely than most people, only longer.) Sanjay knows almost all there is to know about genes and blood. Indeed, he has the exile's air of knowing all there is to know about everything. Yet he has been here for nearly thirty years, is a citizen, and, unlike Rita's jittery clients, seems very much at home. His face has taken on a West Coast transparency. His courtly speech is sprinkled with the local argot. Still, Rita suspects, even knowing all there is to know about her, he sees her as his entryway to the land of dreams. His bridge. His American girl.

Rita's present life is, in her grandfather's view, one of disobedience (like her nightmares), but as a small child she was quite obedient. She submitted when he found her costuming paper dolls in her bedroom on a Saturday afternoon and unhooked the scissors from her thumb and forefinger, reminding her that Jews do not cut on the Sabbath. Nor do they color in coloring books, trace pictures from magazines, turn on the lights, the toaster, the radio, or the television, use the phone, cook, sew, drive. . . . The way Sol explains it, they are defined by what they are forbidden. There are things they must not eat and not wear, not do and not utter. The most constricted people are the most holy, relieved from confronting the daily unknown with bare instinct, for happily, every conceivable pattern of human event and emotion was foreseen centuries ago and the script is at hand, in old books in an old tongue. She submitted. But she was allowed to read. *A Little Princess* was her favorite story, where the orphaned and hungry heroine is forced to live in a lonely freezing garret, until a kindly Indian gentleman feeds her and lights a fire in her room and finally rescues her altogether, restoring her to a life of abundance.

For the most holy people, the most holy season is fall, the most beautiful. Also the most allusive and most amenable to introspection, with its amber light, its sounds of leaves scuttling, brittle as death, on the pavement, its eerie chills at sundown, and its holidays calling for renewal, guilt, atonement, remembrance, hope, and pride, one after the other in breathless succession. It is the season to think over your past deeds and ask forgiveness of anyone you might have injured, for only after asking a fellow creature's forgiveness may you ask God's. God has a big book and keeps his accounts: Your fortunes in the year to come depend on your actions in the year just passed. (Karma, thinks Rita years later, when she knows Sanjay.) It is the season when Rita is required to get out of her jeans and beads and into a dress. Shoes instead of sneakers. Sweating great beads of boredom, resistance seeping from every pore to form a second skin beneath her proper clothing, she trails her grandfather to synagogue to sit with the women in the balcony (so as not to distract the men) and listen to him sing the prayers in a language she cannot understand.

Her grandmother the atheist also conforms, sits in the women's balcony behind a curtain and fasts on the Day of Atonement, and this not merely out of obedience, like Rita. Sonia finds her identity in opposition. She conforms in order to assert her difference in the New World, as in the Old World others asserted it for her, in the form of ostracism and pogroms. But within the family's little conforming circle she has to assert her difference too, and so while her husband is out at the synagogue she fixes herself a forbidden glass of tea. Her wiry body moves quickly around the kitchen, as if charged with electrical current. Snickering like a child, she raises the steaming glass by the rim and drinks, immensely pleased with her mischief, her high cheekbones gleaming.

"You might as well have a sandwich while you're at it," says Rita, at eleven years old not yet required to fast, to choose between her grandparents, obedience in bed with defiance.

A sandwich would be going too far. They destroy the evidence, wash and dry the glass and spoon and put them away; luckily he doesn't count the tea bags, hardly the province of a holy man.

What is the province of a holy man? God, of course. Wrong. Rules. Sanjay could have told her that. His family's rules fill at least as many books. Rita's grandfather loves rules, constrictions, whatever narrows the broad path of life and disciplines the meandering spirit for its own good. The lust to submit is his ruling passion. It is part of the covenant with God: Obey all the rules and you will be safe. Sol takes this literally. He seeks out arcane rules to obey and seizes upon them, appropriates them with the obsessiveness of a Don Juan appropriating new women. Nor is that enough; his passion requires that others obey them too. His wife. His granddaughter. For the family is the pillar of society. The family is the society. And if a member disobeys, strays too far beyond the pillars, he becomes an outcast. At risk in the wide world, the world of the others. "Them."

So Rita rarely hears him speak of God. And Sonia mentions God with contempt, as one would speak of the meanest enemy, too mean even to contend with. "What God says I'm not interested in!" she shouts bitterly when Sol nags her back onto the little path of submission. "I'm interested in what people do right here on earth!" Alone together, Sonia and Rita never tire of cataloguing the discrepancies between God's reputation and his manifest deeds. They, obey in their hearts? It is to laugh. And laugh they do, showing their perfect teeth, as enduring as rocks. Of course they are women, their minds fixed on the specific. Perhaps they cannot grasp the broader scheme of things.

"What would be sins?" Rita asks her grandfather, thinking of Sonia's tea.

He pats his soft paunch thoughtfully with both hands. "Lying to your grandparents. Thinking wicked thoughts. Being unkind to people."

This sounds fairly mild. She tries to enumerate her greater sins but can think of none that any God worthy of the name would take notice of. With a new assassination almost yearly, the portraits of the dead promptly appearing on the walls at school, can God care that she listens to the Supremes on a Saturday afternoon, she and the radio muffled under a blanket? She asks her grandmother about sins but Sonia waves her arm dismissively, an arc of contempt scything the air. Rita infers that God, rather than mortals, has a lot to answer for, though she doesn't know what in particular is on her grandmother's mind besides the general wretchedness abounding. Poor people ride to Washington on mules. Long-haired students in Chicago get beaten by police. Rita passes the time in the balcony constructing cases against God on their behalf. Her father was a lawyer, she has managed to glean; she invokes his help. The cases are very good, watertight, with evidence starting from Abraham; no, Abel. But no matter what the jury decides, God remains. That is his nature, she gathers, to be there watching and judging, always alert for a misstep, but not helping.

Light is coming in at the window, a Pacific coast autumn light, creamy, soft-edged. As it slides up his face, Sanjay wakes, and Rita tells him about her bad dream, for she cannot shake it. She tells him how in the dream her father's father, the most obedient servant of his Lord, is taken, even so. How his obedience did not shield him in the end, and how she, by her disobedience rooted in a certain juxtaposition of genes, causes a shocking event, rivaling the one that convulsed the family twenty-six years ago.

"Heredity," says Sanjay sleepily, "doesn't work that way. You make too much of it." He has exchanged the faith in karma for the science of genetics. And he wants to help. He wants her to turn around and live facing front. Odd, since he comes from a country imprisoned in history, while she is the young West Coast lawyer. Sometimes it seems they have changed places.

"And don't you make much of it? Don't you tell me you get glimpses of your father's face in the mirror when you shave, but with a peeled, American expression? I feel my mother when I brush my hair. In the texture of the hair."

"That's different. You can inherit hair but not destinies."

He sounds so sure. . . . "I think in the dream he was trying to sing. Did I ever tell you that my grandfather used to sing in the synagogue?"

"I thought your mother was the singer."

"Her too. That was a different kind of song. He ran the store all week, but on Saturday mornings he was a cantor, he led the prayers. Then when I was about seventeen, he had some minor surgery in his throat and he never sang again."

"Why, what happened?"

"Nothing. He was afraid."

"Of what?"

"Well that's exactly it. Something cosmic. That his head might burst, I don't know. It was just too risky. The absurd thing was, he had the operation to restore his voice. We never heard him sing again. So what do you make of a man who loves to sing and sings for the glory of God, then refuses to sing out of fear?"

"In his heart he still sings. He sings, Safe, safe." Sanjay composes a little tune on the word.

Rita smiles. "I thought immigrants always sang, Free, free."

"Not always. We"—he means his brother and himself, who came here to be educated and returned home only to visit—"we sing, Away, away. New, new." He yawns, and then, in a lower key, "Guilt, guilt."

All the indigenous American tunes, thinks Rita. But she is still smiling. He has a way of making heavy things feel lighter. He has a mild grace that buoys him through life. Maybe she should marry him after all. She is so malleable an American, she could become anyone with ease. And it would be a way to live; it would be safe, safe. She might even let her hair grow long and smooth it down with coconut oil, start frying wheat cakes and clarifying butter and stepping delicately down the hills of San Francisco as Sanjay's wife did, holding up her long skirts.

That was how Rita first saw them, the Indian gentleman and his wife. It was the day of her graduation from college, which her grandparents flew west to attend. Afterwards, she took them across the bay to San Francisco, to show them her new apartment. For she was staying on. Through a friend, she had found a summer job in a Spanish record store, and in the fall she would start law school.

While Sonia tore through the rooms like a high wind, Sol stood at the front window, holding the curtain to one side and peering out as though he were in a hostile country, a place you could get yourself killed. Though not much of a traveler, he had been here once before, briefly.

"Who are your neighbors?" he asks, gesturing with his chin.

"I don't know. Which ones?" Rita comes over to peer out too.

It is an Indian couple, the man tall and broad, with heavy eyebrows and longish hair, dressed impeccably, even a bit flamboyantly, in a light gray suit. Rita likes the suit and likes his walk, stately, meditative, achieving a look that is both scholarly and debonair. By his side is a slight woman in a green and gold sari, holding his arm. Her head is lowered, so Rita can barely see her face. She holds the sari up skillfully, climbing the hill.

"I guess they're an Indian couple."

"Indians?" Her grandfather's voice rises. Bows and arrows?

"From India. You know, Gandhi, Nehru, no eating cows. That's what the women wear."

"I know what India is. I read the papers too, Rita. I'm not as ignorant as you think."

"Sorry, Papa."

"How do they live? Nice?"

She shrugs. "I guess so."

"Yes. They're not the same as the colored."

"Oh, Papa, don't start."

The Indian couple is moving unusually slowly, their heads cast down. They look like a devoted pair; they walk in step, rhythmically. As they turn into the front yard next door, to the left, he swings the gate open for her.

Much later, when Rita tells Sanjay about the first time she saw him, he says they might have been coming from the doctor; it was the month when his wife had some tests. The tests said yes, but it would probably not get really bad till the end.

It is strange, Rita thinks now, that she was with her grandfather when she first saw Sanjay.

A scene from one of Rita's silences: Her great-uncle Peter, her grandfather's twin brother, is a philanthropic dentist—he fills the cavities of Orthodox Jewish orphans for free. Also he checks Rita's teeth. Her grandmother drives her to his office for a checkup every six months, on a Sunday morning. The tiny waiting room is crowded with old people—fifty years old at least; where are the orphans of legend? They wait in the little waiting room which smells of dental supplies—sweet, medicinal, like wintergreen—until all the paying customers have had their turns, which may take an entire Sunday morning. Rita and Sonia share many qualities of temperament, notably the impatience gene. They wait with difficulty. Though they like to talk, they find no solace in the small talk that accompanies waiting. They leaf through magazines, they go to the superbly clean bathroom smelling of mouthwash, they pace the tiny waiting room. Sonia, unable to be confined, goes out to walk around the block. Rita cannot take such liberties since it's her mouth waiting to be examined, and her uncle might take a notion to sneak her in between the creaky patients. Her grandmother walks fast, round and round the block; Rita imagines her tense, bony body crackling like November twigs. Sonia's short auburn hair is alive in the breeze, and her fierce mind works on the fabric of the past, ripping stitches, patching.

At last it is Rita's turn. Her great-uncle, bald and moon-faced, rotund in his sparkling white jacket, round-collared like a priest's, beckons, the outstretched hand making a swift fluttering motion, giving the impression that she has been dilatory, that she has kept him waiting. He greets her using a Hebrew name that no one ever uses. She feels he is talking to some invisible person in the room. "What a pretty complexion," he says, in a way that suggests perhaps it is not, a consoling way. And, "What strong white teeth!" In a stage whisper, over her head: "She must get those from her mother."

"I have strong white teeth too," Sonia says with savage energy. "When have you ever had to fix anything in my mouth?"

Sonia dislikes her brother-in-law passionately. All the dislike she cannot expend on her husband she transfers to his twin brother. Peter and Sol are cautious people, supremely timid in the face of life. Yet they came to the New World as infants and know only by hearsay what they escaped. Sonia, who came later, remembers, and finds their timidities an indulgence. Her family are extravagant-tempered Russians whom Russians never accepted as such, which is why they journeyed so far. Genetically defiant people with hyperactive brains, willful, angry, ebullient. Their bones snap, the veins in their temples throb. There is nothing they cannot feel passionate about, and so they lavish huge and frightful energies on life and live long, propelled by their exuberant indignation. Rita is fascinated by them and bored by her grandfather's docile family. She sees the two sides of the family as opposing teams, opposing stances towards life. When she is older she sees her grandparents in an incessant game of running bases: they throw the ball back and forth—the ball is truth, how to live—and she, Rita, must run between them, pulled now to the safety of rules and traditions, now back to the thrills of defiance and pride.

Once she is in the funny chair, Peter gives her avuncular rides up and down, chattering affectionately, almost too affectionately, as if he is trying extra hard. There are whispered words with her grandmother, exchanges Rita doesn't grasp except that Sonia wants none of his proffered commiseration. "You can't trust one of them, not one," he mumbles. "That's the way it is, that's the way it will always be."

"Shh, shh," Sonia hushes him in disgust. "Just do her teeth, no speeches." Sonia always sticks up for her; with crackling Sonia she is utterly safe.

"Such beautiful dark hair." He does seem to like her, in the brief time he has available. Yet he calls her by the wrong name, which you do not do to someone you like. That's not who I am, Rita wants to cry out, but there is something peculiar and mysterious about who she is that keeps her silent, open-mouthed like an idiot. She sometimes gets glimmerings of losses below the surface, like sunken jewels that divers plunge and grope for in vain. They might be memories of a different climate, or the feel of an embrace, or a voice, feelings so fleeting and intangible she can hardly call them memories. But they have been with her since she can remember—wispy vapors of another way she might once have been, another mode of feeling the world, as believers in reincarnation sense their past lives.

That's not who I am, she wants to cry out, but she can offer no more, she knows nothing more, and anyway he is all frothing joviality and patter, while his hands nimbly prepare the instruments. Rita is enthralled by the rows of false teeth lined up on the cabinet, pink gums and ivory teeth, the many different shapes waiting like orphans to be adopted, for mouths to come by and take them in, ready to be pressed into service chewing and forming the dental consonants. Unspoken words and stories are hiding in the teeth.

"So. Are you going to play Queen Esther this year?"

"No." She rinses and spits. "The teacher said I should be Vashti."

"Well, Vashti is good too. She was very beautiful."

"She gets killed in the beginning. I was Vashti last year."

"Finished?" asks Sonia impatiently.

Fortunately Rita's teeth are excellent, she can be disposed of in five minutes. Rocks, he says every time. She has rocks in her head. And he tells her that her teeth, like her grandmother's, will last a lifetime. Good news. Sharp and hard, they bite, they grip, grind, gnash, and clench. They make the words come out clear. Sonia grinds her teeth all night, Sol remarks at breakfast. Good, Rita thinks. They will be useful in times of stress. They will help her chew hard things and grind them down, make them fit for swallowing.

When Sanjay's wife died, Rita paid a neighborly call, as her grandfather taught her to do. Solomon was conscientious about visiting the bereaved. He would enter their houses with no greeting (that was the rule), seat himself in a corner, open a book, and pray as though he were alone in the room and the universe, which in a sense he was, for all around him people continued to speak, eat, and even make merry as survivors will.

The rules behind her, no book to guide her, Rita brings a rich, fruity cake to Sanjay and greets him. They have exchanged greetings on the street, she has inquired with concern about his wife, but she has never been in his house before. She notices he has some Indian things—a big brass tray, a lacquered vase with an array of peacock feathers, and several photos of Allahabad, his home town, a very holy place, he tells her, where two holy rivers meet. One photo shows masses of people, the tops of heads, mostly, bathing in a holy river banked by two fantastical buildings, castles out of a tale of chivalry. Otherwise it is a San Francisco kind of house—airy, with thriving plants and colorful pillows. It smells spicy.

They become friends. They go to an occasional movie, a restaurant. He asks her advice about relatives who need green cards. She asks if he can fix her dishwasher. She loves the way he moves, his great weight treading softly, the smooth sound of his voice and the way after all these years he keeps pronouncing certain words in the British fashion—"dance," "record," "laboratory"—his slow, very inquisitive eyes and hard mouth.

Finally, after several months of decorous behavior they meet by chance on the street one evening and get to talking. Something feels different. Ripe. His eyes and his speech are slower, more judicious than usual, almost ponderous. He asks her into his house and she smells the sharp spices. He gives her some stuffed chappattis his daughter brought over that morning; he insists on warming them in the oven first. Delicious. The bread is important; it is, she understands, part of the seduction. Standing very erect, shoulders squared, like a man about to deliver a speech, he says, "Well, Rita, I have never courted an American young woman before, so you'll have to forgive my . . . ineptness. But it seems time, to me. And you? Will you?" She nods. He looks so safe.

Upstairs, the furniture in the bedroom is weighty, built for the ages. It reminds her of the furniture in her grandparents' apartment. Married furniture. The first thing Sanjay does is turn his wife's photograph to the wall.

Rita lets herself be undressed. "Oh. Oh," he says, touching her. When he takes her in his arms she feels an immense relief—at last!—as if she has been freezing for years and suddenly a fur coat is thrown over her, the kind of coat shown in photos of Russian winters, and she realizes she has wanted him from the moment she saw him from the window three years ago, looking out with her grandfather. She can feel his immense relief too, but that, she imagines, is because he has not held anyone in his arms in months. Oh God, she hopes it will not be . . . like that.

No, he is in no hurry. He proves to know a lot about women. Maybe in a past incarnation he was a woman—she can almost believe it. Also, from the way he touches her, she feels how he must have loved his wife. She wonders if she feels like his wife, if maybe all women feel alike, after a certain point. In his arms, Rita forgets who she is. She could almost be his wife. And then she falls immediately asleep.

When she wakes, the bedside lamp is on and Sanjay is weeping into the pillow. He looks up and sees her watching.

"I'm sorry. Forgive me." He stops abruptly.

Is this all she will ever be, a link to the beloved dead?

"Really, I'm terribly sorry, Rita. I thought you were sleeping."

"It's all right, Sanjay, it's all right." What else can she say?

She does not sleep much that night but watches him sleep. For hours, it seems. She has shielded herself so far, but now it envelops her like a shower of gold threads, of red powder, and she sees that love is the greatest defiance of all. She is afraid of it.

She has to leave early, go home to the other side of the wall and change, pick up her cap and gown. She is graduating from law school that very day. Sanjay says he wants to be there, so she gives him a ticket—she has them to spare since her grandparents are not flying out this time. Sol's heart is too irregular.

Just before she leaves to take her place in the line, he slips her a tiny candy wrapped in silver paper. "For luck."

She starts to unwrap it.

"No, no. You eat the paper too."

She trusts him infinitely. She eats the paper. Silver, sweet, delicious. Bits of it stick in her teeth, making the taste linger.

When he announces months later that he loves her and wants to marry her, that he has thought it over and waited to speak until he was quite sure, she takes the information skeptically.

"Why? Can't you believe that I loved her and now I love you?"

"I don't know."

"You must have loved other people. I don't think about them."

"But I haven't."

"Maybe, maybe not. You do love me, though," Sanjay says. "I know. Must I see a problem in that, perhaps?" This is comical, she thinks, this interrogation. He can be so matter-of-fact, even imperious. There is a sliver of amusement in his eyes, too. Whatever he is, she loves.

"I never felt this before. I don't know what to make of it."

"Come now. You must have. American girls . . ."

"I was busy with other things."

"What things?"

She can't tell him how she spent her college years. It's too crazy. Not yet, anyway. So instead she says something hurtful. "You're too old for me."

He seems impervious, tilts his head carelessly. "That can't be helped. And anyway, you don't really mind."

It's true, she doesn't. Quite the contrary.

Rita and Sanjay find that their backgrounds have a number of things in common. A preponderance of rules for proper behavior is one, especially rules about not consorting—eating or sleeping—with members of another caste. This, like pioneers, they have both left behind. Arranged marriages is another. This one does not seem so far behind.

"So you never really knew her before you were married?"

"We knew each other, but not in the way that you mean. The families met several times. We spoke. It's not really so preposterous. The idea is that you come to love each other. We trust in proximity to breed love."

Rita frowns. He is still trusting.

"It sounds very unromantic, I know. But it doesn't exclude romance of a kind."

"Does it work? I mean, for most people?"

"Well, more than you'd expect. Some love each other with a good-will kind of love. Some even have passionate love. But there are other ways to love besides those, more ways than are recognized here. You can love someone simply because she's yours, part of you. You've accepted each other and you don't question it. My parents were like that. Are still like that."

"And what about you? What kind of love was it?"

He closes his eyes. The pain of loss, regret? Or merely impatience. "Why do you keep asking? You know the answer."

She knows. The goodwill kind, the passionate kind, the totally accepting kind. Often, those first three years, she saw them walking arm in arm down the street, their steps falling together in rhythm. Belonging.

"You were lucky. Did she know, the first night, what she was supposed to do?"

"Not precisely. She was a very sheltered girl."

"But you knew, I presume?"

Sanjay takes a deep breath and his face begins a little performance—his face has a great repertoire of expressions. His eyes roll, his forehead wrinkles, his lips curl. "What do you think?"

"Was she appalled?"

"No."

Rita would like to know, in graphic detail, exactly how Sanjay made it clear what was expected. She is not a voyeur by nature; rather, she is mystified by the transmutations of love—how indifference turns into love, love into indifference and even worse. But it is useless to ask. He doesn't tell. It must be too precious. Yes, because he does love to tell stories about his parents, his brothers and sisters and cousins. She has heard comic stories about bicycles capsized in the mud and a flirtatious widowed aunt, stories of school pranks and festival antics, and painful stories about a baby sister who died of diphtheria on the day Gandhi was shot. But no stories about his wife.

"I know what you're thinking. But people can love more than once, Rita. After all . . ."

"I know, I know." Yet she knows only in the abstract. She feels generally ignorant on the subject. She thinks that what she saw, growing up, was not love but a species of belonging.

Her grandparents' marriage took place in 1927 and was also arranged, though not as strictly as Sanjay's. The couple was introduced; they took several walks together over the Brooklyn Bridge; they went to a few movies and even to an opera, *Madame Butterfly*. This was all quite ordinary. But the wedding itself was extraordinary. The father of the groom had collapsed and died two days before. No matter; the rules say ceremonies must take place as scheduled, like Broadway shows. And the bride did not refuse; she had not yet learned how. But she had her doubts, surely, Rita thinks. For it is hard to imagine the Sonia she knows being so compliant. Surely she must have been astounded, felt that such a beginning did not augur well and maybe she had better pull out before it was too late? But it was already too late.

"Can you picture that wedding?" she queries Sanjay.

"Well, quiet, I'd imagine. Very quiet."

No doubt. A dearth of dancing, the musicians laboring to rouse an unappreciative crowd. Rita's various aunts and uncles, disguised as young people, gathered around linen-covered tables, eating sweetbreads and drinking sweet wine while salt streams down their faces. The children fretful and confused—no one is urging delicacies on them or swinging them through the air. Her own father not yet an outcast, not even born, a gleam, as they say, in his father's very gleaming eye. As her grandparents toast their life together, the groom weeps under the harshness of his own discipline. He can barely drink and cannot eat. He does not need to eat. Self-pity and self-satisfaction are his feast—for this ordeal will make him a better person, bring him favor in the eyes of his God. What kind of eyes could they be?

Very quickly the couple has an indissoluble connection, a son. Sonia's first decade of marriage is a depression, then comes the war.

Throughout their married life there are many changes in the world. The maps of Europe, Africa, and Asia change drastically. There are immense shifts of population, new technologies, cures for diseases; wonders and horrors as usual. The twentieth century. But— and she has to admire his tenacity—Rita's grandfather's world remains the world he grew up in, a small world left over from the youth of the century, a bit cramped and crowded, like a room to which new pieces are added but from which nothing is ever thrown away, a thoroughly benign and safe world, according to his stories—for he is, yes, a storyteller, with a magnetic eye, bluest of blues, and a magnetic voice.

"Our house was the place where all immigrants stopped first," he says. "And no matter how crowded we were, when they opened the door, whoever came in I welcomed them with open arms. I was only a child. But I felt the call of blood."

Open arms. He lives, Rita comes to understand, by appropriation. He takes in, processes, categorizes, labels, and provides a commentary. To have any act unexplained or unexcused, anyone left out of the scheme, can put the world in an imbalanced state, as taunting and intolerable as an unresolved chord in his singer's ear.

So he narrates the fortunes of each arrival, one by one: loves, travels, business ventures, progeny. And in his stories—long, highly dramatized, and gripping—never a harsh word is spoken between sister and brother, parent and child, husband and wife, only happy grateful immigrants making good in the promised land, learning the customs and the lingo. He has an instinctive way of skimming over pain or crisis, alighting mostly on moments of epiphany when generosity and breadth of spirit are revealed, moments when virtue triumphs over self-interest. What everyone fled from is never mentioned above a whisper, and never at all in the presence of "them," the others, the ones who can never be trusted, who pursue and destroy. The moral is always the same: The family is the pillar of society. There are no distinctions when it comes to family. A cousin? "Like my own brother!" (A granddaughter? "Like my own daughter!") And when a member strays beyond the pillars he becomes an outcast. Formerly appropriated, now vomited up.

Since Sol's stories extol righteousness, Rita asks why, then, he and his brother don't go out, this minute, and work for civil rights and for an end to the war in Vietnam. If they fled from the draft on one continent, shouldn't they protest it on another? Sol listens because she is a clever speaker, and when she becomes too annoying he waves her away like a mosquito. Her uncle the dentist points out that all the boys in the immediate neighborhood are going to college, not Asia. Once, her great-aunt, the dentist's wife, loses patience. "Protest, protest!" she mocks, eyeing Rita as she would a stranger who has jumped the line at the bakery. "She should be glad she has a roof over her head."

What could it mean? Rita knows her parents are . . . well . . . dead, it must be. The subject is taboo. It is as if she is Sol's and Sonia's child. This is her roof, isn't it? Her grandfather tells his sister-in-law to shut her big mouth. Sonia goes further and throws her out of the house, and the incident is closed. Everyone goes to bed with a headache.

Undaunted, at fourteen years old Rita thinks she too can appropriate the world, make it over to fit her vision. Not all immigrants are so well assimilated, she finds out. She feels for those beyond the pillars, maybe because she is darker than any Jew she knows and has never had a chance to play Queen Esther. With an adolescent's passion to convert, she wants her grandfather to feel for them too, and to agree that breadth of spirit does not mean obeying the most rules but scorning them all, except for the rules of the heart. She wants him to thrill to the uneven rhythms of heroic outcasts, anarchists: "I might have lived out my life talking at street corners, to scorning men. I might have died unmarked, unknown, a failure. Now we are not a failure. This is our career and our triumph. Never in our full life could we hope to do so much work for tolerance, for justice, for man's understanding of man as we do now by accident. Our words— our lives—our pains—nothing! The taking of our lives—lives of a good shoemaker and a poor fish-peddler—all! That last moment belongs to us—that agony is our triumph!" She finds this in a book about famous trials of the century, and shivers with passion.

But Solomon hears it impassively, and in response, launches into one of his own speeches—clears his throat and prepares his oratorical voice. "Ours, Rita, is a religion of ethics. A man's devotion to God is shown in how he treats his fellow man, beginning with his own— his children, his grandchildren"—he smiles fondly, justly pleased with himself on this score—"his neighbors." (Sonia puts down the skirt she is hemming, tosses aside her glasses and stalks out of the room.) "In other words, *mamaleh*, charity begins at home."

Very well, and where is home? Everywhere, she lectures him in turn. He calls her a bleeding heart. Whatever he cannot appropriate, whatever refuses to go down and be assimilated—outsiders, heinous deeds, gross improprieties—he ignores, which means it ceases to exist.

He has been unable to appropriate, for instance, his son's marriage to a Mexican immigrant, which took place in far-off San Francisco, California, in 1955. This Rita learns through piecing together family whispers. If Sol had had his way, ostracism—the tool of his enemies—would not have sufficed; according to the rules, his son would have been interred in absentia and mourned for a week, and neighbors would have visited him and Sonia while they sat on wooden boxes, wearing bedroom slippers, with the mirrors in the house covered by bed sheets. But he didn't have his way. Sonia refused to do it. It was the beginning of her refusals.

That her mother was Mexican is one of four or five facts Rita knows about her. Her name was Carmen. She was a singer—strangely enough, like Rita's grandfather, but singing a different kind of song. Rita would like to know what kind of love her parents had and how they came to marry, but she never will. It was certainly not arranged.

Rita's dream foresees her grandfather's funeral because he is not well, Sanjay suggests reasonably. Perhaps; she shrugs. She is not really seeking explanations. It is certainly true that Sol's fears have caught up with him, and that there are not enough rules to cover them adequately. Once sturdy, he has become in old age what he calls "nervous." He sees death coming, and his nervous system is in a twit. He has spells of weakness, shortness of breath, panic; all activities have to be gauged in advance as to how taxing they will be and the chance of mishaps. He monitors his vital signs with loving care, as solicitous of himself as a mother. The path has narrowed till on the vast new continent there is hardly room to place one foot in front of the other. Safe, safe. Rita hates the way he lives. She wants him to get up and do something—sing, pray, sell sportswear, anything but pave the way for death, be the advance man.

But for safety he must keep himself as confined as possible, especially since Rita and Sonia have slipped out of his control. He would not be so "nervous," he claims, if he could oversee what they were doing at all times. Of course, this cannot be. Rita is far away, doing God knows what and with whom, and Sonia has to manage the store. Sonia began to elude him long ago anyhow. For the first three decades of their marriage she obeyed, and then something happened. It was as if she had sealed up her disobedience the way pioneer women canned fruits and vegetables for a later season, and then she broke it out in abundance, jar after jar releasing its briny fumes. Years ago, members of the congregation reported that they saw the cantor's wife, her granddaughter beside her, driving his car on the Sabbath, a cigarette in her invincible teeth! Where could they be going? There was even talk of replacing him, but it came to nothing—they pitied him, first his great tragedy with his son and now unable to control his family.

Sonia, once tame, has reverted to the ways of her family. Anarchists, though not the grand kind. No, they fit very well into the elastic New World. Except that they argue passionately with the clerks of bureaucracies, they walk on the grass, they refuse to wait on lines, they smoke in nonsmoking areas, they open doors labeled authorized personnel only, they zip through traffic jams on the shoulders of roads or in lanes blocked off by orange stanchions. It is part of their passion, their brand of civil disobedience. Sol is horrified and Rita is amused, even though these are gestures only, to show they will not take the law from anyone, for they know who the lawgivers are. Clay like all the rest. They obey what they like, laws unto themselves. They are in fact (some of them, at any rate) lawyers. They came here in installments, three boys and three girls from Kiev. The girls became seamstresses, the boys lawyers. The girls went to factories, to sit on a cushion and sew a fine seam, while the boys were sent to school—the New World not so unlike the Old in that regard.

Three dressmakers make three lawyers: stitch, stitch. The dressmakers live in small apartments in Jewish ghettos with their husbands, small businessmen like Rita's grandfather, while their brothers prosper in modern assimilated suburbs. Then in 1959, the only child —a son—of one of the girls is stabbed to death in far-off San Francisco, California. That is truly lawless. The family, convulsed, will grieve in unison. That is not the kind of lawlessness, the kind of anarchy they intended, no, never, never! His mother will stop recognizing the world, any world, New, Old, all the same to her.

The family fears she may never return to the realm of the living. Days go by while she sits on a hard kitchen chair with her eyes fixed on nothing. She will not change her clothing or eat or sleep. When spoken to she will not respond, or else shakes her head, or at the most says, "Not now." It seems she is waiting for something, someone. Perhaps she is remembering how she refused to mourn her son when he married out of his faith—was it for this, so she could mourn him now?

Meanwhile her husband, accompanied by his twin brother the dentist, will fly out to the unknown western territories to settle his son's affairs and see that justice is done—a most adventurous trip, which he would not undertake for any other reason, but shock has made him a father again. The former outcast as a corpse is unobjectionable. And what, of all things, will he discover in the shadow of the Golden Gate but a child! Just two years old. If he had known, maybe . . . The child has been staying with her maternal uncle and his wife (her mother being in no condition to take care of her), but really, it is very difficult. They own a bar, a nightclub, actually—he is the bartender, his wife the waitress. (And there Rita's mother sang her Spanish songs. A vision in sequins? A floozy? She will never know.) No place for a baby. Without a moment's hesitation, Solomon transcends himself (possibly for the baby's blue eyes, which reflect his own), to perform the one daring act of his life—he takes her back. He takes her in. It is an act that could speak best for itself, but he cannot resist the ready phrase, a Jewish Polonius.

"It was the call of blood," he explains to Sonia as he enters carrying the child on one arm, suitcase and briefcase dangling from the other. She stares at him in the stupor that has become her mode of existence. Nothing surprises her. "Here," he says more naturally, holding out his burden like an offering. "Better take her to the bathroom. Her name is Rita." He thrusts her at Sonia. "Take a look at her eyes. Like skies."

A good name, Rita. It can derive from either set of genes. And there are plenty of dark Jews, her grandfather will declaim, presenting her to the family and the neighbors, the little bilingual prodigy. Yemenites. Ethiopians. The sons of Ham. Anyway, she is not all that dark. Some regular Jews are swarthy. Anyway, there she is, and her grandmother takes her to the bathroom, feeds her, clothes her, and lo, a miracle sprung from tragedy, Sonia returns to life like Sarah in Genesis, fertilized in old age. Soon the neighborhood women start coming back to the house for fittings. They stand stiffly, only their mouths moving, as she pins folds of fabric around them, the pins stuck in her tough teeth. Rita plays with dolls at their feet, and not all her dolls are blonde. One is quite dark, with glossy black hair— Sonia understands the demands of a pluralistic society. That doll is not Rita's best baby, however. Her best baby is a blue-eyed blonde she calls Nita, to rhyme. The clients fuss over her, how cute, how bright, congratulate her grandmother on this unexpected boon, but their tone is very odd, not utterly pure. Ambiguous, like Rita.

For Sonia, though, there is no ambiguity. She accepts their goodwill with nonchalance—the pins in her mouth make it hard to speak in any case—and in their presence ignores Rita. When they leave she clasps her close, then talks, talks, low and fast like someone who has saved up words over a lifetime. She talks as if she is talking to herself—much of it a small child can hardly understand. So many things that she thinks and feels, but not the one thing. Of Rita's parents she never speaks, but she returns to life, and best of all, learns to drive. She neglects the housework that exasperates her, and together they breeze through the tangled city like tourists. Even when Rita is a big schoolgirl, she will wait for her and greet her at the door at three-fifteen: "Let's take a ride, okay?"

They ride through exotic neighborhoods of Greeks, Asians, blacks, Hispanics, Russians—there they eat pirogen and caviar and borscht. A passionately discontented woman, angular and veiny,

Sonia is most content at the wheel of the dark green Pontiac. A born voyager. Short, straight-backed, she sits on a pillow and stretches her neck like a swan to peruse the traffic. Her driving style is aggressive, arrogant, anarchic. And Rita by her side is her natural passenger. Nothing can shock or frighten her, so thoroughly does she trust her grandmother, so closely are they twined, having accepted each other on first sight with no questions asked, like Sanjay's parents—neither the U-turns in tunnels nor the sprinting across intersections nor the sparring with buses and trucks. Sonia is omnipotent, fearless. Queen of the Road. Defying the rules about the Sabbath, she takes Rita to, of all places, the beach, where in all kinds of weather they wet their feet in the surf and build sand castles and Sonia tells stories—not morality tales like Sol's but true stories without morals—of what lies across the openness of the Atlantic, and she tells Rita that they came here to be free, free.

Now Rita longs for those forbidden afternoons at the edge of the Atlantic. Like a child, she would like to incorporate her grandmother, swallow her, as her grandfather lived by appropriating. Appropriation is the tactic of the lost and the scared. Oh, if only Rita could swallow her whole, if only she would go down, she could have Sonia forever with her. Safe at last. Then she would never clutch her heart and die as in the nightmare, leaving Rita standing alone, severed.

While Sanjay and Rita are watching a Fred Astaire and Ginger Rogers movie on television one evening, her phone rings. Rita speaks to her friend who still works in the Spanish record store in the Mission district. When she hangs up she says, "I've just been invited to a wedding. Rosalia's brother Luis. Would you like to come?"

"I never knew you could speak Spanish like that." They have been lovers for almost a year.

"Oh. Well, I need it, you know, for my clients."

"But you speak it like a native. I thought you were only two years old . . ."

"I learned when I was in college. Do you want to go to the wedding? It'll be fun. Lots of music and dancing."

"Sure."

She sits down and touches his hand. "I used to go out with her brother, years ago. He's very nice. Gentle, you know, like Rosalia. I'm glad he's getting married."

"You never mentioned it before."

"Well, it was nothing, really. We were kids. There's no way it should bother you."

"It doesn't. Only I sometimes realize I know so little about you. You tell me so little."

Sanjay develops an interest in her past loves. Like her curiosity about his wife, his is not lascivious in nature. Rather, he wants coherent social history. What has her life been all about? And generically, what are young American women's lives all about? a question that has never occupied him before.

She is not a typical case, Rita tries to explain. But it's a matter of optics, of the precision of the lens. To a fifty-year-old naturalized Indian widower, she is representative enough. He wants his American girl, Rita thinks. And he wants the real thing.

"Did you ever sleep with any of your clients?"

"No! Anyway, by the time I had clients I already knew you."

"Well, what about at law school?"

"One student." She grins, teasing. "One professor."

"A professor!"

"Is there any more paratha?"

Sanjay reaches for the plate on the floor. "Yes, but they're cold by now."

All during these absurd conversations they eat his daughter's food. Rita feels funny about that, but Sanjay says nonsense, his daughter made it to be enjoyed. Food is for whoever is hungry.

"I don't mind them cold. Thanks. You'll be relieved to know I wasn't in his class at the time."

"But a law professor. A jurist! He must have been so much older."

"He was seven years older, Sanjay. What about you?"

"I may be old, but at least I'm pure!" He laughs loud belly laughs. His whole body shakes. The bed shakes. Rita feels safe, wrapped up warm in his laughter. He is so domesticated, so easy to entertain. Pure: he says he never knew any women besides his wife. Before he was married, two prostitutes. They don't count.

"We'd better start at the beginning. What about in college?"

"This is getting very silly. Stop."

"Aha! Now we're getting somewhere."

"Just Luis, for a while."

"Why a Chicano?"

"Why not? Now stop. Really. It's annoying."

"Because there's something you're not telling me. Why won't you marry me? You're footloose. Then you'd know where you belong."

The Indian gentleman next door wants to rescue the poor orphan girl, give her food and warm clothes and light a fire in her garret. And she would not be cast out if she married him, as her father was. It's thirty years later. And it's Rita. What can you expect? They are prepared for almost anything from her. They believe in nature, not nurture, and she believes with them.

But she has never told anyone. She shakes her head.

"Is it terrible?" Sanjay asks. He is not fooling around anymore. She sees his age in the set of his face. His lips are parted. His cheeks are sagging in a kind of resigned expectation.

"Yes."

He hands her more stuffed bread. "Well, eat something while you tell me, then." To her surprise, his eyes, however old and sympathetic, have turned lustful. He is waiting to hear about a frenzied, tragic love affair. Rita stares right into them as she speaks.

She was seventeen. There was talk in the house about where she would be sent to college. Oh, how she kept them young, kept them abreast of things. She said to her grandmother in the kitchen, making the fish for Friday night, "You have to tell me now. Or I'll go away forever, I swear it."

"Big shot!" Sonia says, her fingers plunged deep in the bowl of chopped fish. "Where will you go? And with what?"

"There's always a way for a girl to make a living, Grandma. This is 1974, after all," and she smirks brazenly. "I know plenty of places I can stay."

A look of doom streaks over Sonia's face, and it is not so much prostitution she is thinking of as certain types of irregular living conditions: dope fiends, drifters, hippies, pads. Rita is bad enough already, with her ideas, her gypsy clothes, her unexplained forays into Manhattan, her odd-looking inky newspapers, the closely typed petitions she brings home indefatigably for them to sign; but at least she sleeps in her bed every night and takes showers. . . . At the same time, the vision of such irregularity holds a fascination for her grandmother, Rita can tell. She sees enticement seasoning the horror in her eyes, orange flecks against the green. Sonia might have tried it herself if she hadn't been so tired, sewing in the factory. Sometimes she even signs the petitions, after Sol goes to bed.

"You're not going anywhere," Sonia says confidently, blinking away her enticement, slapping the fish into ovals, and she shoves the bowl in Rita's direction for help. "Just to college like all your cousins."

"But I'm not the same as them. I have a right to know what I am, don't I? All these years you would never answer me. But I'm not a child anymore. It's my life."

There is something different, this time, in the way she says it, or maybe Sonia is simply worn down—Sol will be going to the hospital for his throat operation very soon; there have been doctors' appointments, consultations; he lays down the law in an ever hoarser voice. "You can't ask this of me!" she groans, but they both understand she means the opposite. Rita waits, her hands growing cold in the bowl of fish. She forms an oval and places it in the baking pan.

"They were separated. They never could get along. I knew. I used to speak to him all the time. No one could stop me from using the phone." She looks at Rita curiously. "I even knew about you."

"What about me?"

"That they had you! But I didn't tell him. That's what he wanted, not to know anything. Like he was dead. So let him not know, I thought." Sonia sits silent, not moving, a hostile witness in the box.

"So?"

She sighs as though she had hoped for a reprieve, that this much would be enough. "So he went over there to get something. They had an argument."

"And?"

She wipes her hands carefully on a dish towel. Then she takes the towel and holds it up to her face, covering her face. Her words come muffled through the towel. "She stabbed him."

"She what?"

"With a knife." She weeps behind the towel.

Rita is weirdly calm. Of all the scenes she has invented, never anything like this. Much more romantic, her visions were. Lost at sea. Activists kidnapped by the Klan. Wasting disease. Cult suicide. Yes, her nights have been busy, but all wrong. "I don't believe it."

"Don't, then. You asked. You pestered me for years."

"It's not possible. He must have been stronger than her."

"But he didn't have the knife," she wails. "Oh, my baby." Shoulders heaving, towel over her face.

Suddenly Rita cannot bear that towel anymore and snatches it away. Her grandmother's hollowed face is wet and blotched and smells of fish. "No. That can't be the whole story. He must have attacked her first."

Sonia gives the maddest laugh, a witch's cackle. "He? The gentlest boy who ever breathed?"

Rita could almost laugh too. Their child, gentle! But she also knows they do not attack. A picture is coming into focus, a kitchen, a hysterical woman who looks like an older version of herself, waving a bread knife; a pale man trying to wrest it from her. But she's too quick, too fierce. . . . Oh God, already she's becoming a type, a caricature. Leave her be. Leave that room altogether, before it gets bloody. . . . What about the baby . . . ? The baby is in another room, mercifully sleeping, yes. Go back, try again, try it in the living room. The scene has endless possibilities, bloody ones, Rita could labor over it for years. Give up the rest of her life to screening it every possible way: He said . . . No, she said . . . She grabbed . . . No, he . . .

"Wasn't there a trial? Didn't the facts come out at the trial? I bet she was a battered wife." Yes, lately even juries have learned to sympathize. Her poor mother, black and blue? Sonia looks baffled—this is beyond her imaginings. "I'll find out the truth," Rita shouts. "I'll visit her in jail." Where she languishes, thinking only of her lost baby.

"She's not in jail."

"No?"

"Finished. Six years and out. Good behavior! Rita, everyone said it, even her brother, what kind of woman she was, how she treated him so terrible. He was a good man, the brother. He wrote us a letter about . . . I felt sorry for him."

The outrage. She killed Rita's gentle father and she walks the streets free. "She never looked for me?" Now, now, she feels tears. This is the real outrage. Sonia feels it too.

"We wouldn't have given you up anyway. You were my reason to go on living. Two years I waited to see you." She covers her face again, this time with her hand and only for an instant. "And then I got you for good." As she gazes at Rita, her brow, for once, is calm. "You're just like him."

Me! thinks Rita, with my murderer's face? It must be a torment to have me around, reminding everyone. And what is just like him? They never say. Now more than ever she wants so badly to see him, it is almost like a sexual longing—she will die, just shrink and evaporate, if she cannot see him, touch him. She does not recognize the feeling till much later, though, when she knows Sanjay.

("When I know you," she says. "When I know you.")

For her mother Rita does not long—she feels she has her already, in her bones, her blood, the coarseness of her hair. In some essential, inescapable way, she carries her around.

"Why did they get married?" she whispers to Sonia. Why does anyone?

"Ha!" Sonia is recovered now, is getting back to her work. She must know these spasms of grief intimately after so many years, the way people know their attacks of epilepsy or asthma—the shape of their parabolas, and the intensity. She must have learned how to assimilate them into her days and proceed. It strikes Rita that she has never seen her grandmother idle. From dawn onwards Sonia scurries about, shopping, cooking, sewing, driving. Then at ten o'clock she falls exhausted into her old stuffed chair in the living room to read novels under a solitary lamp, while Sol calls every ten minutes, "Come to bed already!"

"Why did they have me?"

"Come on with the fish, Rita. It'll be midnight at this rate before we eat."

There is only one place she wants to go to college: Berkeley. Her grandfather is sure it is because they have the most hippies there. Her grandmother knows better, but in the end Rita gets her way. They are old and weary, no match for her in her new wisdom. For what scope and vision she suddenly possesses! Now she understands why her grandfather cleaves to the rules and her grandmother cleaves to him, all the while raging against God and driving like a maniac. She understands why the family, those stolidly decent people, look at her with a blend of pity and suspicion—it's not the color she is, no, it's that at any moment she may show her true colors. . . . She understands so much, it feels at night as if her head will burst with understanding and with blood. Only the one thing she wants to understand she doesn't.

She will find her and make her tell how it was. How to think about it. Until she knows, between her and the rest of the world is a wall of blood, ever fresh, never clotting, and she will never cross it into a life.

Her mother must have been a Catholic; as a girl she must have knelt and confessed to puny childish sins—lying, being unkind, thinking wicked thoughts. Maybe the Christ in her village church dripped with crimson paint and so she got used to spilled blood, it didn't seem alien and horrifying. It doesn't to Sanjay; he is used to handling it, but what does it tell him?

("Stop torturing yourself. It's only a physical substance, a liquid. It carries things, but not the kinds of things you mean. Don't tell me I traveled halfway across the world to find a mystic."

He's getting to sound like a Jew, thinks Rita. They are changing places.)

When she goes away to school her grandparents are afraid she will become a hippie, a druggie, but instead she spends her free time in San Francisco, the Mission district, where the Mexicans and Chicanos live, looking and waiting. A deranged sort of looking— she doesn't really want to find. She wants to be found. She learns Spanish—relearns—and it nestles lovingly in her mouth. Her tongue wraps around the syllables like a lover returning from exile to embrace his beloved, feeling the familiar contours. People say she sounds like a native speaker. She learns it so she can ask around for her, but she never asks. She doesn't even know her mother's name. Carmen, yes, but not her last name. Useless to ask for her own last name. Her mother does not seem one of the family. She would not have kept it.

("How did you expect to find her? What did you think you were doing?" Sanjay is incredulous. The Rita he knows is so sane, so sensible, aside from the nightmares. So presentable. It would be his pleasure to bring her home to meet his family, once they had gotten used to the idea of a half-Jewish, half-Mexican American lawyer twenty-two years younger.)

What did she think she was doing? Wandering around the Mission looking for a woman who looked like her, who would be looking in turn for a girl like Rita. Only the woman isn't looking. She has never looked. Luncheonettes, candy stores, bars—Rita can't get to like the food she buys as her excuse for being there, heavy and beany, maybe because for her it is the food of despair. She reads the names of singers on posters outside cafés, she reads the personal ads in newspapers, she even studies the names alongside doorbells in dingy, flaking old buildings. Crazy, she knows it. No explanation or story could change the fact. Like God in the trials she staged as a child, it remains: One lives having killed the other. It would be the same fact if the roles were reversed.

Nothing ever happens except some men try to pick her up, and once her pocket is picked in a movie line, and she makes friends with a girl who works in a record store and goes out with her brother for a few months. Rita is drawn by the easy friendliness of the family. She sees a life there that she might retreat into, but she would have to tell so many lies, and even so she would never fit in, never feel quite right. By what right is she anywhere, she the most contingent of contingencies, a superfluous mystery? So she breaks it off. And with that, the quest breaks off as well. Enough. She is worn out, like a soldier after battle, like a battleground in the night. For a month, over Christmas vacation of her junior year, she goes home to do nothing but sleep, grinding her teeth.

When Sonia asks anxiously what she plans to do after college, she says she will apply to law school. Because she is tired of her obsessions, tired of the parents she can't remember and who have left her this hard inheritance to swallow, tired of breaking her teeth on it. However hard she gnaws, the mystery won't crack. World without end, she is two years old, and in the next room is some kind of dreadful racket going on that will not let her sleep, some kind of screeching not at all like the singing she is used to, and maybe it is all a bad dream, but the next thing she knows she is in an airplane with two strange men who are interchangeable and who weep, and it is a miserable trip, she wets her pants, she throws up.

"Rita, Rita." Sanjay takes her in his arms. "Lie down and rest. Give it up."

Lying there, Rita wonders once again who she would be had she been left with her aunt and uncle in the bar. Maybe then her mother would have rushed to her when she got out of jail, like a doe flying to her fawn, and sheltered her and told her . . . everything. Or would she have done as the mother eel, who flees to the other end of the world and leaves its young behind, groping in slime? Maybe she could have become a nightclub singer too? But she has no voice— she would probably work in a store like Rosalia. Or go off to New York to search for her father's family, who would appear exotic and a little alluring. She might speak English with a rippling musical accent and move and dress and feel about the world in a different way. She could be almost anyone, and anywhere. Even now, there are times when she thinks of her name and who it stands for, and it feels like looking in a mirror and seeing a blank sheet, the sheet covering a mirror in a house of the bereaved. But she is this, and here, this person in Sanjay's arms.

She thought he would be horrified, repelled by her. Instead he has fallen asleep holding her, his arm draped across her middle like a sash. She watches him sleep for a while, then gets up and tiptoes around the bedroom. She takes a good look at the photograph of his wife. Yes, there is a certain resemblance. The result of nature, history, the migrations of people, and love.

It is strange that with all the hours she has spent in this bedroom she has never poked around. She opens the dresser drawers, one after another, but all she sees are Sanjay's socks and underwear and hand-kerchiefs neatly and predictably folded. Then, on a shelf in the closet she finds a pile of saris, also neatly folded, all colors, generous, deep colors, gold threads running through the fabrics. She chooses a red one, the bridal color. But she can't figure out how to get it on right. It is fun, this dressing up; she did it as a child. Vashti. Finally she gets the sari on in a makeshift fashion, not the way Sanjay's wife used to wear it. In the bottom drawer of the night table she finds little jars of powders—red, amber, green, blue—and she plays with them, dabs them on her hands, puts some green on her eyelids. She has seen women with a spot of red in the center of the forehead, but she is not sure what it means, maybe a symbol of Hindu caste or rank; she doesn't dare do it. She appraises herself in the mirror. Queen Esther, at last. Behind her in the mirror she sees Sanjay roll over and open his eyes. He blinks and the color drains away, leaving him yellowish.

"Rita? What are you doing?"

"How do I look?"

"That's not how it goes. Don't, anyway. Take it off. It's not right."

She steps to the edge of the bed, presenting herself. "Fix it. You must know how it goes. You must have seen it done a million times."

"I don't. Do you know how to tie a tie?"

She tries to dab some red powder on him, but he moves out of reach. He won't play. "Please, Rita. Stop."

She yanks off the red sari, the bridal color, rolls it into a ball, and weeps into it.

"But I love you," he protests, a frightening look of middle-aged acceptance on his face. He does not show any shock at what she has told him—that is what is frightening. Will time do that to her too, and then what will she have left? "I do, Rita." If she didn't know him, his smile might seem simpleminded. "You don't have to masquerade for me to love you."

But she cannot believe it. It costs so much.

The Subversive Divorce

THEY HAD expected to stay married, that is, to live in a plague-ridden land uninfected, immune to the prevailing currents. In their early youth, divorce had been a germ confined to movie stars and misfits, and over the years marriage, like a layer of fuzzy insulation, had kept them wrapped in that safe climate. Till from their own involuntary clawing the insulation grew frayed, and let in the tainted air.

The trouble was a mutual and consistent failure to say or do the right thing at the right time. It was a failure, they recognized in less feverish moments, springing from the premise of marriage itself, which licensed the expectation that each would say and do the right thing in all seasons. In bouts of hoarse shouting and tears, the air between them whipped by gusts of words, they tried to transform each other into more fitting people, without the slightest effect, save that they came to take a perverse pleasure in thwarting expectation.

Then would come a truce. They would recklessly reveal the ingredients of an ideal mate like chefs revealing a secret recipe, and each one would try to cook it up out of the provisions at hand, would try even to procure the absent ingredients from the air. But like inept loaves, their efforts fell flat; like cuts of meat, they were overdone or underdone, with sauces too thick or too thin. When they served these failed dishes there were stinging scenes of reproach. By the end, even if one of them did happen by instinct or accident to say or do the right thing at the right time, the thing was unacceptable, coming as it did from someone already proven to be wrong.

The words of reproach were made more terrible by their banality. For in a process of verbal erosion, theirs became a primitive language, a once-advanced civilization reduced to scratching stick figures, rock scraping rock. I can't take this anymore, it's ruining me, how did I get into such a mess. If one of the teen-aged twins was around, the words would be hissed through teeth scored by nighttime grinding. Go, then, go. I'm not keeping you.

Despite the evident meanings of the words, married life would continue: dinners, children, jobs, recreation, domestic maintenance, and even making love as usual. They liked each other; what they loathed was the distortion of identity marriage produced, marriage so public and powerful, marriage imposing its rites, grinding away the personal in the service of an inferred higher good. Making love by its nature does not permit very much distortion of identity, yet insofar as they were simultaneously married and making love, a certain element of distortion, of institutional service, crept in.

Then one evening when both their son and their daughter were out, leaving them to rant unrestrained, at the instant that he shouted, I can't take this anymore, and she responded, Go, then, go, she realized that this time she meant it. Why right then is a mystery, the pretext being no more virulent than most. She knew only that if she consented to mean what she said, she would never again need to take part in this fevered dialogue.

They both quieted, a welcome hush like the sudden cessation of a truck grinding garbage just outside the window. They had been standing, the better to rage; they sat down to gaze at each other across a coffee table like harmless, relieved strangers who have rushed to the same sheltered doorway in a downpour. Okay, okay, he said in an astonished calm.

Divorce, they well knew, began with physical separation. But she had never, even in the most noxious of spells, felt she had the right to uproot him from his family, nor had he any more wished to be so uprooted. And certainly she could never leave her children. No more could he, but . . . a mother is a mother, he conceded in this polite conversation of strangers in a doorway.

Look around, she said. There's no hurry, now that we've decided. And after a pause, feeling an embryonic wifely panic, added, Meanwhile, we might as well keep our system running as usual. To avoid total disorder?

The domestic system, aspiring to justice, had been meticulously and with great boredom worked out during the era of working such things out. It was not, to her, a thing to be tossed aside lightly, even in the face of divorce.

The system, he said judiciously, existed to support a marriage, which no longer exists. A system runs on expectations, and if we're divorced we hardly have the right to expect very much of each other, do we? That is the whole idea.

His reasoning saddened her, given the climate, heavily scented with sweet expectation, in which they had been married. Though it was less saddening than the prevailing weather.

Look, I don't want total disorder either, he said more sweetly. I'll abide by the system. I promise! This more sweetly still.

But can you still promise? If we're divorced?

They would have to approach the divorce from another path. Money, which made them groan. What money they had was all commingled. The money was as married as they were, if not more so, and how to disentangle it seemed beyond any household remedy. Why not let it remain commingled for the moment? After all, the money was not quarreling uncontrollably, it was not weeping in the shower or behind the wheel of the car with the radio tuned to rock lyrics which, however inane, managed to strafe the exposed heart. And neither one of them was likely to abscond or, heaven forbid, contemplating remarriage. Well, what luck! they exclaimed. Too good to be true! smiling like strangers in a mood of wonder becoming friends in the doorway, sensing some tenuous future connection. So many divorces snagged on money, turning good people vindictive. While in theory, divorce might remove all need for vindication. The war would be over by decree, and like the clouding dust of combat, marriage would settle; you could see the enemy plainly, and draw up plans for coexistence.

What about . . . ? He hesitated. I suppose you're expecting me to sleep here on the couch?

She looked hurt. If that's what you want . . .

Not at all. I'm just trying to . . . You understand, if we're going to be free . . .

Free, she echoed nostalgically, though whether it was nostalgia for her marriage or for her earlier freedom would have been hard to say. A fleeting vision of adulterous adventure next brightened her eyes, until she realized there could be no adulterous adventure, once divorced. I'm not relegating you to the couch, she replied. I never suggested anything so extreme.

They studied each other like strangers who have arranged to have a cup of coffee together after the storm passes, a gaze of acknowledgment, of anticipation of something risky yet promising, at the very least something as opposed to nothing.

Living in sin, she said.

These days they call it simply living together.

It's not quite the same as living together after we've raised two children, is it?

Well . . . He rearranged his body in the chair, shifting into a new phase of the divorce. Now that that's settled, how shall we tell the children?

They'll be sick over it.

Yes indeed. It will seem most peculiar to everyone we know.

And we shall have to explain and I hate to explain.

No one ever had to be sick over our marriage, he said, except us. Somehow marriages, unlike divorces, do not need to be explained, merely announced.

Their eyes caught and held. Do you think . . . maybe we don't have to tell anyone? Until you really move out, that is?

It was his turn to look hurt. Actually there'll be plenty of room here when they go to college, he muttered like a married man.

Maybe we don't have to tell anyone just now, she repeated, bypassing his mutterings like a wife.

He recovered the graciousness of the single. I don't mind. You do as you like.

You really don't mind if I'd rather not tell anyone?

I haven't any right to mind what you do anymore, do I? If we're divorced?

You have a right to mind when it's something that concerns you.

Everything you do concerns me.

No longer, she protested. We're divorced. And yet she was touched, even pierced, very nearly impaled by that slender arrow of love, which recalled why they had gotten married to begin with.

Noticing, he said, Marriage begins to appear as a state of mind.

I suspect marriage is something more fragile yet, namely an illusion. Divorce, whatever its snags and constraints, appears a less illusory state.

But the curious limbo of this hour may be a possible state too.

This is a fairly affable conversation we're having, isn't it? The most affable in many a moon. Like unmarried people. Or previously married people. Or . . . something.

And yet they all complain so piteously of their state, without, however, envying ours.

Frankly, he pursued, what I dislike most about divorce is the word. I would like to propose that we simply think we are . . . not married.

At this point, she said, that is far too ambitious. The moment one of us rises out of our chair to perform any significant act, our relation will want to be defined. No, we have to get divorced now, despite the vulgarity of the word, for the same reasons that we had to get married years ago and not just think we were.

What were those again? he asked slyly.

Ha ha. The true marriage we imagined . . . Yet true marriage, she mused aloud, a thing that cannot exist because of the nature of human nature, would be like salt dissolving in water to make brine, like the action of wind on rock which makes sand, like red and black making brown, like a peach and a plum making a nectarine. All that fury in our marriage was the wind wailing its weariness of beating against the rock and the rock shrieking as it was pulverized, the peach crying for its fuzz and the plum for its dripping pink sweetness, the red and the black moaning as their brilliances muddied, streaming together, the salt drowning in the water and the water becoming tears, tears, tears. Thus true marriage is a brown dusty salty weeping fruit, an anomaly, a contradiction in terms, an impossibility.

But if marriage means that, he said, it would also mean sperm and egg making a child. And then the only true and beautiful and possible marriage is a child. That we have accomplished. Two. That you cannot deny.

Yes, we have served the institution. We have had our marriage.

And this is the place to leave off, for most likely this hour suspended between marriage and divorce, this so brief escape from any defined or decreed connection, affable strangers winging it in a doorway during a downpour, became the hour in which they were the least distorted and the apogee of their lives in common.

What I Did for Love

TOGETHER WITH Carl I used to dream of changing the power structure and making the world a better place. Never that I could end up watching the ten o'clock news with a small rodent on my lap.

He was the fourth. Percy, the first, was a bullet-shaped, dark brown guinea pig, short-haired as distinct from the long-haired kind, and from the moment he arrived he tried to hide, making tunnels out of the newspapers in his cage until Martine, who was just eight then, cut the narrow ends off a shoebox and made him a real tunnel, where he stayed except when food appeared. I guess she would have preferred a more sociable pet, but Carl and I couldn't walk a dog four times a day, and the cat we tried chewed at the plants and watched us in bed, which made us self-conscious, and finally got locked in the refrigerator as the magnetic door was closing, so after we found it chilled and traumatized we gave it to a friend who appreciated cats.

Percy had been living his hermit life for about a year when Martine noticed he was hardly eating and being unusually quiet, no rustling of paper in the tunnel. I made an appointment with a vet someone recommended. On the morning of the appointment, after I got Martine on the school bus, I saw Percy lying very still outside the tunnel. I called the vet before I left for work to say I thought his patient might be dead.

"Might be?"

"Well . . . how can I tell for sure?"

He clears his throat and with this patronizing air doctors have, even vets, says, "Why not go and flick your finger near the animal's neck and see if he responds?"

Since I work for a doctor I'm not intimidated by this attitude, it just rolls off me. "Okay, hold on a minute. . . ." I went and flicked.

"He doesn't seem to respond, but still . . . I just don't feel sure."

"Raise one of his legs," he says slowly, as if he's talking to a severely retarded person, "wiggle it around and see if it feels stiff." He never heard of denial, this guy. What am I going to tell Martine?

"Hang on. . . ." I wiggled the leg. "It feels stiff," I had to admit.

"I think it's safe to assume," he says, "that the animal is dead."

"I guess we won't be keeping the appointment, then?" I'm not retarded. I said it on purpose, to kind of rile him and see what he'd say.

"That will hardly be necessary."

To get ready for the burial, I put Percy in a shoebox (a new one, not the tunnel one), wrapped the tissue paper from the shoes around him, and added some flowers I bought on the way home from work, then sealed it up with masking tape. Carl and I kept the coffin in our room that night so Martine wouldn't have to be alone in the dark with it. She didn't cry much, at least in front of us. She keeps her feelings to herself, more like me in that way than Carl. But I knew she was very attached to Percy, hermit that he was. The next morning, a Saturday, the three of us set out carrying the box and a spade and shovel we borrowed from the super of the building. Carl's plan was to bury him in the park, but it was the dead of winter, February, and the ground was so frozen the spade could barely break it.

"This isn't going to work," he said.

Martine looked tragic. She's always been a very beautiful child, with a creamy-skinned face and an expression of serene tragic beauty that, depending on the situation, can make you want to laugh or cry. At that moment I could have done either. We were huddled together, our eyes and noses running from the cold, Martine clutching the shoebox in her blue down mittens.

"I know what," Carl said. "We'll bury him at sea."

Martine's face got even more tragic, and I gave him a funny look too. What sea? It was more than an hour's drive to Coney Island and I had a million things to do that day.

"The river. It's a very old and dignified tradition," he told her. "For people who die on ships, when it would take too long to reach land. In a way it's nicer than an earth burial—in the course of time Percy's body will drift to the depths and mingle with coral and anemone instead of being confined in—"

"Okay," she said.

So we walked up to the 125th Street pier on the Hudson River. This is a desolate place just off an exit of the West Side Highway, where the only buildings are meat-processing plants and where in the daytime a few lone people come to wash their cars, hauling water up in buckets, and even to fish, believe it or not, and at night people come to buy and sell drugs. I looked at Martine. She handed me the box like she couldn't bear to do it herself, so I knelt down and placed it in the river as gently as I could. I was hoping it would float for a while, at least till we could get her away, but my romantic Carl was saying something poetic and sentimental about death and it began to sink, about four feet from where we stood. It was headed south, though, towards the Statue of Liberty and the open sea, I pointed out to her. Free at last.

We got her another guinea pig, a chubby buff-colored one who did not hide and was intelligent and interested in its surroundings, as much as a guinea pig can be. We must have had it—Mooney, it was called—for around a year and a half when Carl began talking about changing his life, finding a new direction. He was one of those people—we both were—who had dropped out of school because it seemed there was so much we should be doing in the world. I was afraid he would be drafted, and we had long searching talks, the way you do when you're twenty, about whether he should be a conscientious objector, but at the last minute the army didn't want him because he had flat feet and was partially deaf in one ear. Those same flat feet led all those marches and demonstrations. Anyhow, he never managed to drop back in later on when things changed. Not that there was any less to do, but somehow no way of doing it anymore and hardly anyone left to do it with, not to mention money. You have to take care of your own life, we discovered. And if you have a kid . . . You find yourself doing things you never planned on.

He started driving a cab when Martine was born and had been ever since. It's exhausting, driving a cab. He spent less and less time organizing demonstrations and drawing maps of the locations of nuclear stockpiles. Now he spent his spare time playing ball with the guys he used to go to meetings with, or reading, or puttering with his plants, which after me, he used to say, were his great passion. It was not a terrible life, he was not harming anyone, and as I often told him, driving a cab where you come in contact with people who are going places was more varied than what I do all day as an X-ray technician, which you could hardly call upbeat. Most of the time, you find the patients either have cancer or not, and while you naturally hope for the best each time, you can't help getting to feel less and less, because a certain percentage are always doomed regardless of your feelings. Well, Carl was not satisfied, he was bored, so I said, "Okay, what would you do if you had a totally free choice?"

"I would like to practice the art of topiary."

"What's that?"

"Topiary is the shaping of shrubberies and trees into certain forms. You know, when you drive past rich towns in Westchester, you sometimes see bushes on the lawns trimmed to spell a word or the initials of a corporation? You can make all sorts of shapes—animals, statues. Have you ever seen it?"

"Yes." I was a little surprised by this. You think you know all about a person and then, topiary. "Well, maybe there's someplace you can learn. Take a course in, what is it, landscape gardening?"

"It's not very practical. You said totally free choice. I don't think there could be much of a demand for it in Manhattan."

"We could move."

"Where, Chris?" He smiled, sad and sweet and sexy. That was his kind of appeal. "Beverly Hills?"

"Well, maybe there's something related that you can do. You know those men who drive around in green trucks and get hoisted into the trees in little metal seats? I think they trim branches off the ones with Dutch elm disease. Or a tree surgeon?"

This didn't grab him. We talked about plants and trees, and ambition, and doing something you cared about that also provided a living. Finally he said it was a little embarrassing, but what he really might like, in practical terms, was to have a plant store, a big one, like the ones he browsed in down in the Twenties.

"Why should that be embarrassing?"

"When you first met me I was going to alter the power structure of society and now I'm telling you I want to have a plant store. Are you laughing at me, Chris? Tell the truth."

"I haven't heard you say anything laughable yet. I didn't really expect you to change the world, Carl."

"No?"

"I mean, I believed you meant it, and I believed in you, but that's not why I married you." Lord no. I married him for his touch, it struck me, and the sound of his voice, and a thousand other of those things I thought I couldn't exist without. It also struck me that I had never truly expected to change the power structure but that I had liked hanging out with people who thought they could. It was, I would have to say, inspiring.

"Do you think I'm having a mid-life crisis?"

"No. You're only thirty-three. I think you want to change jobs."

So we decided he should try it. He could start by getting a job in a plant store to learn about it, and drive the cab at night. That way we could save some money for a small store to begin with. He would have less time with me and Martine, but it would be worth it in the long run. Except he didn't do it right away. He liked to sit on things for a while, like a hen.

That summer we scraped together the money to send Martine to a camp run by some people we used to hang out with in the old days, and since it was a camp with animals, sort of a farm camp, she took Mooney along. Her third night away she called collect from Vermont and said she had something very sad to tell us. From her tragic voice, for an instant I thought they might have discovered she had a terminal disease like leukemia, and how could they be so stupid as to tell her—they were progressive types, maybe they thought it was therapeutic to confront your own mortality—but the news was that Mooney was dead. Someone had left the door of the guinea pigs' cage open the night before and he got out and was discovered in the morning in a nearby field, most likely mauled by a larger animal. I sounded relieved and not tragic enough, but fortunately Carl had the right tone throughout. At the age of eleven she understood a little about the brutalities of nature and the survival of the fittest and so on, but it was still hard for her to accept.

Martine is a peacefully inclined, intuitive type. She would have felt at home in our day, when peace and love were respectable attitudes. We named her after Martin Luther King, which nowadays seems a far-out thing to have done. Not that my estimation of him has changed or that I don't like the name, only it isn't the sort of thing people do anymore. Just as, once we stayed up nights thinking of how to transform the world and now I'm glad I have a job, no matter how boring, and can send her to camp for a few weeks.

Anyway, the people running the camp being the way they were, they immediately bought her a new guinea pig. Aside from her tragedy she had a terrific time, and she came home with a female pig named Elf, who strangely enough looked exactly like Mooney, in fact if I hadn't known Mooney was dead I would have taken Elf for Mooney. I remember remarking to Carl that if things were reversed, if Mooney had been left at home with us and died and we had managed to find an identical bullet-shaped replacement, I might have tried to pass it off as Mooney, in the way mothers instinctively try to protect their children from the harsher facts of life. But Carl said he wouldn't have, he would have told her the truth, not to make her confront harsh reality but because Martine would be able to tell the difference, as mothers can with twins, and he wouldn't want her catching him in a lie. "You know she has such high standards," he said.

In the dead of winter, even colder than in Percy's era, Martine told us Elf wasn't eating. Oh no, I thought. *Déjà vu.* The stillness, then the stiffness, wrapping it in the shoebox, burial at sea . . . Nevertheless, what can you do, so I made an appointment with the vet, the same old arrogant vet—I didn't have the energy to look for a new one. I was feeling sick when the day arrived, so Carl took off from work and went with Martine and Elf.

"There's good news and bad news," he said when they got home. "The good news is that she doesn't have a dread disease. What's wrong with her is her teeth."

I was lying in bed, trying to sleep. "Her teeth?"

"You've got it. Her top and bottom teeth are growing together so she can't eat. She can't separate them to chew." He gave me a demonstration of Elf's problem, stretching his lips and straining his molars.

"Please, this is no time to make me laugh. My stomach is killing me."

"What is it? Your period?"

"No. I don't know what."

"Well, listen—the bad news is that she needs surgery. Oral surgery. It's a hundred twenty-five including the anesthetic."

"This is not the least bit funny. What are we going to do?" Martine was putting Elf back in her cage, otherwise we would have discussed this with more sensitivity.

"Is there a choice? You know how Martine feels—Albert Schweitzer Junior. I made an appointment for tomorrow. She'll have to stay overnight."

"I presume you mean Elf, not Martine."

"Of course I mean Elf. Maybe I should call a doctor for you too."

"No, I'll be okay. What's a stomachache compared to oral surgery?"

"I don't want you getting all worked up over this, Chris." He joined me on the bed and started fooling around. "Thousands of people each year have successful oral surgery. It's nothing to be alarmed about."

"I'll try to deal with it. Ow, you're leaning right where it hurts." Martine came into the room and Carl sat up quickly.

"She's looking very wan," she said.

"Two days from now she'll be a new person," Carl said.

"She's never been a person before. How could she be one in two days?"

"Medical science is amazing."

"I have no luck with guinea pigs." She plopped into a chair, stretched out her legs, and sat gazing at her sneakers. I noticed how tall she was growing. She was nearly twelve and beginning to get breasts. But she wasn't awkward like most girls at that stage; she was stunning, willowy and auburn-haired, with green eyes. There was sometimes a faint emerald light in the whites of her eyes that would take me by surprise, and I would stare and think, What a lucky accident.

"Maybe none of them live long," I said. "I doubt if yours are being singled out."

"They have a four-to-six-year life span. I looked it up in the encyclopedia. But in four years I've gone through almost three."

That night I had such terrible pains in my stomach that Carl took me to the emergency room, where after a lot of fussing around—they tried to send me home, they tried to get me to sleep—they found it was my appendix and it had to come out right away. It was quite a few days before I felt like anything resembling normal, and I forgot completely about Elf's oral surgery.

"Chris, before we go inside, I'd better tell you something." Carl switched off the engine and reached into the back seat for my overnight bag. He was avoiding my eyes.

"What happened? I spoke to her on the phone just last night!" I was about to leap out of the car, but he grabbed my arm.

"Hold it a minute, will you? You're supposed to take it easy."

"Well what's wrong, for Chrissake?"

He looked at me. "Not Martine. Jesus! Elf."

"Elf." I thought I would pass out. I was still pretty drugged.

"She got through the surgery all right. We brought her home the next day. But . . . I don't know whether she was too weak from not eating or what, but she never started eating again. And so . . ."

"I never liked that doctor. How did Martine take it this time?"

"Sad but philosophical. I think she's used to it by now. Besides, she was more concerned about you."

"I'm glad to hear that. So where is the corpse? At sea again?"

"Well, no, actually. That's why I wanted to tell you before you went in the apartment. The temperature has been near zero. The river is frozen."

"Just give it to me straight, Carl."

"She's wrapped in some plastic bags on the bathroom windowsill. Outside. The iron grating is holding her in place. I was going to put her in the freezer with the meat, but I thought you might not care for that."

"Couldn't you find a shoebox?"

"No. I guess nobody's gotten new shoes lately."

"And how long is she going to stay there?"

"They're predicting a thaw. It's supposed to get warm, unseasonably warm, so in a few days we'll take her out to the park. Anyway, welcome home. Oh, there's another thing."

"I hope this is good."

It was. He had found a job working in the greenhouse at the Botanical Garden.

Since Martine never brought the subject up again after the thaw and the park burial, I assumed the guinea pig phase of her life was over. Two weeks after she returned from camp that summer, the super who had loaned us the spade and shovel for Percy came up to say there was a family in the next building with a new guinea pig, but their baby was allergic to it and couldn't stop sneezing. Maybe we wanted to do them a favor and take it off their hands?

Martine and I turned to each other. "What do you think?" I said.

"I'm not sure. They're a lot of expense, aren't they?"

"Not so bad. I mean, what's a little lettuce, carrots . . ."

"The medical expenses. And you don't like them too much, do you, Mom?"

I tried to shrug it off with a blank smile. I looked at Mr. Coates—what I expected I'll never know, since he stood there as if he had seen and heard everything in his lifetime and was content to wait for this discussion to be over. I wondered how much of a tip he would get for the deal. Nothing from us, I vowed.

"I've noticed," Martine said. "You don't like to handle them. You don't like small rodents."

"Not a whole lot, frankly." They looked to me like rats, fat tailless rats. For Martine's sake I had wished them good health and long life, but I tried not to get too close. When she was out with her friends and I had to feed them, I used to toss the lettuce in and step back as they lunged for it. I didn't like the eager squeaks they let out when they smelled the food coming, or the crunching sounds they made eating it. And when I held them—at the beginning, when she would offer them to me to stroke, before she noticed how I felt about small rodents—I didn't like the nervous fluttery softness of them, their darting squirmy little movements, the sniffing and nipping and the beat of the fragile heart so close to the surface I could feel it in my palms. "But they don't bother me so long as they're in the cage in your room." Which was true.

"You could go over and take a look," said Mr. Coates finally. "I'll take you over there if you want."

"Maybe I'll do that, Mom. Do you want to come too?"

"No. I know what guinea pigs look like by now."

"What color is it?" Martine was asking him on the way out.

"I don't know the color. I ain't seen it myself yet."

I didn't pay any more attention to Rusty, named for his color, than I had to the others. I made sure to be in another room while Martine and Carl cut his nails, one holding him down, the other clipping—they took turns. Martine started junior high and got even more beautiful, breasts, hips, the works, with a kind of slow way of turning her head and moving her eyes. She also started expressing intelligent opinions on every subject in the news, test tube babies, airplane hijackings, chemicals in packaged foods, while Carl and I listened and marveled, with this peculiar guilty relief that she was turning out so well—I guess because we were not living out our former ideals, not changing the world or on the other hand being particularly upwardly mobile either. Carl was happier working in the greenhouse, but we still hadn't managed to save enough to rent a store or qualify for a bank loan.

At Martine's thirteenth birthday party in May, we got to talking in the kitchen with one of the mothers who came to pick up her kid. I liked her. She was about our age, small and blonde, and she had dropped out of school too but had gone back to finish and was even doing graduate work.

"What field?" I asked. I was scraping pizza crusts into the garbage while Carl washed out soda cans—he was very big on recycling. In the living room the kids were dancing to a reggae song called "Free Nelson Mandela," and the three of us had been remarking, first of all, that Nelson Mandela had been in prison since we were about their age and in the meantime we had grown up and were raising children and feeling vaguely disappointed with ourselves, and secondly, that dancing to a record like that wouldn't have been our style even if there had been one back then, which was unlikely. Singing was more our style. And the fact that teen-agers today were dancing to this "Free Nelson Mandela" record at parties made their generation seem less serious, yet at this point who were we to judge styles of being serious? The man was still in prison, after all.

"Romance languages," she said. She was playing with the plastic magnetic letters on the refrigerator. They had been there since Martine was two. Sometimes we would use them to write things like Merry Xmas or, as tonight, Happy Birthday, and sometimes to leave real messages, like Skating Back at 7 M. The messages would stay up for the longest time, eroding little by little because we knocked the letters off accidentally and stuck them back any old place, or because we needed a letter for a new message, so that Happy Birthday could come to read Hapy Birda, and at some point they would lose their meaning altogether, like Hay irda, which amused Martine no end. This woman wrote, "Nel mezzo del cammin di nostra vita."

"What does that mean?" Carl asked her.

" 'In the middle of the journey of our life.' It's the opening of *The Divine Comedy*. What it means is, here I am thirty-five years old and I'm a graduate student."

"There's nothing wrong with that," said Carl. "I admire your determination. I'm driving a cab, but one day before I die I'm going to learn to do topiary, for the simple reason that I want to."

She said what I knew she would. "What's topiary?"

He stopped rinsing cans to tell her.

I never read *The Divine Comedy*, but I do know Dante goes through Hell and Purgatory and eventually gets to Paradise. All the parts you ever hear about, though, seem to take place in Hell, and so a small shiver ran up my spine, seeing that message on the refrigerator above Happy Birthday. Then I forgot about it.

In bed that night I asked Carl if he was serious about learning topiary. He said he had been thinking it over again. Since he had gotten a raise at the greenhouse, maybe he might give up the cab altogether, he was so sick of it, and use the money we'd saved for the store to study landscape gardening.

"Well, okay. That sounds good. I can work a half day Saturdays, maybe."

"No, I don't want you to lose the little free time you have. We'll manage. Maybe there's something you want to go back and study too."

"I'm not ambitious. Why, would I be more attractive, like, if I went to graduate school?"

"Ha! Did I hear you right?" He let out a comic whoop. "I don't even remember her name, Chris. Listen, you want me to prove my love?"

That was the last time. The next day he came down with the flu, then Martine and I got it, and just when we were beginning to come back to life he had a heart attack driving the cab. He might have made it, the doctor said, except he was alone and lost control of the wheel. They told me more details about it, just like a news report, more than I could bear to listen to, in fact. I tried to forget the words the minute I heard them, but no amount of trying could make me stop seeing the scene in my mind. They offered me pills, all through those next insane days, but I wasn't interested in feeling better. Anyhow, what kind of goddamn pill could cure this? I asked them. I also kept seeing in my mind a scene on the Long Island Expressway when Martine was a baby and we were going to Jones Beach. About three cars ahead of us over in the right lane, a car started to veer, and as we got closer we could see the driver slumping down in his seat.

Before we could even think what to do, a state trooper appeared out of nowhere and jumped in on the driver's side to grab the wheel. Sirens started up, I guess they took him to the hospital, and a huge pile-up was averted. Watching it, I felt bad about how we used to call cops pigs. That sounds a little simpleminded, I know, but so was calling them pigs. And now I wondered how come a miracle in the form of a cop happened for that person and not for Carl, which is a question a retarded person might ask—I mean, an out-of-the-way street in Queens at eleven at night . . . It happened the way it happened, that's all. A loss to all those who might have enjoyed his topiary. I do think he would have done it in his own good time. If only we had had a little more time, I could have taken care of him. I wouldn't have been a miracle, but I would have done a good job. The way he vanished, though, I couldn't do a thing, not even say goodbye or hold his hand in the hospital or whatever it is old couples do—maybe the wife whispers that she'll be joining him soon, but I have no illusions that I'll ever be joining him, soon or late. I just got a lot less of him than I expected. Another thing is that the last time we made love I was slightly distracted because of the graduate student he admired for her determination, not that anything transpired between them except some ordinary conversation, but it started me wondering in general. Stupid, because I know very well how he felt, he told me every night. Those words I don't forget. I let them put me to sleep. I lie there remembering how it felt with his arms and legs flung over me and can't believe I'm expected to get through decades without ever feeling that again.

So I did end up working half days on Saturdays. In July Martine was supposed to go back to the camp run by the progressives and pacifists, where she had always had such a great time except for her tragedy with Mooney, and I didn't want to begin my life alone by asking for help.

"I don't have to go," she said. "If we don't have the money it's all right. I don't think I even feel like going anymore." My beautiful child with the tragic face. Now she had something worthy of that face.

"You should go, however you feel. When you get there you'll be glad."

"Except there's a slight problem," she said.

"What's that?"

"Rusty. I'm not taking him. Not after what happened to Mooney."

"No," I agreed.

"Which means . . ."

"Oh God! All right, I can do it. How bad can it be? A little lettuce, cabbage, right? A few handfuls of pellets . . ."

"There's the cage to clean too."

"The cage. Okay."

It was hard, her going off on the bus, with the typical scene of cheery mothers and fathers crowding around waving brown lunch bags, but I forced myself through it and so did she. I would force myself through the rest of my life if I had to.

First thing every morning and before I went to bed I put a handful of pellets in Rusty's bowl and fresh water in his bottle, and when I left for work and came home I dropped a few leaves of something green into the cage. Since I never really looked at him I was shocked, the fourth night after Martine left, when Mr. Coates, who had come up to fix the window lock in her room, said in his usual unexcited way, "Your pig's eye's popping out."

The right eye was protruding half an inch out of the socket and the cylindrical part behind it was yellow with gummy pus, a disgusting sight. "Jesus F. Christ," I said.

"He won't be no help to you. You need a vet."

The thought of going back to that arrogant vet who I always suspected had screwed up with Elf was more than I could take, so I searched the yellow pages till I found a woman vet in the neighborhood. When I walked in the next day carrying Rusty in a carton, I knew I had lucked out. She had curly hair like a mop, she wore jeans and a white sweatshirt, and she seemed young, maybe twenty-nine or thirty. Her name was Doctor Dunn. Very good, Doctor Dunn, so there won't be all that other shit to cope with.

To get him on the examining table I had to lift him up by his middle and feel all the squirminess and the beat of the scared delicate heart between my palms.

"It looks like either a growth of some kind pushing it forward, or maybe an abscess. But in either case I'm afraid the eye will have to go. It's badly infected and unless it's removed it'll dry up and the infection will spread and . . . uh . . ."

"He'll die?"

"Right."

159

Seventy-five dollars, she said, including his overnight stay, plus twenty-five for the biopsy. Terrific, I thought, just what I need. It was lower than the other vet's rates, though.

"I want to explain something about the surgery. He's a very small animal, two pounds or so, and any prolonged anesthesia is going to be risky. What this means is, I can't make any guarantees. I'd say his chances are . . . seventy–thirty, depending on his general condition. Of course, we'll do everything we can. . . ."

"And if I don't do it he'll die anyhow?"

"Right."

Squirming there on the table was this orange rat whose fate I was deciding. I felt very out of sync with reality, as if I was in a science fiction movie and how did I ever arrive at this place. "Okay. I guess we'd better do it."

The receptionist I left him with told me to call around four the next day to see how he came through the surgery. *If* was what she meant. That evening out of habit I almost went in to toss him some celery, then I remembered the cage was empty. There was no reason to go into Martine's room. But I decided to take the opportunity to clean the cage and the room both. I had found that the more I moved around the more numb I felt, which was what I wanted.

On the dot of four, I called from work. Doctor Dunn answered herself.

"He's fine! What a trouper, that Rusty! We had him hooked up to the EKG the whole time and monitored him, and he was terrific. I'm really pleased."

"Thank you," I managed to say. "Thank you very much." In one day she had established a closer relationship with him than I had in a year. That was an interesting thought. I mean, it didn't make me feel emotionally inadequate; I simply realized that's why she went through years of veterinary school, because she really cared, the way Carl could have about topiary, I guess.

"Can you come in and pick him up before seven? Then I can tell you about the post-op care."

Post-op care? I had never thought of that. I had never even thought of how the eye would look. Would it be a hole, or just a blank patch of fur? Would there be a bandage on it, or maybe she could fix him up with a special little eye patch?

I found Rusty in his carton on the front desk, with the receptionist petting him and calling him a good boy. "We're all crazy about him," she said. "He's quite a fella, aren't you, Rusty-baby?"

Where his right eye used to be, there was a row of five black stitches, and the area around it was shaved. Below the bottom stitch, a plastic tube the diameter of a straw and about an inch long stuck out. That was a drain for the wound, Doctor Dunn explained. He had a black plastic collar around his neck that looked like a ruff, the kind you see in old portraits of royalty. To keep him from poking himself, she said.

"Was he in good condition otherwise?" I thought I should sound concerned, in this world of animal-lovers.

"Oh, fine. Now . . . The post-operative care is a little complicated, so I wrote it down." She handed me a list of instructions:

1. Cold compresses tonight, 5–10 minutes.
2. Oral antibiotics, 3× a day for at least 7 days.
3. Keep collar on at all times.
4. Feed as usual.
5. Call if any excessive redness, swelling, or discharge develops.
6. Come in 3–4 days from now to have drain pulled.
7. Call early next week for biopsy results.
8. Make appointment for suture removal, 10–14 days.
9. Starting tomorrow, apply warm compresses 5–10 minutes, 2× a day for 10 days.

"Here's a sample bottle of antibiotics. Maybe I'd better do the first dose to show you how." She held him to her chest with one hand, while with the other she nudged his mouth open using the medicine dropper and squeezed the drops in, murmuring, "Come on now, that's a good boy, there you go." As she wiped the drips off his face and her sweatshirt with a tissue, I thought, Never. This is not happening to me. But I knew it was, and that I would have to go through with it.

When I went to get some ice water for the cold compress that night, I saw the message the graduate student mother had left on the refrigerator near Happy Birthday, which was now Happ Brhday. "Ne mezz l camn di nstr vita," it read. I knew some letters were missing though not which ones, and those that were left were crooked, but I remembered well enough what it meant. I sat down to watch the ten o'clock news with Rusty on my lap and put the compress on his eye, or the place where his eye used to be, but he squirmed around wildly, clawing at my pants. Ice water oozed onto my legs. I told him to cut it out, he had no choice. Finally I tried patting him and talking to him like a baby, to quiet him. Don't worry, kiddo, you're going to be all right—stuff like that, the way Carl would have done without feeling idiotic. It worked. Only hearing those words loosened me a little out of my numbness and I had this terrible sensation of walking a tightrope in pitch darkness, though in fact I was whispering sweet nothings to a guinea pig. I even thought of telling him what I'd been through with my appendix, a fellow sufferer, and God knows what next, but I controlled myself. If I freaked out, who would take care of Martine?

I figured seven and a half minutes for the compress was fair enough—Doctor Dunn had written down 5–10. Then I changed my mind and held it there for another minute so if anything happened I would have a clear conscience when I told Martine. I held him to my chest with a towel over my shirt, feeling the heart pulsing against me, and squirted in the antibiotic. I lost a good bit, but I'd have plenty of chances to improve.

In the morning I found the collar lying in the mess of shit and cedar chips in his cage. I washed it and tried to get it back on him, but he fought back with his whole body—each time I fitted it around his neck he managed to squirm and jerk his way out, till beyond being repelled I was practically weeping with frustration. Two people could have done it easily. Carl, I thought, if ever I needed you . . . Finally after a great struggle I got it fastened in back with masking tape so he wouldn't undo it. But when I came home from work it was off again and we wrestled again. The next morning I rebelled. The drops, the compresses, okay, but there was no way I was going to literally collar a rodent morning and night for ten days. There are limits to everything, especially on a tightrope in the dark. I called Doctor Dunn from work.

"Is he poking himself around the eye?" she asked. "Any bleeding or discharge? Good. Then forget it. You can throw the collar away."

I was so relieved.

"How is he otherwise? Is he eating?"

"Yes. He seems okay. Except he's shedding." I told her how when I lifted him up, orange hairs fluttered down into his cage like leaves from a tree. When leaves fell off Carl's plants, which I was also try-

ing to keep alive though that project wasn't as dramatic, it usually
meant they were on their way out. I had already lost three—I didn't
have his green thumb. It seemed my life had become one huge effort
to keep things alive, with death hot on my trail. I even had night-
mares about what could be happening to Martine at camp. When I
wrote to her, though, I tried to sound casual, as if I was fine, and I
wrote that Rusty was fine too. Maybe Carl would have given her all
the gory details, but I didn't mind lying. He was going to be fine. I
was determined that pig would live even if it was over my dead body.
Luckily I wasn't so far gone as to say all this to Doctor Dunn. "Is
that a bad sign?"

"Shedding doesn't mean anything," she said. "He doesn't feel
well, so he's not grooming himself as usual. It'll stop as he gets
better."

I also noticed, those first few days, he would do this weird dance
when I put the food in his cage. It dawned on me that he could smell
it but not see it. While he scurried around in circles, I kept trying
to shove it towards his good side—kind of a Bugs Bunny routine.
Then after a while he developed a funny motion, turning his head
to spot it, and soon he was finding it pretty well with his one eye. I
told Doctor Dunn when I brought him in to have the drain removed.
She said yes, they adapt quickly. They compensate. She talked about
evolution and why eyes were located where they were. Predators, she
said, have close-set eyes in the front of their heads to see the prey, and
the prey have eyes at the sides, to watch out for the predators. How
clever, I thought, the way nature matched up the teams. You couldn't
change your destiny, but you had certain traits that kept the game
going and gave you the illusion of having a fighting chance. We talked
about it for a good while. She was interesting, that Doctor Dunn.

A few days later she plucked out the stitches with tweezers while
I held him down.

"I have to tell you," she said, "not many people would take such
pains with a guinea pig. Some people don't even bother with dogs
and cats, you'd be amazed. They'd rather have them put away. You
did a terrific job. You must really love animals."

I didn't have the heart to tell her that although it didn't turn my
stomach anymore to hold him on my lap and stroke him for the com-
presses, he was still just a fat rat as far as I was concerned, but a fat
rat which fate had arranged I had to keep alive. So I did.

"Well, you could say I did it for love."

She laughed. "Keep applying the warm compresses for another day or two, to be on the safe side. Then that's it. Case closed."

"What about the biopsy?"

"Oh yes, the lab report. It's not in yet, but I have a feeling it wasn't malignant. He doesn't look sick to me. Call me on it next week."

In eleven days Martine will be back. Beautiful Martine, with her suntan making her almost the color of Rusty. I'll warn her about the eye before she sees him. It doesn't look too gruesome now, with the stitches out and the hair growing back—soon it'll be a smooth blank space. In fact, if not for the missing eye she would never have to know what he went through. The house will feel strange to her all over again without Carl, because whenever you're away for a while you expect to come home to some pure and perfect condition. She'll be daydreaming on the bus that maybe it was all a nightmare and the both of us are here waiting for her. But it'll be an altogether different life, and the worst thing is—knowing us, sensible, adaptable types— that one remote day we'll wake up and it'll seem normal this way, and in years to come Carl will turn into the man I had in my youth instead of what he is now, my life. I even envy her—he'll always be her one father.

So I'm applying the warm compresses for the last time, sitting here with a one-eyed guinea pig who is going to live out his four-to-six-year life span no matter what it takes, in the middle of the journey of my life, stroking him as if I really loved animals.

The Two Portraits of Rembrandt

I H A V E before me on picture postcards two self-portraits by Rembrandt, one painted in 1629, when he was twenty-three, the other in 1669, the year of his death. I have been eyeing them on and off for a long time, two years, as objects to be decoded. The message would be something beyond the obvious one about experience as registered in the flesh and the trek towards death. They seem to refer to passages, journeys, remote from Rembrandt's; they suggest something closer to home.

"The extraordinary phenomenon of Rembrandt's self-portraits," the critic Jakob Rosenberg tells us, "has no parallel in the seventeenth century or even in the entire history of art." Sixty of them, besides etchings and drawings. Years ago, in an introductory art history class, the instructor asked why, in our opinion, did Rembrandt paint himself so many times. Egotism, I promptly thought, and that was the answer a few jocular students gave. Our instructor was disheartened. "Rembrandt seems to have felt that he had to know himself if he wished to penetrate the problem of man's inner life," Jakob Rosenberg says. How obvious. How could I not have perceived that, even at seventeen?

The figure in both portraits is posed in the same way: upper body on the diagonal, head turned to face the viewer. The right side of the face is lit and the left is in shadow, but this contrast is more pronounced in the early work. In both portraits Rembrandt wears something white around his neck, while the rest of the clothing is black, first a glossy, elegant black, then, forty years later, drab and porous. From the young Rembrandt there radiates a willed elegance, an arrogance nearing defiance—youthful softness masquerading as hardness. His soft brown hair billows around his face, a long, smooth face, smoothly painted. The eyes are dark, soft, and unwelcoming, and a shadowy furrow grooves the bridge of the nose, which is straight and fleshy at the tip; the lips are rosy and curled, with the faintest suggestion of a mustache, the chin is prominent, and the space between lips and chin a shade long, a subtle disproportion adding to the general aloofness. It could be the portrait of a youth too clever for his own good painted by a discerning older person. But the painter is the youth himself, appraising his forced arrogance. A faint wonder ruffles the surface—how dare you presume to capture me, know me?

In the later portrait, all, as one might expect, is changed utterly. Rembrandt is wearing a hat, an amber beret streaked with beige. The hair is wispier, less carefully groomed; the skin has Rembrandt's characteristic mottled texture. No more smoothness, either in the subject or in the manner of presentation. The nose is fleshier and nubbier, the mouth a thin line. The fine slope of the jaw has given way to jowls and double chin: everywhere paunchy, pouchy fleshiness. He looks sad, weary, a man who has been through hard times. As indeed he has: he has seen his popularity and esteem, at their height in his thirties, gradually wane; he has seen three children die at birth; has suffered the loss of his wife, Saskia, and years later of his mistress and housekeeper, Hendrickje Stoffels; has lost his only son, Titus, at the age of twenty-nine; has been bankrupt and lost most of his possessions—enough to leave pouches on anyone's face.

Jakob Rosenberg writes that this last self-portrait exhibits "some decline in the aged artist's expressive power. His painterly skill has not failed him, but the psychological content shows a diminished intensity. The facial expression here is mild and slightly empty, when compared to all the others in the imposing group of late self-portraits," which the same critic calls, variously, mellow, tragic, monumental, reflecting "mythical grandeur and dignity," "philosophic superiority," "a deep consciousness of man's fateful destiny," and so forth.

True, there is little grandeur or majesty here, but the expression is not so much empty as subdued, in the way of a man who has withdrawn his investment in his face and liquidated it, so to speak, who is in the process of ceasing to care.

I have before me also two pictures of my father with about a forty-year interval between them, not paintings but photographs. The first is a standard graduation photo, so old that the cap and gown have almost merged with the dark background. I can just make out one sharp corner of the mortarboard floating above my father's head, pointing forward like a lance. Held flat under the light, though, the photo relinquishes the whole silhouette—gown, hat, and tassel— black eerily detaching itself from sepia. This must have been taken on the occasion of his graduation from Brooklyn Law School, when he was twenty-two or -three, about Rembrandt's age in the first self-portrait. My father sometimes said that if he had had the means— money, social class, correct ethnic background—to attend law school at Harvard or Yale, his life would have gone differently. He was not a complainer; this was a simple fact. It seems to me his life did not go so badly as it was, but what can I presume to know about his aspirations? I do know he wanted to make a lot of money and that from time to time, to my mother's horror, he would invest in risky business deals cooked up with like-minded aspirers, and lose his savings. To the end of his days he kept his dream of striking it rich. Rembrandt, who was a notoriously poor financial manager, as well as hugely extravagant in his youth, was driven in later years to an odd stratagem to stave off creditors. A contract was drawn up in which Hendrickje Stoffels and his son, Titus, were made proprietors of a business, art dealers engaged in selling the works of Rembrandt, who would own nothing himself—save his genius—and be in effect working for them. My father was not a poor manager, in fact he earned his living advising others on prudently managing their businesses, and he was not too extravagant either. But he enjoyed taking risks. Maybe it was not Brooklyn Law School that thwarted him. Maybe he too had entered, tacitly, into a contract wherein his talents were used in the service of his wife and children: an employee of a sort. In any case, the graduation picture is of a man I never knew, who hardly knew himself yet.

The connection, the curious feature, is my father's striking resemblance to the young Rembrandt—I should say my father's graduation photo's resemblance to Rembrandt's self-portrait. Even the poses are similar, though reversed—my father's left side faces the viewer and the right side of his face is shadowed—and the costumes, black relieved by the white collar. Like Rembrandt's, my father's eyes are dark, only instead of being aloof and impenetrable they are penetrating—two little glints of light, like lasers, animate the pupils. The nose, like Rembrandt's, is straight, then fleshy at the tip, the mouth has the same beautiful bow shape and haughty curl, there is the same unsettling length between mouth and prominent chin. An elongated, smooth arrogance, the blank, hard defiance of youth. Both faces are touching in their innocence and at the same time conceal what they might know, as the faces of youth can readily do.

My father did not age as drastically as Rembrandt; his cheeks remain firm in the later photo; the face is more fleshy and molded, but hardly paunchy. Because he did not suffer the wearying effects of self-scrutiny? But why should there be any resemblance, why should the comparison be symmetrical? Granted that faces in their sixties mirror the trajectory of their owners' lives, my father's life had little in common with Rembrandt's. Their similar faces took dissimilar routes to the same end. Maybe in their eighties, when the uniqueness of individual faces is subsumed under the common fate, they might again have looked alike—but neither lived that long. Meanwhile my father never lost children or wife; he was not a painter and not seeking knowledge of man's inner life; he neither achieved wide acclaim in his youth nor lost it; his business reversals were not on so grand a scale, and unlike Rembrandt, he always managed to haul his forces together and venture anew. In this late photograph (a group picture including my mother and four friends) he appears to be a calm, wise, contented man. Still handsome, in his white shirt and gray patterned tie he looks straight into the camera, one eye, as always, open slightly wider than the other, and he is almost smiling, on the verge of a full smile—but he cannot quite yield it up, as he could not quite yield up the tear I once saw in his eye. Even so, he emits benevolence. Judicious, good-tempered. Maybe not "mythical grandeur and dignity," but "philosophic superiority," yes. Is this the "real" man, sage and mellow? Does he know himself at last? I feel that although dead now, he is looking straight at me, that I am looking back at myself.

Perhaps the soul does not depart from the body at the last breath, to fly out the window and rise, but begins departing in the late years and takes its leave gradually, puff by puff, which accounts for the shrinking we notice and grieve over, the "diminished intensity" the critic complains of in the last Rembrandt self-portrait. In the late photo of my father, though, I see no diminishment yet; the face is fully alive with the abiding spirit.

My father's hand would slice the air dismissively at my analyzing pictures. I myself feel a tribal needling: all this trouble for *pictures*?

He lived by the word. Pictures were a crude, provisional mode of representation and communication, happily supplanted by the advent of language. People who still looked at pictures for information were in a pre-verbal state, babies or Neanderthals. The *Daily News*, "New York's Picture Newspaper," was a publication designed for the illiterate, for "morons." Likewise *Life* magazine, which prided itself on its photography; he would not have it in the house. His newspaper of choice, the *New York Times*, contained pictures, but he probably regarded them as a concession to the occasional lapses of its readers, or proof that certain events took place, for instance that the Big Three—Roosevelt, Churchill, and Stalin—really did meet at Yalta. Other printed matter he would not allow in the house were confession magazines and *Classic Comics*, which retold great books in cartoons with captions. My aunt in Brownsville once gave me two *Classic Comics* for my birthday. I flaunted them—he wouldn't outlaw a birthday gift, but he offered to buy me the real books if only I would get the comics out of his sight. In the end I had to admit he was right, they were as nothing next to the real thing, and so for a long time I didn't value pictures either. Like him, I trusted only things that came in the form of or humbly awaited translation into words.

Or numbers. In company he liked to announce his age, a habit my mother deplored. "I'll be fifty-three years old in February!" "I'm fifty-eight years old!" "Sixty-four last February!" he would proclaim, beaming, twinkling, puffing out his chest as if the attainment of such years without showing them deserved a decoration. This was self-knowledge of a kind: he could translate himself into numbers, he kept track. My mother would grumble or slip out of the room. She would never reveal her age. When pressed, she told me she was seven years younger than he—seven must have been the highest number she thought she could offer without suggesting a questionable age gap. But part of family lore was that my parents had met in high school. When I asked how this could be if they were seven years apart, she said my father had been behind in school because he was an immigrant. He must have been very far behind, it seemed to me, maybe even a ludicrous figure?—my own school had some hulking retarded students who turned up in the same classroom perennially, like furniture. . . . Mostly I would contemplate their seven-year age difference and their meeting in high school, two irreconcilable facts, then shove it aside like a shoelace you can't unknot—today, anyway.

My mother was two years younger than my father, I learned much later. My desire to know was frustrated by one type of vanity. My father, even in his immigrant state, was not far behind at all, it turns out; his type of vanity would hardly have liked my thinking he was.

Maybe it was their limitation and finiteness that he disliked about pictures. He loved what was bountiful and boundless and hated anything mean and narrow. (He hated the way he was offered food at the *Classic Comics* aunt's house in Brownsville. " 'You don't want a piece of fruit, do you?' " he would imitate. "What does she expect a person to say? Of course I don't want a piece of fruit.") Pictures were circumscribed by their frames. A house, a tree, a cloud, added up to a landscape, and that was the end of it. The space of pictures is inner space, but he didn't look into, he looked at. Words, though, could go on forever, linear, one opening the door to a dozen others, each new one nudging at another door, and so on to infinite mansions of meditation. Nor was there any limit to what you could say; words bred more words, spawned definition, comparison, analogy. A picture is worth a thousand words, I was told in school. Confucius. But to me, too, the value seemed quite the other way around. And why not ten thousand, a hundred thousand? Give me a picture and I could provide volumes. Meanings might be embedded in the picture, but only words could release them and at the same time, at the instant they were born and borne from the picture, seize them, give them shape and specific gravity. Nothing was really possessed or really real until it was incarnate in words. Show and Tell opened every school day, but I rarely cared to show anything. You could show forever, but how could you be sure the essence had been transmitted, without words? Words contained the knowledge, words *were* the knowledge, the logos, and words verified that the knowledge was there.

Long ago, long before I knew him, my father must have had a foreign accent. I try to imagine how he sounded and hear a stranger. Did my mother, sitting next to him in high school, watch it gradually slip from him, as you watch a swimmer gradually dry in the sun, the drops first showering off, then rolling down slowly, then evaporating imperceptibly? Was there a point at which she told him, "You've got it, relax, you sound like everyone else"? One way or another, his command of the language, like Rembrandt's of his brushes, reached virtuoso proportions. Maybe—and one might suspect this of Rembrandt too, judging from the early self-portrait—he was like those stubbornly perfectionist babies you hear of, who refuse to babble, and speak only when they can produce flawless paragraphs. But fluency alone is not memorable; he was verbally idiosyncratic, selective, in such a way—or to such ears—that he leaves behind most vividly a heap of phrases, as the other left canvases by which to know him.

My father spoke of visits to my mother's family as "going to Williamsburg," "going to Brownsville," "going to Borough Park"—the last pronounced as one word with the accent on the first syllable—rather than going to her mother's or sisters' houses. This made the visit more of a geographical venture than a personal encounter. His mode of being in the world turned on movement, getting from one place to another rather than being anywhere, something that intensified as he aged and became less mobile. Then on a family visit, immediately upon reaching the destination he would check his watch and the car's odometer and announce, "We made very good time." No sooner was he settled in a chair than he would begin calculating when he might start the return trip, plotting, again, how to make the best time. Of course, he was not well in his last years and was most comfortable lying in bed. But all his life he preferred any position to sitting; he lived in physical extremes, either frenetic movement or total repose. After supper he would lie down with the *New York Times* on the red tufted couch in the living room and wonder why my brother, at seven years old, wouldn't stop running around making noise and lie down with him. But he would stand to eat breakfast and stand, or pace, to converse. My brother and sister and I do not much like to sit either. We are most comfortable standing or lying down. Something in our genetic structure does not like to bend.

Williamsburg, Brownsville, and Borough Park were neighborhoods in Brooklyn which because of my father's frequent mention of them ("What's doing in Borough Park?" after my mother telephoned her sister) remain archetypal place names bearing the personalities of my aunts and my grandmother. Now Brooklyn boasts unfamiliar names that sound concocted: Cobble Hill, Carroll Gardens, Boerum Hill. Where are these strange places? I think, and what are their real names? I can see my father's lips compressing scornfully, rejecting the new fatuities. Greenwich Village, once Manhattan's Bohemia, he persisted in pronouncing as spelled rather than the correct "Grennich" Village. Far as he was from Bohemia, he must have heard the words spoken; I think he persisted in the literal pronunciation to protest at least one of the area's many, to him, arty eccentricities.

He spent his first American years on Cherry Street on Manhattan's Lower East Side, and forever after spoke the words "Cherry Street" with a tone of disgust and hostility, a tone in which I could feel the textures of deprivation, of all that was disheveled and ungainly. He would have been appalled to know that a movie called *Hester Street* (near Cherry Street) drew fashionable crowds over fifty years later, that his humiliation was advertised as art. Now on Cherry Street stand tall buildings, low- and middle-income housing. Hispanic people, Chinese people, artists live there, not in squalor. But when I hear the words "Cherry Street" I think, squalor, confinement, and I feel the lust to rise up out of them—as if that had not already been done for me.

In speech and in everything else he liked boldness and swiftness and despised timidity or hesitation, and he promulgated these tastes as absolutes. Fortunately my brother and sister and I came to be loud or swift or bold, most of the time; we picked it up in the atmosphere or had it in the genes or learned it for survival. The faint of heart, the slow, sometimes even the thoughtful, were morally inferior as well as aesthetically displeasing. My father was driving up Utica Avenue in Brooklyn, a steep hill, when an elderly woman, crossing as the light was changing, saw our car approach and stopped midstreet. Then she reconsidered and started to walk again. He slowed down; she stopped. He accelerated; she trotted. Madly working the gearshift, he came to a violent halt and rolled down the window. My innards stiffened at the prospect of what terrible words he would say, how he would mortify her, the epitome of all he scorned. (Rembrandt, too, was reputed to be "a most temperamental man" who tended to "disparage everyone" and make "brusque, ironical remarks.") As she stood in the middle of the street, thoroughly muddled now, he at last hurled out sternly, resoundingly, "Don't falter!"

My mother could be loud and bold and swift when necessary, but in a manner different from the rest of us. Softer, with prettiness and diplomacy. She was what men call "emotional"; her words and judgments arose from feeling and intuition rather than reason, a mode of operation inimical to my father. He would ask her a question, did she want to go here or there at such and such a time, and she would reply with a string of conditional sentences. "Give me a yes or no answer!" he would shout. I admired his quest for clarity and definitiveness; I took it as a categorical imperative. If every question had a yes or no answer there would be fewer problems in the world, no shilly-shallying. Later I learned that this tactic came from a legalistic tradition and was used in the courtroom to interrogate witnesses. So he had not invented it—though it might have been invented expressly for him.

It wasn't obscenities that I feared my father would hurl at the faltering woman—I had never heard him use those. "God-damned" was his adjective in moderate anger, and "Goddamn it to hell" his expletive when he was seriously enraged; he was a man inhabited by rage, who seemed most alive, most recognizably himself, when in a verbal tempest. His furies lashed the stupidity or willfulness of those around him, and in them would blaze forth like lightning the word "moron," his worst epithet. In our household, "moron" was a word of such immense power and inclusiveness, so thoroughly condemning, that the filthier words I learned later are mild in comparison. "Moron" was the worst epithet because brains were the most precious possession, without which a person was of little or no worth. "There's no substitute for brains," he liked to say. Brains were demonstrated by articulate speech, such as his own disquisitions on political and economic topics. He would fix the listener with his glittering brown eyes and address him or her as a hypothetical You. The thesis might be abstract, the workings of the laissez-faire economy or the dynamics of imperialism, but it would usually be illustrated by a concrete example. "Let's say You have half a million dollars to invest. Now supposing You happen upon an extremely advantageous . . ." And so on. Then at some point—perhaps You were about to indulge in a shady deal, to act with less than utter probity— he would reassure his listener, "I mean editorial You, of course, you understand." He never failed to make this explanation about editorial You, an odd scruple in a man who was otherwise quite ready to call people morons.

He was generally pleased with his three children because he judged them intelligent, but women, to be worthy, had to be pretty as well. Those who were not he called "dogs" and found it painful to be in their presence. "She's a dog," he would say with revulsion, but a different kind of revulsion than he used for "Moron!"—a sort of regretful revulsion, as if it were not the woman's fault that her presence

173

pained him, whereas in the case of "Moron!" the person was held responsible. Among my friends, who were perpetually crowding into the house, he liked the ones who were bright, pretty, and lively; he asked them questions so he could enjoy their replies and tease them a bit, and he addressed lectures on politics to them, using editorial You; the others he avoided.

When he felt insufficiently appreciated or when my mother disagreed with his views, he would say with rueful conviction, "A man is never a prophet in his own home town," and till I was grown I mistook the key word for "profit," possibly because he was a businessman as well as a lawyer and often spoke of "the profit motive," for example, as the real reason for the United States' hostility to communism ("Markets! Markets! It's all economics! The profit motive!"). Strangely enough, I attributed almost the right meaning to the adage anyway, though I was puzzled by its semantic awkwardness. Then at some point I realized it was "prophet" he had been uttering all those years. So it was not respect and credit and glory that he sought, but spiritual allegiance. Disciples. In a less exalted sense, company.

He loved company, especially on errands or trips to the doctor and dentist. He cajoled me into watching him get haircuts and have his shoes shined, and on a few Saturdays even took me along to see a client upstate, to have company for the drive. He would present me with aplomb to the barber or client, try to get me to say something clever, then proceed with business. I always brought a book. I, who loved the idea of going places alone and thought it the pinnacle of adulthood, would suspect that, like our government in its hostility to communism, he had an ulterior motive—to get me out of the house or tell me a secret—but he didn't. He truly wanted company.

In turn he would offer to drive us—his children—and our friends to places, and given the way he loved to drive, he would want to drive us to places we preferred to walk to, and would feel slighted when his offers were declined. He had little understanding of walking for pleasure, of allowing time to flow unorganized, of not wishing to "make good time." He took walks, as far as I was aware, only during the summers, in the country, when he would often ask me along for company. We would set out down the dirt road and he would commence beating the bushes on either side for a good walking stick. He couldn't amble along without a purpose, so the purpose became finding the walking stick. I would find a few candidates, but they generally didn't meet his standards, which were unclear. At last he would find just the right one—thick, sturdy, a good height; he would rip the twigs and leaves from it and, holding it in his right hand and stomping it on the ground, walk still more purposefully, trying it out. We went along, talking; he explained things to me, not about the natural surroundings we were in, of which he knew nothing, but political and social things; sometimes I even had the pleasure of being editorial You and having my responses solicited in a Socratic way. Before I was ever satisfied with our walk, he would turn around. It seemed the thrill of the walk was over once he had found the stick and tested it. At the end of the walk he would usually toss it back into the woods, and when the next walk came around he regretted it. "I had such a good walking stick last week—what ever happened to it?" He had a nostalgic turn of mind. Nothing today was as good as it had been yesterday, and nothing was ever as good as it could be.

The world in general showed an offensive, needless disorder. At the refusal of people and events in the world of our household to arrange themselves as he wished and knew to be best, he often called, in alarming tones, for "discipline." He was forever "putting his foot down." "Discipline! Discipline!" and when I was quite young it would frighten me to think of what terrible rules might be forthcoming. But it was only the word. The foot never came down. After such scenes my mother, who was intimidated neither by his pronouncements and threats nor by their volume, would tell me that his father, "the old man," had been a stern disciplinarian, and that while his sons forever resented him for it, they kept the notion that it was the way to be a father. I am hard put to remember any rule he actually laid down. No comic books and no reading at the dinner table are all that come to mind, and the latter we—my sister and I, the offenders—often ignored. This is not to say that his bark was worse than his bite. His bark *was* his bite. To know him meant to have been exposed to his fierceness, fiercely articulate. But even then what did you know, really? Only that he had an immense vat of boiling fury inside, in precarious balance, waiting to be tipped over.

Certain times when his anger was provoked, or when he wished to give the impression that it was, he would stand quite still and say he was "counting to ten." He would press his lips into a hard thin line and I would imagine, pounding inside his head, "One, two, three . . ." Then he would speak quietly, in a tight voice. He took pride in these moments of tantrums controlled notwithstanding great provocation, and even seemed to expect admiration from us, his near victims. But no one congratulated him, for we understood he was only pretending: the provocation lacked the mysterious extra grain that rubbed the equally mysterious sore place in his soul and caused the explosive, intolerable pain, sweeping him past the gates of civilized restraint to a far and savage, solitary place. Then there was no counting to ten. Then he would call volcanically for "peace and quiet." "Will you let me have some peace and quiet!"—holding his head as if it might erupt. At the apogee of the tantrum he would yell at my mother, "You make my life miserable!" and would flee, slamming the front door so the house shook. I would hear the engine starting up in the driveway, sputtering as violently as he, then the whiz of the car escaping down the street. I was sure he would never be back. The next hour or two, alone in my room with the door closed, I would try to decide whom to live with after the divorce, and conjure the scene of myself being consulted in the judge's chambers, a dark room with dark drapes and green carpets and oak furniture, the judge in black robes and gray hair, with a somber countenance, feeling sorry for me in my plight—the whole scene something like a Rembrandt painting, murky, a spiritual murk, redolent of profundity and pain. It was a difficult decision; there were significant pros and cons on either side, but I knew how to give a yes or no answer, and most of the time (not always—not when I was too repelled by his noise) I would decide to go with my father, never doubting that he would request me of the judge: he was easier to live with, his arbitrariness congruent with my own; he set fewer rules and left me more to myself. I felt a temperamental affinity, I understood him, or so I believed. And the absence of my mother would not really be an absence, I felt obscurely. A mother is so close, you can carry her around inside wherever you go. But a father can escape. And then who would talk to me? His presence, like that of all men, was exotic. When he came home at night I would ask what he had done out in the world, and he would tell me. I would have a glimpse of what awaited me.

I felt sorry for my mother for the impending loss of us both (and how baffled she would be at my choice!), but after all, she had provoked him, hadn't she? Yet why did his reaction have to be so violent—why the words so torrentially bitter? Why remove a splinter with pliers? The answer was a mystery known as the family temper, spoken of by my aunts and uncles by marriage with a resignation they might have employed for the genealogical shape of a chin or a hand. No one sought its origin, mired in the bogs of history and the tangle of chromosomes. No one had ever gotten anywhere trying to reform it; you lived with it and navigated your way around it, like a neighbor's savage watchdog.

I don't think my father knew what he was so angry about either. He was not introspective by nature and the habit of introspection had not yet suffused the middle class so that one undertook it as a duty whether or not so inclined. He too must have felt his terrible temper as a hereditary burden no more eradicable than his inherited and tireless heart, which kept cruelly beating when every other organ had failed and when he tried to yank from his chest the patches hooking him to the heart monitoring machine, mistaking them for life-sustaining equipment. And because he was not introspective and his words were spontaneously borne on currents of logic or enthusiasm or impulse or rage, we were not a family who ever "talked things over." When I hear nowadays the psychological language urging family members to settle differences by calm discussion, to reveal their feelings, be "open," when I see snatches of television families "working things through," I get a sense of comic unreality. I try it so that my children do not become thralls to verbal fire and brimstone, but I have a sense of rubbing against the grain, of participating in some faddish, newfangled ritual. I feel like shouting out what I want and hearing others shout back, and slugging it out with ever more pungent insults. . . .

While I drifted in fantasies of our life together, in which I would know instinctively how not to provoke him, the car would pull into the driveway, the door would open and close with a temperate sound. Relief and disappointment: no dramatic change now, no exotic twosome. I never gave a thought to where he might have been during that hour or two. Probably just driving, counting to ten, till the wild sea-green vein in his right temple stopped pulsing.

After these outbursts, my mother could remain cool for days ("belligerent," he would call her; "Why do you walk around with a chip on your shoulder?"), but she sensibly refused to believe she made his life miserable. I, who took all words literally, especially those spoken with passion, still thought it logical and inevitable that one of them should leave. The concept of leaving was not in my mother's repertoire of possibilities, and besides, she regarded the words as no more meaningful than steam or lava. She preferred to give credence to other of his remarks, such as when in company, if she referred to her size—she was a very large woman—and he had had a drink or two, he would say gaily, "I love every inch of it," though most of the time, quite unlike her, he was reserved to the point of prudery about sexual matters. I saw him twist my mother's arm with the playful sadism that was his sign of physical affection, but I never saw a real embrace or a real kiss.

She said too that when they were alone he was another way entirely; he merely had to "show off" in front of others. She was instinctively right about matters of the heart; it was probably this very rightness, those relentless instincts, amiably presented, unsupported by any rational structure, that my father found so exasperating. Also, despite her conventional moral judgments, she had endless sympathy and excuses for wrong-doers. Public Defender, he called her, and this too, I realized only later, was a legal term with a very specific meaning. He might be ready with money, words, car rides, and devotion, but he could not, or would not, comprehend moral ambivalence or extend sympathy for emotional confusion. Once, when I was in my twenties, I tried talking to him about some painful dilemma, which took nerve—we all talked a lot, constantly, but we did not "have talks." As I started to cry he walked out of the room. When he saw it was something no money or car ride could help, that I was not editorial You this time, he was confounded, as confounded as the woman crossing the street.

I never saw but one tear of his: at the funeral of my mother's mother he delicately flicked at his lower lid with his pinkie, smiling cavalierly, pretending it was a speck. My grandmother, she of Williamsburg, was a woman of the sort he loved: feisty, clever, pretty, bold, swift, decisive, and opinionated, and years earlier he had taught her, in Yiddish, to play gin rummy, in which all those qualities could be brought to bear, and had pronounced her an excellent player, which was very unusual, because most of the people he played cards with, including my mother and the five men in his weekly pinochle game, he called morons.

When he was old and sick and I visited him, I brought along many pairs of corduroy pants to hem—I had young children and was busy,

I couldn't waste a minute. He wasn't saying much. But sitting on the back porch, watching me pick up one pair of corduroy pants after another, he did say, "You haven't stopped sewing since you got here." I nodded and kept on. Would it not be sufficient, he was asking, simply to keep him company, even if he could no longer offer the flow of words? He may even have been acknowledging—little as I like to think he knew about such matters—that I couldn't sit still and watch him die, I could hardly sit under the best of circumstances, so I let down hems for growing children. At that moment he was undergoing, as Jakob Rosenberg says of Rembrandt's last portrait, "some decline in . . . expressive power." His face showed "a diminished intensity." His spirit, so amply present in the serene and judicious photo, was leaving puff by puff. He was in the process of ceasing to care.

I have had the graduation photo of my father for almost ten years, since he, raging without words, died, and the picture postcards of the Rembrandts for about two years. Only the other day did the fourth one, my father in his sixties, fall into my hands, completing the group, that is, notifying me that they formed a group. My father would find all this silly and suppositious, especially since I clearly live, as he did, by the word. I would not attempt to explain to him, even if I could, that the pictures have been speaking to me in sentence fragments, subjects only, for a very long time, and that the arrival of the fourth picture was the long-awaited predicate. And then they had to be translated.

Mrs. Saunders Writes to the World

MRS. SAUNDERS placed her white plastic bag of garbage in one of the cans behind the row of garden apartments and looked about for a familiar face, but finding nothing except two unknown toddlers with a babysitter in the playground a short distance off, she shrugged, gazed briefly into the wan early spring sun, and climbed the stairs back to her own door. She was looking for someone because she had a passion to hear her name spoken. But once inside, as she sponged her clean kitchen counter with concentrated elliptical strokes, she had to acknowledge that hearing "Mrs. Saunders" would not be good enough anymore. She needed—she had begun to long, in fact, with a longing she found frightening in its intensity—to hear her real name.

She squeezed the sponge agonizingly over the sink, producing a few meager drops. No one called her anything but Mrs. Saunders now. Her name was Fran. Frances. She whispered it in the direction of the rubber plant on the windowsill. Fran, Franny, Frances. Anyone seeing her, she thought, might suspect she was going crazy. Yet they said it was good to talk to your plants. She could always explain that she was whispering to them for their health and growth. Fran, Franny, Frances, she breathed again. Then she added a few wordless breaths, purely for the plants' sake, and felt somewhat less odd.

There was no one left to call her Fran. Her husband had called her Franny, but he was long dead. Her children, scattered across the country, called her Ma when they came at wide intervals to visit, or when she paid her yearly visit to each of the three. Except for Walter, she reminded herself, as she was fussy over accuracy, except for Walter, whom she saw only about once every year and a half, since he lived far away in Oregon and since his wife was what they called unstable and couldn't stand visitors too often or for too long a period.

Her old friends were gone or far off, and the new ones stuck to "Mrs. Saunders." The young people who moved in and out of these garden apartments thought of themselves as free and easy, she mused, but in fact they had their strange formalities, like always calling her Mrs. Saunders, even though they might run in two or three times a week to borrow groceries or ask her to babysit or see if she needed a lift to the supermarket. She pursed her lips in annoyance, regarded her impeccable living room, then pulled out the pack of cigarettes hidden in a drawer in the end table beside her chair. Mrs. Saunders didn't like these young girls who ran in and out to see her smoking; it wasn't seemly. She lit one and inhaled deeply, feeling a small measure of relief.

It wasn't that they were cold or unfriendly. Just that they didn't seem to realize she had a name like anyone else and might wish to hear it spoken aloud once in a while by someone other than herself in her darkened bedroom at night, or at full volume in the shower, mornings. And though she knew she could say to her new neighbors, "Call me Fran," as simply as that, somehow whenever the notion came to her the words got stuck in her throat. Then she lost the drift of the conversation and worried that the young people might think her strange, asking them to repeat things they had probably said perfectly clearly the first time. And if there was one thing she definitely did not want, she thought, stubbing the cigarette out firmly, it was to be regarded as senile. She had a long way to go before that.

Suddenly the air in the neat room seemed intolerably stuffy. Cigarette smoke hung in a cloud around her. Mrs. Saunders felt weak and terribly unhappy. She rose heavily and stepped out onto her small balcony for a breath of air. Jill was lounging on the next balcony with a friend.

"Oh, hi, Mrs. Saunders. How are you? Isn't it a gorgeous day?" Tall, blond, and narrow-shouldered, Jill drew in a lungful of smoke and pushed it out with pleasure.

"Hello, Jill dear. How's everything?"

"Struggling along." Jill stretched out her long jean-clad legs till her feet rested on the railing. "Mrs. Saunders, this is my friend, Wendy. Wendy, Mrs. Saunders. Mrs. Saunders has been so terrific to us," she said to Wendy. "And she never complains about the kids screeching on the other side of the wall."

"Hi," said Wendy.

"Nice to meet you, Wendy," said Mrs. Saunders. "I don't mind the children, Jill, really I don't. After all, I had children of my own. I know what it's like."

"That's right. Three, aren't there?"

"Yes," Mrs. Saunders said. "Walter, Louise, and Edith. Walter was named after his father."

"We named Jeff after his father too," Wendy remarked.

"Mrs. Saunders sometimes babysits for Luke and Kevin," Jill explained to Wendy. "They adore her. Sometimes they even tell us to go out so she can come and stay with them. I don't know what it is you do with them, Mrs. Saunders."

She smiled, and would have liked to linger with the two young women, but suddenly she had to go in, because a furious sob rose in her throat, choking her. She threw herself down on the bed and wept uncontrollably into the plumped-up pillows. Everyone in the world had a name except her. And it would never change. Nobody here, at this stage in her life, was going to come along and start calling her Fran. Franny, surely never again. She remembered the days—they were never far from her mind—when her husband was sick and dying in the bedroom upstairs in the old house, and fifteen, maybe twenty times a day she would hear his rasping, evaporating voice calling, "Franny, Franny." She would drop everything each time to see what it was he wanted, and although she had loved him deeply, there were moments when she felt if she heard that rasping voice wailing out her name once more she would scream in exasperation; her fists would clench with the power and the passion to choke him. And yet now, wasn't life horribly cruel, she would give half her remaining days to hear her name wailed once more by him. Or by anyone else, for that matter. She gave in utterly to her despair and cried for a long time. She felt she might die gasping for breath if she didn't hear her own name.

At last she made an effort to pull herself together. She fixed the crumpled pillows so that they looked untouched, then went into the bathroom, washed her face and put on powder and lipstick, released her gray hair from its bun and brushed it out. It looked nice, she thought, long and still thick, thank God, falling down her back in a glossy, smooth sheet. Feeling young and girlish for a moment, she fancied herself going about with it loose and swinging, like Jill and Wendy and the other young girls. Jauntily she tossed her head to right and left a few times and reveled in the swing of her hair. As a matter of fact it was better hair than Jill's, she thought, thicker, with more body. Except it was gray. She gave a secretive smile to the mirror and pinned her hair up in the bun again. She would go into town and browse around Woolworth's to cheer herself up.

Mrs. Saunders got a ride in with Jill, who drove past the shopping center every noon on her way to get Luke and Kevin at nursery school. In Woolworth's she bought a new bathmat, a bottle of shampoo and some cream rinse for her hair, a butane cigarette lighter, and last, surprising herself, two boxes of colored chalk. She couldn't have explained why she bought the chalk, but since it only amounted to fifty-six cents she decided it didn't need justification. The colors looked so pretty, peeking out from the open circle in the center of the box—lime, lavender, rose, yellow, beige, and powder blue. It was spring, and they seemed to go with the spring. It occurred to her as she took them from the display case that the pale yellow was exactly the color of her kitchen cabinets; she might use it to cover a patch of white that had appeared on one drawer after she scrubbed too hard with Ajax. Or she might give Luke and Kevin each a box, and buy them slates as well, to practice their letters and numbers. They were nice little boys, and she often gave them small presents or candy when she babysat.

Feeling nonetheless as though she had done a slightly eccentric thing, Mrs. Saunders meandered through the shopping center, wondering if there might be some sensible, inexpensive thing she needed. Then she remembered that the shoes she had on were nearly worn out. Certainly she was entitled to some lightweight, comfortable new shoes for spring. With the assistance of a civil young man, she quickly was able to find just the right pair. The salesman was filling out the slip. "Name, please?" he said. And then something astonishing happened. Hearing so unexpectedly the word that had been obsessing her gave Mrs. Saunders a great jolt, and, as she would look back on it later, seemed to loosen and shake out of its accustomed place a piece of her that rebelled against the suffocation she had been feeling for more years than she cared to remember.

She knew exactly the answer that was required, so that she could find reassurance afterwards in recalling that she had been neither mad nor senile. As the clerk waited with his pencil poised, the thing that was jolted loose darted swiftly through her body, producing vast exhilaration, and rose out from her throat to her lips.

"Frances."

She expected him to look at her strangely—it was strange, she granted that—and say, "Frances what?" And then, at long last she would hear it. It would be, she imagined, something like making love years ago with Walter, when in the dark all at once her body streamed and compressed to one place and exploded with relief and wonder. She felt a tinge of that same excitement now, as she waited. And it did not concern her that the manner of her gratification would be so pathetic and contrived, falling mechanically from the lips of a stranger. All that mattered was that the name be spoken.

"Last name, please." He did not even look up.

Mrs. Saunders gave it, and gave her address, and thought she would faint with disappointment. She slunk from the store and stood weakly against a brick wall outside. Was there to be no easing of this pain? Dazed, she stared hopelessly at her surroundings, which were sleek, buzzing with shoppers, and unappealing. She slumped and turned her face to the wall.

On the brick before her, in small letters, were scratched the words "Tony" and "Annette." An arrow went through them. Mrs. Saunders gazed for a long time, aware that she would be late meeting Jill, but not caring, for once. She broke the staple on the Woolworth's bag, slipped her hand in, and drew out a piece of chalk. It turned out to be powder blue. Shielding her actions with her coat, she printed in two-inch-high letters on the brick wall outside the shoe store, FRANNY. Then she moved off briskly to the parking lot.

At home, after fixing herself a light lunch, which she ate excitedly and in haste, and washing the few dishes, she went back down to the garbage area behind the buildings. In lavender on the concrete wall just behind the row of cans, she wrote FRANNY. A few feet off she wrote again, FRANNY, and added WALTER, with an arrow through the names. But surveying her work, she took a tissue from her pocket and with some difficulty rubbed out WALTER and the arrow. Walter was dead. She was not senile yet. She was not yet one of those old people who live in a world of illusions.

Then she went to the children's playground, deserted at nap-time, and wrote FRANNY in small letters on the wooden rail of the slide, on the wooden pillars of the newfangled jungle gym, and on the concrete border of the sandbox, in yellow, lavender, and blue, respectively. Choosing a quite private corner behind some benches, she crouched down and wrote the six letters of her name, using a different color for each letter. She regarded her work with a fierce, proud elation, and decided then and there that she would not, after all, give the chalk to Luke and Kevin. She was not sure, in fact, that she would ever give them anything else again.

The next week was a busy and productive one for Mrs. Saunders. She carried on her usual round of activities—shopping, cooking, cleaning her apartment daily, and writing to Walter, Louise, and Edith; evenings she babysat or watched television, and once attended a tenants' meeting on the subject of limited space for guest parking, though she possessed neither a car nor guests; she went to the bank to cash her social security check, as well as to a movie and to the dentist for some minor repair work on her bridge. But in addition to all this she went to the shopping center three times with Jill at noon, where, using caution, she managed to adorn several sidewalks and walls with her name.

She was not at all disturbed when Jill asked, "Anything special that you're coming in so often for, Mrs. Saunders? If it's anything I could do for you . . ."

"Oh, no, Jill dear." She laughed. "I'd be glad if you could do this for me, believe me. It's my bridge." She pointed to her teeth. "I've got to keep coming, he says, for a while longer, or else leave it with him for a few weeks, and then what would I do? I'd scare the children."

"Oh, no. Never that, Mrs. Saunders. Is it very painful?" Jill swerved around neatly into a parking space.

"Not at all. Just a nuisance. I hope you don't mind—"

"Don't be ridiculous, Mrs. Saunders. What are friends for?"

That day she was more busy than ever, for she had not only to add new FRANNYs but to check on the old. There had been a rainstorm over the weekend, which obliterated her name from the parking lot and the sidewalks. Also, a few small shopkeepers, specifically the butcher and the baker, evidently cleaned their outside walls weekly. She told Jill not to pick her up, for she might very likely be delayed, and as it turned out, she was. The constant problem of not being noticed was time-consuming, especially in the parking lot with its endless flow of cars in and out. Finished at last, she was amazed to find it was past two-thirty. Mrs. Saunders was filled with the happy exhaustion of one who has accomplished a decent and useful day's work. Looking about and wishing there were a comfortable place to rest for a while, she noticed that the window she was leaning against belonged to a paint store. Curious, she studied the cans and color charts. The colors were beautiful: vivid reds, blues, golds, and violets, infinitely more beautiful than her pastels. She had never cared much for pastels anyway. With a sly, physical excitement floating through her, Mrs. Saunders straightened up and entered.

She knew something about spray paint. Sukie, Walter's wife, had sprayed the kitchen chairs with royal blue down in the cellar last time Mrs. Saunders visited, nearly two years ago. She remembered it well, for Sukie, her hair, nose, and mouth covered with scarves, had called out somewhat harshly as Mrs. Saunders came down the steps, "For God's sake, stay away from it. It'll choke you. And would you mind opening some windows upstairs so when I'm done I can breathe?" Sukie was not a welcoming kind of girl. Mrs. Saunders sighed, then set her face into a smile for the paint salesman.

As she left the store contentedly with a shopping bag on her arm, she heard the insistent beep of a car horn. It was Jill. "Mrs. Saunders, hop in," she called. "I had a conference with Kevin's teacher," Jill explained, "and then the mothers' meeting to plan the party for the end of school, and after I dropped the kids at Wendy's I thought maybe I could still catch you."

Jill looked immensely pleased with her good deed, Mrs. Saunders thought, just as Louise and Edith used to look when they fixed dinner on her birthday, then sat beaming with achievement and waiting for praise, which she always gave in abundance.

"Isn't that sweet of you, Jill." But she was not as pleased as she tried to appear, for she had been looking forward to the calm bus ride and to privately planning when and where to use her new purchases. "You're awfully good to me."

"Oh, it's nothing, really. Buying paint?"

"Yes, I've decided to do the kitchen and bathroom."

"But they'll do that for you. Every two years. If you're due you just call the landlord and say so."

"But they don't use the colors I like and I thought it might be nice to try. . . ."

"It's true, they do make you pay a lot extra for colors," Jill said thoughtfully.

Mrs. Saunders studied the instructions on the cans carefully, and went over in her mind all the advice the salesman had given her. Late that evening after the family noises in the building had subsided, she took the can of red paint down to the laundry room in the basement. She also took four quarters and a small load of wash—the paint can was buried under the wash—in case she should meet anyone. She teased herself about this excessive precaution at midnight, but as it happened she did meet one of the young mothers, Nancy, pulling overalls and polo shirts out of the dryer.

"Oh, Mrs. Saunders! I was frightened for a minute. I didn't expect anyone down here so late. So you're another night owl, like me."

"Hello, Nancy. I meant to get around to this earlier, but it slipped my mind." She took the items out of her basket slowly, one by one, wishing Nancy would hurry.

"Since I took this part-time job I spend all my evenings doing housework. Sometimes I wonder if it's worth it." At last Nancy had the machine emptied. "Do you mind staying all alone? I could wait." She hesitated in the doorway, clutching her basket to her chest, pale and plainly exhausted.

"Oh no, Nancy dear. I don't mind at all, and anyhow, you look like you need some rest. Go on and get to sleep. I'll be fine."

She inserted her quarters and started the machine as Nancy disappeared. The clothes were mostly clean; she had grabbed any old thing to make a respectable-looking load. The extra washing wouldn't hurt them. With a tingling all over her skin and an irrepressible smile, she unsealed the can. Spraying was much easier than she had expected. The *F*, which she put on the wall behind the washer, took barely any time and effort. Paint dripped thickly from its upper left corner, though, indicating she had pressed too hard and too long. It was simple to adjust the pressure, and by the second *N* she felt quite confident, as if she had done this often before. She took a few steps back to look it over. It was beautiful—bold, thick, and bright against the cream-colored wall. So beautiful that she did another directly across the room. Then on the inside of the open door, rarely seen, she tried it vertically; aside from some long amateurish drips, she was delighted at the effect. She proceeded to the boiler room, where she sprayed FRANNY on the boiler and on the wall, then decided she had done enough for one night. Waiting for the laundry cycle to end, she was surrounded by the red, lustrous reverberations of her name, vibrating across the room at each other; she felt warmed and strengthened by the firm, familiar walls of her own self. While the room filled and teemed with visual echoes of FRANNY, Mrs. Saunders became supremely at peace.

She climbed the stairs slowly, adrift in this happy glow. She would collect her things from the dryer late tomorrow morning. Lots of young mothers and children would have been in and out by then. Nancy was the only one who could suspect, but surely Nancy didn't come down with a load every day; besides, she was so tired and harassed she probably wouldn't remember clearly. Mrs. Saunders entered her apartment smiling securely with her secret.

Yet new difficulties arose over the next few days. The deserted laundry room at night was child's play compared to the more public, open, and populated areas of the development. Mrs. Saunders finally bought a large tote bag in Woolworth's so she could carry the paint with her and take advantage of random moments of solitude. There were frequent lulls when the children's playground was empty, but since it was in full view of the balconies and rear windows, only once, at four-thirty on a Wednesday morning, did she feel safe, working quickly and efficiently to complete her name five times. The parking lot needed to be done in the early hours too, as well as the front walk and the wall space near the mailboxes. It was astonishing, she came to realize, how little you could rely on being unobserved in a suburban garden apartment development, unless you stayed behind your own closed door.

Nevertheless, she did manage to get her name sprayed in half a dozen places, and she took to walking around the grounds on sunny afternoons to experience the fairly delirious sensation of her identity, secretly yet miraculously out in the open, sending humming rays towards her as she moved along. Wherever she went she encountered herself. Never in all her life had she had such a potent sense of occupying and making an imprint on the world around her. The reds and blues and golds seemed even to quiver and heighten in tone as she approached, as if in recognition and tribute, but this she knew was an optical illusion. Still, if only they could speak. Then her joy and fulfillment would be complete. After her walks she sat in her apartment and smoked and saw behind her closed eyes parades of brilliantly colored FRANNYs move along in the darkness, and felt entranced as with the warmth of a soothing physical embrace. Only once did she have a moment of unease, when she met Jill on her way back in early one morning.

"Mrs. Saunders, did anything happen? What's the red stuff on your fingers?"

"Just nail polish, dear. I spilled some."

Jill glanced at her unpolished nails and opened her mouth to speak, but apparently changed her mind.

"Fixing a run in a stocking," Mrs. Saunders added as she carried her shopping bag inside. She sensed potential danger in that meeting, yet also enjoyed a thrill of defiance and a deep, faint flicker of expectation.

Then one evening Harris, Jill's husband, knocked on Mrs. Saunders' door to tell her there would be a tenants' meeting tomorrow night in the community room.

"You must have noticed," he said, "the way this place has been deteriorating lately. I mean, when we first moved in four years ago it was brand-new and they took care of it. Now look! First of all there's this graffiti business. You must've seen it, haven't you? Every kid and his brother have got their names outside—it's as bad as the city. Of course that Franny character takes the cake, but the others are running her a close second. Then the garbage isn't removed as often as it used to be, the mailboxes are getting broken, there's been a light out for weeks in the hall. . . . I could go on and on."

She was afraid he would, too, standing there leaning on her door-frame, large and comfortably settled. Harris was an elementary-school teacher; Mrs. Saunders guessed he was in the habit of making long speeches. She smiled and wondered if she ought to ask him in, but she had left a cigarette burning in the ashtray. In fact she had not noticed the signs of negligence that Harris mentioned, but now that she heard, she was grateful for them. She felt a trifle weak in the knees; the news of the meeting was a shock. If he didn't stop talking soon she would ask him in just so she could sit down, cigarette or no cigarette.

"Anyhow," Harris continued, "I won't keep you, but I hope you'll come. The more participation, the better. There's power in numbers."

"Yes, I'll be there, Harris. You're absolutely right."

"Thanks, Mrs. Saunders. Good night." She was starting to close the door when he abruptly turned back. "And by the way, thanks for the recipe for angel food cake you gave Jill. It was great."

"Oh, I'm glad, Harris. You're quite welcome. Good night, now."

Of course she would go. Her absence would be noted, for she always attended the meetings, even those on less crucial topics. Beneath her surface nervousness the next day, Mrs. Saunders was aware of an abiding calm. Buoyed up by her name glowing almost everywhere she turned, she felt strong and impregnable as she took her seat in the community room.

"Who the hell is Franny anyway?" asked a man from the neighboring unit. "She started it all. Anyone here got a kid named Franny?" One woman had a Frances, but, she said, giggling, her Frances was only nine months old. Mrs. Saunders felt a throb of alarm in her chest. But she soon relaxed: the nameplates on her door and mailbox read "Saunders" only, and her meager mail, even the letters from Walter, Louise, and Edith, she had recently noticed, was all addressed to Mrs. F. Saunders or Mrs. Walter Saunders. And of course, since these neighbors had never troubled to ask. . . . She suppressed a grin. You make your own bed, she thought, watching them, and you lie in it.

The talk shifted to the broken mailboxes, the uncollected garbage, the inadequacy of guest parking, and the poor TV reception, yet every few moments it returned to the graffiti, obviously the most chafing symptom of decay. To Mrs. Saunders the progress of the meeting was haphazard, without direction or goal. As in the past, people seemed more eager to air their grievances than to seek a practical solution. But she conceded that her experience of community action was limited; perhaps this was the way things got done. In any case, their collective obtuseness appeared a more than adequate safeguard, and she remained silent. She always remained silent at tenants' meetings—no one would expect anything different of her. She longed for a cigarette, and inhaled deeply the smoke of others' drifting around her.

At last—she didn't know how it happened for she had ceased to pay attention—a committee was formed to draft a petition to the management listing the tenants' complaints and demanding repairs and greater surveillance of the grounds. The meeting was breaking up. They could relax, she thought wryly, as she milled about with her neighbors, moving to the door. She had done enough painting for now anyway. She smiled with cunning and some contempt at their innocence of the vandal in their midst. Certainly, if it upset them so much she would stop. They did have rights, it was quite true.

She walked up with Jill. Harris was still downstairs with the other members of the small committee which he was, predictably, chairing.

"Well, it was a good meeting," Jill said. "I only hope something comes out of it."

"Yes," said Mrs. Saunders vaguely, fumbling for her key in the huge, heavy tote bag.

"By the way, Mrs. Saunders . . ." Jill hesitated at her door and nervously began brushing the wispy hair from her face. "I've been meaning to ask, what's your first name again?"

In her embarrassment Jill was blinking childishly and didn't know where to look. Mrs. Saunders felt sorry for her. In the instant before she replied—and Mrs. Saunders didn't break the rhythm of question and answer by more than a second's delay—she grasped fully that she was sealing her own isolation as surely as if she had bricked up from inside the only window in a cell.

"Faith," she said.

The longing she still woke with in the dead of night, despite all her work, would never now be eased. But when, in that instant before responding, her longing warred with the rooted habits and needs of a respectable lifetime, she found the longing no match for the life. And that brief battle and its outcome, she accepted, were also, irrevocably, who Franny was.

The profound irony of this turn of events seemed to loosen some old, stiff knot in the joints of her body. Feeling the distance and wisdom of years rising in her like sap released, she looked at Jill full in the face with a vast, unaccustomed compassion. The poor girl could not hide the relief that spread over her, like the passing of a beam of light.

"Isn't it funny, two years and I never knew," she stammered. "All that talk about names made me curious, I guess." Finally Jill turned the key in her lock and smiled over her shoulder. "Okay, good night, Mrs. Saunders. See you tomorrow night, right? The boys are looking forward to it."

Grand Staircases

I K N E W a man once—it was like having a disease. He was my disease. Also the wonder drug that relieved it. I felt grand whenever I had my fix, which could be simply his bountiful presence in the room, his voice—he was an inspired talker—but terrible coming down after. The worst of it was, he didn't seem to know the pain he was causing. At least he didn't like to hear about it, naturally enough. Moments when it strained at the leash and I had to let it loose, he would change the subject to something more entertaining. He was a gifted subject-changer. In truth there was no telling how much he knew. For all the bounty of his talking, he had certain remote, inaccessible chambers of secrecy. And he was smart. Like an idiot savant, smart enough to be dumb when he needed to.

One night in my kitchen, after it was officially all over between us, I was telling him in a mild way, over the remains of dinner, how bad he had made me feel, sexless and ugly and dull and at times almost evil, when I had been used to seeing myself as just the opposite, as very like him, as a matter of fact. He made me feel that way because he resisted me. First he stalked me and afterwards he resisted. Not from any perverse strategy, I don't think. He felt he had a reasonable position to defend. He was trying to be faithful to an architect he was in love with, but alas she was away in Eastern Europe for six months, studying grand staircases of the eighteenth century. It was during the second month of her absence that we met. I began as his friend and confidante. He would tell me how much he missed her, loved her. He obviously needed to tell this to someone and I didn't mind, then, being the one. He showed me her picture. Well, there was nothing wrong with that either, at that point. More and more he sought me out, more and more he talked about her. He had the idea that she was some sort of goddess or perfect being, that she would save him, I'm not sure from what, from everything in life men require saving from. I should have known enough to be wary—when men talk to women at length about their earlier women . . . But soon we were talking about many other things as well, hours at a stretch like adolescents, telling everything we had ever done or thought or felt. And I let myself drift. I didn't dream of diverting his love from the architect: he seemed a type I could never fall in love with, hale and hearty, good-humored (until I discovered this was only the facade; behind it he was glum and introspective, just what I liked). Though I suppose I was a diversion, in the other sense.

Later on, when we were together every evening, he still talked about her, but less. After all. I remembered the picture and her alleged supernatural appeal. She was pretty, a little prettier than I but not all that much. She looked gentler perhaps, yet who can really tell from a picture? I wondered what enchantment she possessed that I lacked, and decided after much wondering that more than any magical quality it was her having been there first, at a more propitious moment. A couple of things he told me about her I found funny, for example that she cut out recipes and pasted or typed them on five-by-eight cards to be filed alphabetically in a metal box, but I knew the one thing I must never do was laugh at her. That would be sacrilege. Not that she was any more laughable than anyone else—a couple of things about everyone are funny. I found her interesting actually, orphaned young, jolted in and out of foster homes and so on, which was probably why I first listened. Though it may have been the way he saw her and told about her that made her interesting. He had that transforming power; ordinary things would pass through his mind and come out lustrous. Sometimes I went to movies or read books he had described and found them less vivid than I expected; then I realized it was all in his telling, the enthusiasm and the play of mind, those grand and undulating ascents.

I was picking at the crumbs of the excellent brownies he had brought for dessert and telling him in a friendly way how he had made me feel, without bitterness or accusations, because it was all officially over between us, the torments, the pulling together and pulling apart (his pulling apart), the endless shuffling over whether we were to be just friends or lovers as well (whether our being lovers would destroy him as the decent moral being he claimed he was trying to be), and if lovers, serious or frivolous lovers, and if serious

lovers, serious enough to disrupt the course of each other's lives . . .
for there was always his true love who should not suffer any more
jolting; all over too was the trying to remain friends in spite of it, that
was no longer in question since meanwhile, apart from the shuffling
(or maybe because of the revelations it entailed), we had become
best friends, better friends, we agreed, than most people could ever
dream of being to each other; we were friends of the blood and
of temperament, we could not cease talking or listening, our words
some honeyed elixir passed from mouth to mouth, and we thought
and felt alike on nearly every matter except the matter of us, where
I could not accept why such rare consanguinity shouldn't make us
the best of lovers as well, but then I was not at the same time on an
erotic pilgrimage and so could not appreciate his dilemma, nor the
well-organized architect's imminent return from Eastern Europe to
continue the work of his salvation from I was never quite sure what.
Unexpected and puzzling events like me, perhaps. For after he made
love with me, he said, he was in torment, but at those moments I
could not be terribly sympathetic. Had it not been for her, I would
think, there would be none of this torment and no need for salvation
from it. I could not accept myself as a source of torment: I too had
always thought I was trying to be a decent moral being, and such
beings do not cause torment, or so I thought. Much as I disliked hear-
ing about his torment, I knew his revealing it was a kind of testimony
to our friendship. Not all lovers are such extraordinary friends; con-
ceivably not even he and the architect, which might have contributed
to his torment; it may be, though I would rather not think so, that
the two conditions are mutually exclusive. And sometimes it was in-
deed as if we were two sets of people, a pair of wretched lovers and
a pair of benevolent friends who discuss their tormenting lovers over
long and homey dinners. Yet with all my complaining I never used so
strong a word as torment. It seemed too dangerous, as if that word
like a gust of wind might blow down our fragile little structure, a
house of cards compared to the grandiose structure he had built with
the architect, I gathered.

But all that was over now and we were just friends, as they say. Be-
cause he kept turning up, hungry, bearing tributes of food, even after
she came back with her wealth of information on grand staircases of
the eighteenth century. He said we had something special, I occupied
a special place in his life, he even loved me—this he brought out with

difficulty—and would hate to do without me though he remained deeply in love with the architect.

My telling him how he had made me feel made him very uncomfortable—for he was, to some extent, the decent moral being he aspired to be; I don't wish to give the impression he was heartless, not at all, the problem was the opposite, he indulged in an overextension of the heart—so uncomfortable that he got up and washed our dinner dishes sitting in my sink, just for something to do. This was not one of his more inspired changes of subject; still, it had its merit. He was a man who took the initiative around the house, never an exploiter. The shapers of feminist doctrine would have approved of him, domestically, at any rate. I leaned against a counter near the sink and watched. Over the running water he said, "It's funny you should be telling me this. You should really be telling someone else these things about me, someone who could take your part wholeheartedly and give you some satisfaction."

"You have a point," I said. "But it's so convenient. You know the situation. I don't have to fill you in. And besides, you understand me better than anyone else."

"True. It's because we are true friends, aren't we?" He looked up from the sink anxiously. He was always anxious about this, always wanted reassurance of my friendship and my good opinion. Maybe he feared that someday he would turn up as usual and I would not wish to see him. He knew that would be perfectly logical. Maybe someday I wouldn't.

"Yes, yes, I just told you so. Listen, we'll pretend we're talking about someone else, that it's some other man I'm complaining to you about."

"That's a little hard to do when I know that other man is me."

"Just pretend. See what you can come up with."

"Okay." And he sighed heavily. "Okay, I'll try."

We went into the living room. I sat in the easy chair with my feet up on the coffee table and he lay down on the couch with his hands locked behind his head, as he always did. It was a couch we used to make love on, in the era when we were making love, and inevitably when I saw him lying there I could not help recalling that era. On the couch or else the floor right below, partly under the coffee table unless we took the trouble to push it aside, but it was marble and very heavy. The couch was not especially comfortable as couches go, and floors in general are not. . . . But often when it happened it would happen fast and there was no time to spare to get up and walk to the bedroom. It would happen so fast because he had been resisting the impulse for so long, hours maybe, floating high on words, being the best of friends, resisting exactly this happening, and then all of a sudden—he might even be getting up to say good night and priding himself on a virtuous evening—he would have no more resistance. Or maybe it was a game he liked, a private spiritual battle where till the very last moment the outcome is touch and go. It was not my game, but then lovers do play separate games. And maybe he would be thinking about the traveling architect all through it, but I never asked. Not that I didn't feel free to, but I was afraid of hearing the possible truth, the complexities of it—how I might have been standing in for her like an understudy giving so fine a performance the audience almost forgets its disappointment; or more likely how the architect and I both in body and spirit might have been merging and unmerging in his mind in some far subtler way like chemicals or, better still, representations of the real and the ideal, each of us partaking of both but in different aspects, with now one and now the other of our images advancing to the foreground and receding; and, most of all, I was afraid of how interesting he would make it sound—it was painful enough already. For afterwards he would hate himself and not be too enamored of me either, since I was the provocation, merely by existing. But he knew too it wasn't entirely my doing and so he'd feel guilty for turning away; between his guilt towards the architect and his guilt towards me and whatever others dragged along from the past, he had constructed a nice cozy little cell of guilt where he could be all alone after his indulgences, which is perhaps what he really wanted. Of course it was not always like that; thankèd be fortune it hath been otherwise, as in Wyatt's famous poem of love and rage, twenty times better, naked in my chamber, something in that vein; many times we even made it to the bedroom, but that was mostly at the beginning. Later it was as if, given the time it would take to walk to my chamber, he might change his mind.

He had made himself a cup of coffee and set it on the marble table, and now and then I took a sip. Coffee makes me sick but sometimes I get a yen for just a little. I liked to drink out of his cup and he never minded. He was good that way. A generous soul, not fastidious. Never chary of those forms of intimacy.

"Okay," he said. "This other man." And he looked at me with great brown sad dog eyes. "I'll tell you what I think. This other man you're talking about is a fop, a cad, a pretentious, self-indulgent joker."

He kept staring, and I could see that he meant it. I could see in the lush brown of his eyes the torment he used to speak of but no longer did. And in the recesses of the irises, grand staircases to remote, inaccessible chambers. I couldn't speak. Our bodies had touched each other and interpenetrated in nearly every imaginable way, but I felt this moment was the most naked we had ever had. And I felt vastly sorry for him, more sorry, finally, than I did for myself.

He grinned; it was hesitant and shy, like a boy's grin. "Why are you looking at me that way?"

I told him what I had been thinking, about the nakedness and closeness.

"Do you really think so?" he said.

"Yes, I do. And maybe you're right, what you said. Maybe he is all that. But the thing is, you see, I liked him. I was crazy about him."

The Middle Classes

T H E Y   S A Y memory enhances places, but my childhood block of small brick row houses grows smaller every year, till there is barely room for me to stand upright in my own recollections. The broad avenue on our corner, gateway to the rest of the world, an avenue so broad that for a long time I was not permitted to cross it alone, has narrowed to a strait, and its row of tiny shops—dry cleaners, candy store, beauty parlor, grocery store—has dwindled to a row of cells. On my little block itself the hedges, once staunch walls guarding the approach to every house, are shrunken, their sharp dark leaves stunted. The hydrangea bush—what we called a snowball bush—in front of the house next to mine has shrunk; its snowballs have melted down. And the ledges from each front walk to each drive-way, against whose once-great stone walls we played King, a kind of inverse handball, and from whose tops we jumped with delec-table agonies of fear—ah, those ledges have sunk, those leaps are nothing. Small.

In actuality, of course, my Brooklyn neighborhood has not shrunk but it has changed. Among the people I grew up with, that is under-stood as a euphemism meaning black people have moved in. They moved in family by family, and one by one the old white families moved out, outwards, that is, in an outward direction (Long Island, Rockaway, Queens), the direction of water—it seems not to have occurred to them that soon there would be nowhere to go unless back into the surf where we all began—except for two of the old white families who bravely remained and sent reports in the outward directions that living with the black people was fine, they were nice people, good neighbors, and so these two white families came to be regarded by the departed as sacrificial heroes of sorts; everyone admired them but no one would have wished to emulate them.

The changes the black families brought to the uniform block were mostly in the way of adornment. Colorful shutters affixed to the front casement windows, flagstones on the walkways leading to the porch steps, flowers on the bordering patches of grass, and quantities of ornamental wrought iron; a few of the brick porch walls have even been replaced by wrought-iron ones. (Those adjacent porches with their low dividing walls linked our lives. We girls visited back and forth climbing from porch to porch to porch, peeking into living room windows as we darted by.) But for all these proprietary changes, my block looks not so very different, in essence. It has remained middle class.

Black people appeared on the block when I lived there too, but they were maids, and very few at that. Those few came once a week, except for the three families where the mothers were schoolteachers; their maids came every day and were like one of the family, or so the families boasted, overlooking the fact that the maids had families of their own. One other exception: the family next door to mine who had the snowball bush also had a live-in maid who did appear to live like one of the family. It was easy to forget that she cleaned and cooked while the family took their ease, because when her labors were done she ate with them and then sat on the porch and contributed her opinions to the neighborhood gossip. They had gotten her from the South when she was seventeen, they said with pride, and when her grandmother came up to visit her the grandmother slept and ate and gossiped with the family too, but whether she too was expected to clean and cook I do not know.

It was less a city block than a village, where of a hot summer evening the men sat out on the front porches in shirtsleeves smoking cigars and reading newspapers under yellow lanterns (there were seven New York City newspapers) while the wives brought out bowls of cherries and trays of watermelon slices and gossiped porch to porch, and we girls listened huddled together on the steps, hoping the parents would forget us and not send us to bed, and where one lambent starry summer evening the singular fighting couple on the block had one of their famous battles in the master bedroom—shrieks and blows and crashing furniture; in what was to become known in local legend as the balcony scene, Mrs. Hochman leaned out of the open second-floor casement window in a flowing white nightgown like a mythological bird and shouted to the assembled throng, "Neighbors,

neighbors, help me, I'm trapped up here with a madman" (she was an elocution teacher), and my mother rose to her feet to go and help but my father, a tax lawyer, restrained her and said, "Leave them alone, they're both crazy. Tomorrow they'll be out on the street holding hands as usual." And soon, indeed, the fighting stopped, and I wondered, What is love, what is marriage? What is reality in the rest of the world?

The daughters of families of our station in life took piano lessons and I took the piano lessons seriously. Besides books, music was the only experience capable of levitating me away from Brooklyn without the risk of crossing bridges or tunneling my way out. When I was about eleven I said I wanted a new and good piano teacher, for the lady on Eastern Parkway to whose antimacassared apartment I went for my lessons was pixilated: she trilled a greeting when she opened the door and wore pastel-colored satin ribbons in her curly gray hair and served tea and excellent shortbread cookies, but of teaching she did very little. So my mother got me Mr. Simmons.

He was a black man of around thirty-five or forty recommended by a business acquaintance of my father's with a son allegedly possessed of musical genius, the development of which was being entrusted to Mr. Simmons. If he was good enough for that boy, the logic ran, then he was good enough for me. I was alleged to be unusually gifted too, but not quite that gifted. I thought it very advanced of my parents to hire a black piano teacher for their nearly nubile daughter; somewhere in the vast landscape of what I had yet to learn, I must have glimpsed the springs of fear. I was proud of my parents, though I never said so. I had known they were not bigoted but rather instinctively decent; I had known that when and if called upon they would instinctively practice what was then urged as "tolerance," but I hadn't known to what degree. As children do, I underestimated them, partly because I was just discovering that they were the middle class.

Mr. Simmons was a dark-skinned man of moderate height and moderate build, clean-shaven but with an extremely rough beard that might have been a trial to him, given his overall neatness. A schoolteacher, married, the father of two young children, he dressed in the style of the day, suit and tie, with impeccable conventionality. His manners were also impeccably conventional. Nice but dull was how I classified him on first acquaintance, and I assumed from his demeanor that moderation in all things was his hallmark. I was mistaken: he was a blatant romantic. His teaching style was a somber intensity streaked by delicious flashes of joviality. He had a broad smile, big teeth, a thunderous laugh, and a willing capacity to be amused, especially by me. To be found amusing was an inspiration. I saved my most sophisticated attitudes and phraseology for Mr. Simmons. Elsewhere, I felt, they were as pearls cast before swine. He was not dull after all, if he could appreciate me. And yet unlike my past teachers he could proclaim "Awful!" with as much intrepidity as "Beautiful!" "No, no, no, *this* is how it should sound," in a pained voice, shunting me off the piano bench and launching out at the passage. I was easily offended and found his bluntness immodest at first. Gradually, through Mr. Simmons, I learned that false modesty is useless and that true devotion to skill is impersonal.

Early in our acquaintance he told me that during the summers when school was out his great pleasure was to play the piano eight hours in a row, stripped to the waist and sweating. It was January when he said this, and he grinned with a kind of patient longing. I recognized it as an image of passion and dedication, and forever after, in my eyes, he was surrounded by a steady, luminous aura of fervor. I wished I were one of his children, for the glory of living in his house and seeing that image in the flesh and basking in the luxuriant music. He would be playing Brahms, naturally; he had told me even earlier on that Brahms was his favorite composer. "Ah, Brahms," he would sigh, leaning back in his chair near the piano bench and tilting his head in a dreamy way. I did not share his love for Brahms but Brahms definitely fit in with the entire picture—the hot day, the long hours, the bare chest, and the sweat.

Mr. Simmons had enormous beautiful pianist's hands—they made me ashamed of my own, small and stubby. Tragicomically, he would lift one of my hands from the keyboard and stare at it ruefully. "Ah, if only these were bigger!" A joke, but he meant it. He played well but a bit too romantically for my tastes. Of course he grasped my tastes thoroughly and would sometimes exaggerate his playing to tease me, and exaggerate also the way he swayed back and forth at the piano, crooning along with the melody, bending picturesquely over a delicate phrase, clattering at a turbulent passage, his whole upper body tense and filled with the music. "You think that's too schmaltzy, don't you?" laughing his thunderous laugh. The way he pronounced "schmaltzy," our word, not his, I found very droll. To admonish me when I was lazy he would say, "*Play* the notes, *play* the notes," and for a long time I had no idea what he meant. Listening to him play, I came to understand. He meant play them rather than simply touch them. Press them down and make contact. Give them their full value. Give them yourself.

It seemed quite natural that Mr. Simmons and I should come to be such appreciative friends—we were part of a vague, nameless elite—but I was surprised and even slightly irked that my parents appreciated him so. With the other two piano teachers who had come to the house my mother had been unfailingly polite, offering coffee and cake but no real access. About one of them, the wild-eyebrowed musician with the flowing scarves and black coat and beret and the mock-European accent, who claimed to derive from Columbia University as though it were a birthplace, she commented that he might call himself an artist but in addition he was a slob who could eat a whole cake and leave crumbs all over the fringed tapestry covering her piano. But with Mr. Simmons she behaved the way she did with her friends; I should say, with her friends' husbands, or her husband's friends, since at that time women like my mother did not have men friends of their own, at least in Brooklyn. When Mr. Simmons arrived at about three forty-five every Wednesday, she offered him coffee—he was coming straight from teaching, and a man's labor must always be respected—and invited him to sit down on the couch. There she joined him and inquired how his wife and children were, which he told her in some detail. That was truly dull. I didn't care to hear anecdotes illustrating the virtues and charms of his children, who were younger than I. Then, with an interest that didn't seem at all feigned, he asked my mother reciprocally how her family was. They exchanged such trivia on my time, till suddenly he would look at his watch, pull himself up, and with a swift, broad smile, say, "Well then, shall we get started?" At last.

But my father! Sometimes my father would come home early on Wednesdays, just as the lesson was ending. He would greet Mr. Simmons like an old friend; they would clap each other on the shoulder and shake hands in that hearty way men do and which I found ridiculous. And my father would take off his hat and coat and put down his *New York Times* and insist that Mr. Simmons have a drink or at least a cup of coffee, and they would talk enthusiastically about—

of all things—business and politics. Boring, boring! How could he? Fathers were supposed to be interested in those boring things, but not Mr. Simmons. After a while Mr. Simmons would put on his hat and coat, which were remarkably like the hat and coat my father had recently taken off, pick up his *New York Times*, and head for his home and family.

And my father would say, "What a nice fellow that Mr. Simmons is! What a really fine person!" For six years he said it, as if he had newly discovered it, or was newly astonished that it could be so. "It's so strange," he might add, shaking his head in a puzzled way. "Even though he's a colored man I can talk to him just like a friend. I mean, I don't feel any difference. It's a very strange thing." When I tried, with my advanced notions, to relieve my father of the sense of strangeness, he said, "I know, I know all that"; yet he persisted in finding it a very strange thing. Sometimes he boasted about Mr. Simmons to his friends with wonder in his voice: "I talk to him just as if he were a friend of mine. A very intelligent man. A really fine person." To the very end, he marveled; I would groan and laugh every time I heard it coming.

Mr. Simmons told things to my father in my presence, important and serious things that I knew he would not tell to me alone. This man-to-man selectivity of his pained me. He told my father that he was deeply injured by the racial prejudice existing in this country; that it hurt his life and the lives of his wife and children; and that he resented it greatly. All these phrases he spoke in his calm, conventional way, wearing his suit and tie and sipping coffee. And my father nodded his head and agreed that it was terribly unfair. Mr. Simmons hinted that his career as a classical pianist had been thwarted by his color, and again my father shook his head with regret. Mr. Simmons told my father that he had a brother who could not abide the racial prejudice in this country and so he lived in France. "Is that so?" said my mother in dismay, hovering nearby, slicing cake. To her, that anyone might have to leave this country, to which her parents had fled for asylum, was unwelcome, almost incredible, news. But yes, it was so, and when he spoke about his brother Mr. Simmons' resonant low voice was sad and angry, and I, sitting on the sidelines, felt a flash of what I had felt when the neighbor woman being beaten shrieked out of the window on that hot summer night—ah, here is reality at last. For I believed that reality must be cruel and harsh and densely complex. It would never have occurred to me that reality could also be my mother serving Mr. Simmons home-baked layer cake or my father asking him if he had to go so soon, couldn't he stay and have a bite to eat, and my mother saying, "Let the man go home to his own family, for heaven's sake, he's just done a full day's work." I also felt afraid at the anger in Mr. Simmons' voice; I thought he might be angry at me. I thought that if I were he I would at least have been angry at my parents and possibly even refused their coffee and cake, but Mr. Simmons didn't.

When I was nearing graduation from junior high school my mother suggested that I go to the High School of Music and Art in Manhattan. I said no, I wanted to stay with my friends and didn't want to travel for over an hour each way on the subway. I imagined I would be isolated up there. I imagined that the High School of Music and Art, by virtue of being in Manhattan, would be far too sophisticated, even for me. In a word, I was afraid. My mother wasn't the type to press the issue but she must have enlisted Mr. Simmons to press it for her. I told him the same thing, about traveling for over an hour each way on the subway. Then, in a very grave manner, he asked if I had ever seriously considered a musical career. I said instantly, "Oh, no, that sounds like a man's sort of career." I added that I wouldn't want to go traveling all over the country giving concerts. He told me the names of some women pianists, and when that didn't sway me, he said he was surprised that an intelligent girl could give such a foolish answer without even thinking it over. I was insulted and behaved coolly towards him for a few weeks. He behaved with the same equanimity as ever and waited for my mood to pass. Every year or so after that he would ask the same question in the same grave manner, and I would give the same answer. Once I overheard him telling my mother, "And she says it's a man's career!" "Ridiculous," said my mother disgustedly. "Ridiculous," Mr. Simmons agreed.

Towards the end of my senior year in high school (the local high school, inferior in every way to the High School of Music and Art in Manhattan), my parents announced that they would like to buy me a new piano as a graduation present. A baby grand, and I could pick it out myself. We went to a few piano showrooms in Brooklyn so I could acquaint myself with the varieties of piano. I spent hours pondering the differences between Baldwin and Steinway, the two pianos most used by professional musicians, for in the matter of a piano—unlike a high school—I had to have the best. Steinways were sharp-edged, Baldwins more mellow; Steinways classic and traditional, Baldwins romantically timeless; Steinways austere, Baldwins responsive to the touch. On the other hand, Steinways were crisp compared to Baldwins' pliancy; Steinways were sturdy and dependable, while Baldwins sounded a disquieting tone of mutability. I liked making classifications. At last I decided that a Baldwin was the piano for me—rich, lush, and mysterious, not at all like my playing, but now that I think of it, rather like Mr. Simmons'.

I had progressed some since the days when I refused to consider going to the High School of Music and Art in Manhattan. If it was to be a Baldwin I insisted that it come from the source, the Baldwin showroom in midtown Manhattan. My mother suggested that maybe Mr. Simmons might be asked to come along, to offer us expert advice on so massive an investment. I thought that was a fine idea, only my parents were superfluous; the two of us, Mr. Simmons and I, could manage alone. My parents showed a slight, hedging reluctance. Perhaps it was not quite fair, my mother suggested, to ask Mr. Simmons to give up a Saturday afternoon for this favor. It did not take an expert logician to point out her inconsistency. I was vexed by their reluctance and would not even condescend to think about it. I knew it could have nothing to do with trusting him: over the years they had come to regard him as an exemplar of moral probity. Evidently the combination of his being so reliable and decent, so charming, and so black set him off in a class by himself.

I asked the favor of Mr. Simmons and he agreed, although in his tone too was a slight, hedging reluctance; I couldn't deny it. But again, I could ignore it. I had a fantasy of Mr. Simmons and myself ambling through the Baldwin showroom, communing in a rarefied manner about the nuances of difference between one Baldwin and another, and I wanted to make this fantasy come true.

The Saturday afternoon arrived. I was excited. I had walked along the streets of Manhattan before, alone and with my friends. But the thought of walking down Fifty-seventh Street with an older man, clearly not a relative, chatting like close friends for all the sophisticated world to see, made my spirits as buoyant and iridescent as a bubble. Mr. Simmons came to pick me up in his car. I had the thrill of sliding into the front seat companionably, chatting like close friends with an older man. I wondered whether he would come around and open the door for me when we arrived. That was done in those days, for ladies. I was almost seventeen. But he only stood waiting while I climbed out and slammed it shut, as he must have done with his own children, as my father did with me.

We walked down broad Fifty-seventh Street, where the glamour was so pervasive I could smell it: cool fur and leather and smoky perfume. People looked at us with interest. How wondrous that was! I was ready to fly with elation. It didn't matter that Mr. Simmons had known me since I was eleven and seen me lose my temper like an infant and heard my mother order me about; surely he must see me as the delightful adult creature I had suddenly become, and surely he must be delighted to be escorting me down Fifty-seventh Street. I would have liked to take his arm to complete the picture for all the sophisticated world to see, but some things were still beyond me. I felt ready to fly but in fact I could barely keep up with Mr. Simmons' long and hurried stride. He was talking as companionably as ever, but he seemed ill at ease. Lots of people looked at us. Even though it was early April he had his overcoat buttoned and his hat brim turned down.

We reached the Baldwin showroom. Gorgeous, burnished pianos glistened in the display windows. We passed through the portals; it was like entering a palace. Inside it was thickly carpeted. We were shown upstairs. To Paradise! Not small! Immensely high ceilings and so much space, a vista of lustrous pianos floating on a rich sea of green carpet. Here in this grand room full of grand pianos Mr. Simmons knew what he was about. He began to relax and smile, and he talked knowledgeably with the salesman, who was politely helpful, evidently a sophisticated person.

"Well, go ahead," Mr. Simmons urged me. "Try them out."

"You mean play them?" I looked around at the huge space. The only people in it were two idle salesmen and far off at the other end a small family of customers, father, mother, and little boy.

"Of course." He laughed. "How else will you know which one you like?"

I finally sat down at one and played a few timid scales and arpeggios. I crept from one piano to another, doing the same, trying to discern subtle differences between them.

"Play," Mr. Simmons commanded.

At the sternness in his voice I cast away timidity. I played Chopin's "Revolutionary Etude," which I had played the year before at a recital Mr. Simmons held for his students in Carl Fischer Hall— nowadays called Cami Hall—on Fifty-seventh Street, not far from the Baldwin showroom. (I had been the star student. The other boy, the musical genius, had gone off to college or otherwise vanished. I had even done a Mozart sonata for four hands with Mr. Simmons himself.) Sustained by his command, I moved dauntlessly from Baldwin to Baldwin, playing passages from the "Revolutionary Etude." Mr. Simmons flashed his broad smile and I smiled back.

"Now you play," I said.

I thought he might have to be coaxed, but I was forgetting that Mr. Simmons was never one to withhold, or to hide his light. Besides, he was a professional, though I didn't understand yet what that meant. He looked around as if to select the worthiest piano, then sat down, spread his great hands, and played something by Brahms. As always, he *played* the notes. He pressed them down and made contact. He gave them their full value. He gave them himself. The salesmen gathered round. The small family drew near to listen. And I imagined that I could hear, transmogrified into musical notes, everything I knew of him—his thwarted career, his schoolteaching, his impeccable manners, his fervor, and his wit; his pride in his wife and children; his faraway brother; his anger, his melancholy, and his acceptance; and I also imagined him stripped to the waist and sweating. When it was over he kept his hands and body poised in position, briefly, as performers do, as if to prolong the echo, to keep the spell in force till the last drawn-out attenuation of the instant. The hushed little audience didn't clap, they stood looking awed. My Mr. Simmons! I think I felt at that moment almost as if he were my protégé, almost as if I owned him.

We didn't say much on the way home. I had had my experience, grand as in fantasy, which experiences rarely are, and I was sublimely content. As we walked down my block nobody looked at us with any special interest. Everyone knew me and by this time everyone knew Mr. Simmons too. An unremarkable couple. At home, after we reported on the choice of a piano, Mr. Simmons left without even having a cup of coffee. He was tired, he said, and wanted to get home to his family.

Later my mother asked me again how our expedition had been.

"Fine. I told you already. We picked out a really great piano. Oh, and he played. He was fantastic, everyone stopped to listen."

My mother said nothing. She was slicing tomatoes for a salad.

"I bet they never heard any customer just sit down and play like that."

Again no response. She merely puttered over her salad, but with a look that was familiar to me: a concentrated, patient waiting for the proper words and the proper tone to offer themselves to her. I enjoyed feeling I was always a step ahead.

"I know what you're thinking," I said nastily.

"You do?" She raised her eyes to mine. "I'd be surprised."

"Yes. I bet you're thinking we looked as if he was going to abduct me or something."

The glance she gave in response was more injured than disapproving. She set water to boil and tore open a net bag of potatoes.

"Well, listen, I'll tell you something. The world has changed since your day." I was growing more and more agitated, while she just peeled potatoes. Her muteness had a maddening way of making my words seem frivolous. She knew what she knew. "The world has changed! Not everyone is as provincial as they are here in Brooklyn!" I spit out that last word. I was nearly shouting now. "Since when can't two people walk down the street in broad daylight? We're both free—" I stopped suddenly. I was going to say free, white, and over twenty-one, an expression I had found loathsome when I heard my father use it.

"Calm down," my mother said gently. "All I'm thinking is I hope it didn't embarrass him. It's him I was thinking about, not you."

I stalked from the room, my face aflame.

I went to college in Manhattan and lived in a women's residence near school. For several months I took the subway into Brooklyn every Wednesday so I could have a piano lesson with Mr. Simmons, it being tacitly understood that I was too gifted simply to give up "my music," as it was called; I slept at home on my old block, then went back up to school on Thursday morning. This became arduous. I became involved with other, newer things. I went home for a lesson every other Wednesday, and soon no Wednesdays at all. But I assured Mr. Simmons I would keep renting the small practice room at school and work on my own. I did for a while, but the practice room was very small and very cold, and the piano, a Steinway, didn't sound as lush as my new Baldwin back home; there was an emptiness to my efforts without the spur of a teacher; and then there were so many other things claiming my time. I had met and made friends with kindred spirits from the High School of Music and Art, and realized that had I listened to my mother I might have known them three years sooner. The next year I got married, impulsively if not inexplicably; to tell why, though, would take another story.

Naturally my parents invited Mr. and Mrs. Simmons to the wedding. They were the only black people there, among some hundred and fifty guests. I had long been curious to meet Mrs. Simmons but regrettably I could not get to know her that afternoon since I had to be a bride. Flitting about, I could see that she was the kind of woman my mother and her friends would call "lovely." And did, later. She was pretty, she was dressed stylishly, she was what they would call "well-spoken." She spoke the appropriately gracious words for a young bride and one of her husband's long-time students. In contrast to Mr. Simmons' straightforward earnestness, she seemed less immediately engaged, more of a clever observer, and though she smiled readily I could not imagine her having a thunderous laugh. But she fit very well with Mr. Simmons, and they both fit with all the other middle-aged and middle-class couples present, except of course for their color.

Mrs. Simmons did not know a soul at the wedding and Mr. Simmons knew only the parents of the boy genius and a few of our close neighbors. My mother graciously took them around, introducing them to friends and family, lots of friends and lots of family, so they would not feel isolated. I thought she overdid it—she seemed to have them in tow, or on display, for a good while. I longed to take her aside and whisper, "Enough already, Ma. Leave them alone." But there was no chance for that. And I knew how she would have responded. She would have responded silently, with a look that meant, "You can talk, but I know what is right to do," which I could not deny. And in truth she was quite proud of knowing a man as talented as Mr. Simmons. And had she not introduced them they certainly would have felt isolated, while this way they were amicably received. (Any bigots present successfully concealed their bigotry.) My mother

was only trying to behave well, with grace, and relatively, she suc-
ceeded. There was no way of behaving with absolute grace. You had
to choose among the various modes of constraint.

For all I know, though, the Simmonses went home and remarked
to each other about what lovely, fine people my parents and their
friends were, and how strange it was that they could spend a pleas-
ant afternoon talking just as they would to friends, even though they
were all white. How very strange, Mr. Simmons might have said,
shaking his head in a puzzled way, taking off his tie and settling
down behind his newspaper. It is a soothing way to imagine them,
but probably false.

I had always hoped to resume my piano lessons someday, but
never did. And so after the wedding Mr. Simmons disappeared from
my life. Why should it still astonish me, like a scrape from a hidden
thorn? There were no clear terms on which he could be in my life,
without the piano lessons. Could I have invited the Simmonses to our
fifth-floor walk-up apartment in a dilapidated part of Manhattan for
a couples evening? Or asked him to meet me somewhere alone for a
cup of coffee? At what time of day? Could my parents, maybe, have
invited the Simmonses over on a Sunday afternoon with their now
teen-aged children and with my husband and me? Or for one of their
Saturday night parties of mah-jongg for the women and gin rummy
for the men and bagels and lox for all? Could Mr. Simmons, too,
have made some such gesture? Possibly. For I refuse to see this as a
case of *noblesse oblige*: we were all the middle classes.

But given the place and the time and the dense circumambient air,
such invitations would have required people of large social imagi-
nation, and none of us, including Mr. and Mrs. Simmons, had that.
We had only enough vision for piano lessons and cups of coffee and
brief warm conversations about families, business, politics, and race
relations, and maybe I should be content with that, and accept that
because we were small, we lost each other, and never really had each
other, either. Nonetheless, so many years later, I don't accept it. I
find I miss him and I brood and wonder about him: where is he and
does he still, on summer days, play the piano for eight hours at a
stretch, stripped to the waist and sweating?

Francesca

I THOUGHT I knew what my life was. Through most of it I have been sober and single-minded, for the last twenty-odd years studying the curious eruptions of wayward cells, cancer cells. Most of them cause turbulence and ruin, while a few, especially in older bodies, nestle harmlessly in a corner where they can be virtually ignored, though we forget them at our peril. But then something happened. It seems my passage through the world has been generating trails I could never have imagined, and which might be better ignored as well. After all, so much of human history, private history, goes unacknowledged. Yet I find myself unwilling to let this particle rest. It refuses to, in any case. It has reappeared through a turn of fate, and in a troubling, even terrifying form.

I should note, by way of preface, that I have never been a man who had difficulties with women, or who had hurting ways. Now two women are hurt on my account and they will never know why.

Twenty-four years ago, I spent a semester of my senior year of college in Rome, on one of those programs abroad which have become so common. At the time, it was, if not a rarity, at least more of a special privilege than it is today. And so the dozen of us who were chosen set foot in Italy with a giddiness, an almost unreal elation, sharpened and sustained by our knowing—the men, that is— we might well be drafted and sent to Vietnam soon after graduation. Now or never: we must cram all our youth into those five months. And what better place? Our group made some side trips, to Florence, Siena, Ravenna, a few other cities. But mostly we stayed in Rome, which even without any threat of imminent danger provides giddiness and elation enough. With all that, I have to say I was on the stodgy side, for a young man in those unstodgy years. Not by choice but through shyness and inhibition.

The program was in art history. I was doing a double major—art history and biochemistry. I had trouble making up my mind, though I was leaning towards biochemistry. It was more practical, and I thought my bent for the meticulous and measurable would serve me better there. Still, I kept up the art history major, partly because I wanted the trip. I wanted something to shake me out of my stodginess—I knew it would take shaking from outside. And since my family was poor and I spent my summers working, there was little chance I would get abroad any other way.

An Italian professor of art history at the University of Rome was attached to our group. He had a long, difficult name we had trouble pronouncing; it sounded to me more Greek or Romanian than Italian. He would walk around the city with us, expounding on its architecture, its churches, its history, as well as amble through the museums, murmuring with nonchalant erudition about the paintings, and finally, he conducted a weekly seminar which convened in his large, ornately cluttered apartment in a small street just off the Piazza Navona, where, he explained, gladiatorial contests, chariot races, and all sorts of rowdy festivities were held in ancient days.

This Roman professor, tall, stout, and rather imposing, with thick strong features, an unruly black mustache, thinning hair, and a genial bemused manner—as if he found us lovable, benign aliens—must have been forty or so, though we naturally saw him as advanced in age. He had an American wife eight or ten years younger than himself, a rangy, firm-boned woman with hair the color of honey and an imperturbably ironic manner, and on seminar nights she would serve us elaborate, rum-drenched pastries with wonderfully muddy coffee in thimble-like cups—translucent white with a rim of gold at the top—and later, dense, sweet, tart anisette liqueur. She had two young daughters, fair-haired like herself, maybe three and five, who would cavort among us babbling in incomprehensible Italian, so that very soon we realized the seminars would not be excessively scholarly or purposeful: we should regard them instead as a way to get an inside look at a real Roman family. Though as one of the girls in our group pointed out, it was hardly a typical Roman family since the wife and mother was American, like us.

She—Janet was the wife's name—did not seem American. So far as I could tell, her clothes, her mannerisms and gestures were all Roman: decisive, dramatic, mellow. She appeared to have taken on, effortlessly, the coloration of her chosen environment, and when she spoke Italian to the children, which at first we understood only in bits and pieces, she sounded to us like a native, but of course we were not the best of judges.

She was only ten or so years older than we were, yet it was enough of a gap to make us treat her deferentially, as the professor's wife, the role in which she was presented. One evening one of the more outspoken girls asked how she and the professor had happened to meet and marry.

"I was a student here in a program like yours," she said. Her English had a very faint tinge of otherness, not an accent exactly, for she was a native speaker, but a hint that the words and inflections were seldom used, taken out on special occasions like fine linen— crisp and slightly self-conscious. "The professor was doing the seminars, the tours, the whole bit. At the end I . . . just stayed. We got married. That's the story." She smiled ironically and shrugged, the way the girls in our group sometimes smiled and shrugged, as if to imply they possessed more information and wisdom than we men could dream of, and withheld it out of a teasing, challenging perversity. At that instant I saw her as having been one of us, the young and unsettled, rather than as a grown up, established, foreign sophisticate. She became a person who had taken a risky turn, surprised and perhaps even dismayed her family. Tricked fate, as it were. A palpable illustration that we might do the same.

Often at the end of the seminar the professor would disappear for lengthy telephone calls, or to say goodnight to the children, or on unknown errands, and Janet would sit with us. I thought she was simply fulfilling her duty, till after a while I saw she was genuinely interested. More than interested—on the lookout for something. I don't know how I sensed it: she didn't seem bored with her own life—there was a shimmering animation about her, a sense of being richly present—but she was restless too; she enjoyed stirring things up and inducing revelation. She would ask questions that coaxed our awkward self-doubts to the surface, and she managed to do this without being rude or overbearing, but by being charming. Once she had made us speak of our uncertainties they seemed no longer awkward but brimming with possibility.

Gradually I became the one she spoke to most often. Looking back, I think perhaps I seemed most in need of being shaken loose, released from the claws of naiveté. We would sit in the glow of the fireplace as she interrogated me like a curious, unconventional aunt from far away. What did I think about my past, did I like my parents, what were my ambitions, what did I want to find out about the world?

"How things work," I said hesitantly.

"What things, for instance?"

"Well, cells."

"Cells," she repeated. She got me to talk about a fairly commonplace senior project I had undertaken in the lab, involving crossbreeding in fruit flies, and though she was attentive there was a playful note to her attention, as if, while these were important matters, we must not take them too seriously. I found her easy to talk to, but confusing.

One late afternoon I met her in the Borghese Gardens, where I would often wander on my own, semi-intoxicated with the mere idea of being where I was. After chatting for a moment I was about to continue on my way, but she suggested a coffee. I was impressed with the way she ordered the waiter about in typically imperious Roman fashion, and tossed back the dark brew in one gulp. I expected we would talk in our usual manner; I was still acting the boy prepared to be questioned, to indulge my fantasies in her adult attentiveness. But after a few moments of this she said, "Don't you have any curiosity about what's around you? Do you ever feel the need to ask questions?" I was puzzled. Mired in deference, I had little experience in talking to adults on equal terms.

"Well, sure. How come you went so far from home?" I asked.

She laughed. "I came here to get away from people like you." She spoke in a friendly way, a way that invited further questions, but in my puzzlement I said nothing. "From innocence," she added, as if I had urged her on. "American innocence."

I had an inkling, then, of what she had in mind, for even the most untried young man senses, if nothing else, a sexual challenge. But I simply couldn't believe it. She went on to tell me she had grown up on a farm in Nebraska—not all that far from my own small Minnesota town, yet I doubted that I could ever grow so comfortably urbane. Even after three years I was not quite at ease in my Ivy League college, which I attended thanks to a scholarship. As a matter of fact I am not quite at ease even now.

As she talked that afternoon, she would occasionally touch my arm or wrist. Just before we got up to leave, she let her fingers rest on my arm for an unsettling time. I knew, but was still afraid to trust my instinct. Or my luck, as a college boy would doubtless have put it then.

"Why don't we walk for a while?" she said. "Or are you rushing off to pursue your studies?"

Of course I agreed to walk. By now I was desperate to touch her, my hands were drawing into fists, the blood was rushing through me—all of which she surely knew. But I was afraid. Italians were famously demonstrative, affectionate: if she were simply doing as the Romans do I might be making a shameful mistake. I could end up in trouble, be sent home in disgrace. What would my parents say? It sounds ludicrous now, I know. Young Americans are no longer so ignorant or inept.

"Do you have a girlfriend here yet?" she asked. "An Italian? Or is that all happening within the group?"

"No," I said. "There's very little of that going on, unfortunately. We haven't had a chance to meet too many Italians so far. And we're mostly just friends."

"Just friends," she mocked. "What wholesome young people."

We were walking up towards the Pincio—for the view, she suggested. It was about five o'clock on a March afternoon, still fairly cold. At the top of the hill we stopped to look down at the traffic and hubbub circling the great column in the Piazza del Popolo, and in the distance, in the fading light, the ruins. Hugging her shoulders against the wind, she turned to me in such a teasing way that even a dolt such as I knew I was supposed to kiss her. If before I had feared it might be a disgrace to kiss her, now I knew I would be disgraced if I didn't. And I wanted to very badly anyway.

What followed is easily imagined—how I was initiated into the intrigue of secret meetings and deceptions, how I felt this to be the great adventure of my life (as indeed it was). She was not only a restless woman, I discovered, but a beautiful and rare one. I had hardly noticed her beauty and rarity—I was so predisposed to see her as the professor's wife. Naturally I felt guilty throughout, above all when the professor spent time helping me with a term paper, or when, after the seminars, he said, "Janet, would you bring us the coffee, please?" I would watch her, deft and gracious, the very picture of an elegant faculty wife, serving the coffee without taking any particular notice of me.

Guilty, but also boundlessly thrilled and excited: it was at those moments, in the presence of the group, in the presence of her husband, that I craved her the most. One night I couldn't bear it, and followed her into the kitchen on the pretext of carrying some cups and saucers, to run my hand along her back and hips. She looked over her shoulder as if I were a mad vulgarian, as if our intimate hours were a boy's dream.

"What on earth do you think you're doing?" Like a boy, I quickly drew my hand back. I almost apologized, but I was not that much of a boy anymore. The next day, when we were alone, she said, "That simply isn't how you go about things. You're ruined if you start taking those chances."

"Oh, do you do this often? You sound like you have the routine down pat," I said, seized with jealousy.

"No," she said. "Just once, a few years ago."

"Also a student? Do you specialize?"

"Not a student," she said, and wouldn't say more except, "Don't be nasty, don't spoil everything."

"And will you do it again?"

She laughed. "How can I tell?"

"Why with me?"

"Do you really need to ask?"

"I guess I do."

"I liked you. You seemed the right sort."

"What sort is that?"

"Oh," and she pretended to think it over, or perhaps really did think it over. "Decent. Clever." I was flattered then, but later dismayed. Decent and clever? Not exactly stirring declarations to an ardent lover.

I assumed she must be miserable with the professor: why else would she have sought me out? But she laughed this off as another sign of my conventional ignorance. She said nothing disparaging about him, never talked of him at all, except to answer, when I inevitably asked, that they made love infrequently. I realize by this time how many women say that to their lovers, yet I believe it was true. I believed everything she said—there was such an air of conviction about her—though while she told the truth, it could not have been the whole truth. Possibly she thought I was not ready to hear the whole truth, or possibly, as in my own research, truth can never be told in its entirety.

I asked if she minded being summoned to serve coffee to students week after week and she said not at all, there was no indignity in serving coffee. Besides, it was part of the bargain. What bargain, I wanted to ask, but was too uneasy and suspected she wouldn't answer anyway. Explanation was hardly her style. She liked talking to the students, was all she volunteered; it gave her a chance to speak English.

"But this person who made the bargain, the person you are with him—is that really you?"

"It's no more false than this. I can be any number of people. Don't you find that?" Not a new notion by any means, but the first time I had seen it enacted. "Do you think," she said tauntingly, "that the person you see is the only 'real' me? Do you think there are real and unreal selves?" I had in fact thought so, but from her ironic tone it would have been mortifying to confess it.

I found her a riddle. Later, of course, I would see her as a complex, self-willed woman, and such types tend to be inscrutable to men. But back then she was older than anyone I had ever known, far older than her age—a thirty-one-year-old woman with the mind of an eighty-year-old. It was she who described herself that way, and I came to feel she was right. She lived as though she had seen and assessed everything and had had the time to put it into perspective, and now had very little time left and need answer only to herself.

When the semester ended I scrambled to find a way to stay for the summer. For her. She urged me to stay, but I didn't need much urging. The professor was going to Holland and Germany for several months to do research. I managed to get a job as a waiter in a cafe. I knew enough Italian, by then, to take the imperiously snapped orders. We made love whenever we could, when the children were napping, or late at night, or weekends when Janet could leave them with her in-laws. However unique and indescribable it felt to me, our love clearly belonged to a well-documented genre: brief, heedless, intense, and transforming. But my story is not about the loss of innocence or the discovery—it felt like the invention—of passion, or about loving in an unidealistic, futureless, encapsulated, carnal way,

which may be what loss of innocence is. The real story takes place
two decades later.

After I returned home and finished college I was drafted, as ex-
pected. I spent two months in Vietnam surviving in a way I could not
in a million years recount. In truth I have done all I could to forget
it. I was wounded early on, in the shoulder, and luckily spent the rest
of my time at a desk. I seldom watched the news reports or read the
papers about it, afterwards. I was no soldier and no activist. I am not
interested in politics but in science. I know how irresponsible that
sounds—I have often been lectured about it. And when I am, I say
nothing, just remind myself that I work, however marginally, on a
cure for cancer: that should be enough.

Graduate studies in science are among the most laborious and de-
manding: you can get to be thirty or more before you assume a real
position, draw a respectable paycheck and feel like an adult. Most of
the students came from more comfortable backgrounds than mine.
My family had a hard time figuring out why, in my late twenties and
after so many years in school, I was still writing a dissertation and
earning a workman's wage. They said that with the same efforts I
might have gone to medical school and become a prosperous doctor.
It wasn't their fault that they couldn't see how specific my interests
were. When I was finally done I wanted some ease. I wanted not
to have to account for myself all the time. I married a woman with
whom that would be possible. A nurse—I met her in the Emergency
Room when I was badly bruised hitting the chain link fence as I
reached for an impossibly high ball. She was, and is, a stocky, pretty,
able woman with pale brown boyishly-cut hair. I loved her and still
do, even if it is not the kind of love pictured in books or films, or
that I knew with Janet. It is love all the same, and arguably stronger
than what I knew with Janet, possessing a structure and endurance.
This sounds unfair to my wife, perhaps, now that I see it set down
so baldly, and yet she enjoys a good life. We have our children and
our house and our work and our friends, and we sleep close together
at night still.

Several months ago, in an Italian scientific journal, I came across
a series of articles on migratory cells. With my dregs of Italian I
could see they might be crucial to my research, but returning to a
long-lost language is not, alas, like riding a bicycle, where no matter

how long ago, they say, you remember how. A colleague suggested I call the Romance Languages Department: they could send over a graduate student to translate, who would be glad of the extra money. The secretary called back promptly to say she had just the person, a very bright Italian student who was bilingual—her mother was British or American or something—besides being punctual, reliable, and so forth. I was rushing to class and didn't ask her name, just said to send her over the next morning during my office hours. I didn't really think of her as a person at all, then. I was excited about what I might learn and couldn't wait to see the translation. The student was merely a step on the way to satisfying my curiosity.

She arrived promptly at ten: tall, slim, pale and auburn-haired, wearing a soft gray wool skirt, a green sweater and leather boots, not the usual jeans and sweatshirt uniform. She wanted to appear professional, I thought. Her manner was un-student-like as well. Students are usually shy and fumbling or else excessively candid and enthusiastic, which comes to the same thing. This one seemed reserved, not shy. She presented herself in an economical way, just as much as necessary for the purpose. All in all, she was extremely self-possessed.

"I've come about the translation work," she said, and announced her name. Francesca. The last name—well of course that is obvious by this time. Life, like science, is full of the coincidences that unleash discovery.

I was glad to be seated, because I might have toppled over. I had the oddest sense that my face was escaping me, I was losing control over it. I felt a jumble of wonderment, panic, curiosity—I had no idea what might be happening on the surface. I tried to smile and be polite, but for all I knew I looked stunned.

How could I be sure so quickly? The name, as I have said, was unusual even for Mediterranean names with their syllabic frills and furbelows. There couldn't be many with that name. Still, I needed to be absolutely certain.

"I spent some time in Rome when I was a student." I tried to sound casual though my mind teemed with memories and frantic calculations. I hoped my worst suspicion wasn't so, and yet I hoped it was. "On an art history program."

"Really," she said mildly.

What did I expect? Thousands must have done the same. I made myself stumble on. "One of my professors had your name. His first name was Federico."

She showed no great surprise. "That's my father. He's a professor of art history."

"Is that so?" Now it was legitimate to sound a bit excited, so my feelings had some release. "Isn't that a coincidence! I knew both your parents. They used to have the students over all the time. That little street near the Piazza Navona. Did you grow up there?"

"Yes, I remember the students. They were coming over until quite recently." She smiled indulgently, as if hosting American students was a lovable eccentricity of her quaint parents.

"What a coincidence!" I said again.

"Well, really not that strange. They must have entertained hundreds of American students. What did you think of them, my parents, that is?"

That sort of abrupt slashing through pleasantries was exactly her mother's style and unsettled me for an instant, like hearing the rustlings of a ghost. But I was not a boy now; I had had the beneficent experience of her mother. "I found them wonderful people. They made us feel so at home, especially your mother. How is your mother?"

"Mother died last fall." She looked down to get away from me. This was private, delicate territory. She was still grieving. And I, I could not even tell what I was feeling, apart from grim surprise and a pressing warmth behind my eyes. I fended it off. I needed all my forces just to speak casually to the girl. I was not permitted to express anything out of the ordinary. I would take the news home with me, for later.

"I'm so sorry. She must have been still relatively young, as I remember. What—what was it?"

"It's all right, you can ask. She had cancer. Lymphoma."

"Ah."

"It was pretty quick. She wasn't sick very long."

"And you—" I felt slightly dizzy and gripped the edge of the desk to anchor myself. "I wonder if you were one of the little girls I used to see playing? I don't think there was a Francesca, though. One was Elsa, I remember. Rosa?"

"Very good." She smiled as though I were a clever child. "There's Elsa and Rosalia, then me, then Pietro—he's two years younger."

"I see. Well, I was there in 'sixty-six . . ."

"A year too soon for me. I was twenty-three just last week, in fact."

"April."

"April, yes." She frowned ironically, then laughed. The eyes, green and witty, were her mother's. "Why, do you follow astrology, like your former president? Americans are so amusing sometimes. The cruelest month, as one of your poets says."

If they know nothing else, I have found, the students all know that line; in that respect, she was generic. Then I realized her knowledge would be more than superficial: my daughter was a student of literature. For as I feared and hoped, I was looking at my own daughter. I wanted to leap up and embrace her. I wanted to do all sorts of things at once, laugh, weep, mourn her mother, find out about the family, even reveal myself. For a moment I thought I might do this—not right away, but some day in the future. But only for a moment.

Still, could I be sure, one may ask? Oh, I was sure. Even if the dates hadn't worked out, even if it wasn't true that Janet rarely made love with the professor, this girl was mine. I could see it. She had my coloring. My hair, before it faded and started going gray. My family's body, tall and narrow and energetic, though her movements had an un-American mellowness. She reminded me of my mother and my older sister. I wondered if they would notice, were they to see her. Could I ever manage to introduce her? How could I explain her? Yet all the while I knew this would never come to pass. I wouldn't mind shocking my family at this point, but I could not shock her, Francesca. She had her father—she didn't need another.

"No," I laughed. "I don't follow astrology. In your mother's case April was a lucky month, I'd say. And how is your father?"

She passed over my compliment. "He's fine. He just retired from the university but he still writes papers. Of course it was terrible for him, my mother . . . They were so devoted. So close. You must have noticed. But he has lots of friends. And my sisters live nearby and keep an eye on him. My brother is in school at Berkeley. We both flew back when Mother was sick. Well, you don't need to hear all this. Would you like to tell me about the translation?"

"No, no, I really do want to hear. I remember them so vividly."

She smiled. "There's nothing more to tell."

"When you write will you give him my regards?"

"Sure. But there were so many, you know . . . The house was like a—a port of call. My mother was constantly serving them coffee and listening to their problems. I guess you know."

"Yes." I couldn't stop staring at her, trying to find traces of my children, my other children. She was beautiful in a way it took a while to appreciate, even more so than her mother, whom she did not resemble except for the eyes and the cool, self-possessed manner. Like Janet's, her statements were assertions, with a tinge of irony.

She was also, like Janet, decisively, provocatively polite. "About the translation . . ." she prompted.

"It's only natural," I mused, "that this should be an amazing co-incidence for me, while for you . . . . I mean, to come upon an old acquaintance of your parents, all the way across the ocean—no big deal, right?"

"On the contrary, it's a pleasure to meet you."

What I felt at that moment was pride, I must admit. Paternal pride. Few Americans of twenty-three would speak with such aplomb. And her speech was not diluted with the nervous meaningless tics, the "likes" or "you knows" which disjointed the talk of even the bright-est students. Well, God knows I had had nothing to do with it. Credit her mother. "But it can't be quite the same pleasure."

"Nothing is quite the same as anything else, is it?"

"How true." I laughed faintly. "Well, let me tell you what I need to have done." I showed her the articles. "Do you think you'll have trouble with the technical terms?"

She didn't answer right away, but leafed through the pages. "I don't think so. It's the technical terms that are similar in both lan-guages. Besides, that's what dictionaries are for, aren't they?" She gave me a rather impish grin, and suddenly I felt something new stirring in the room. I was grown now—it no longer took me weeks to identify it. The girl, I was almost sure, was flirting with me. She had sensed my interest and was responding. I would have to be more careful.

"It's about cancer cells."

"So I see."

"I hope that's not—I mean, will it upset you?"

She gazed at me as her mother used to, as if I were ludicrously inept. "I've already had the reality. There's not much the words can add."

"Yes, I see. I'm sorry. So, when do you think you can have this ready? Is three weeks too soon?"

"No, that's all right."

I arranged to pay her fifteen dollars an hour, which she seemed to find generous. "Then we're all set, uh—do you mind if I call you Francesca?"

Again she smiled coolly. "What else?"

"Well, I might call you Signorina." I didn't mean to encourage her but couldn't help myself. I was at a loss. I only wanted to get closer to her, befriend her.

"I don't think we have to be quite that formal. Professor." This time there was no doubt. She flung her tweed coat over her shoulders and was gone.

I locked the door, then sat down, bent my head to the desk and allowed myself my grief. It could not wait to be taken home. And nothing about Janet belonged at home.

When at last I looked up I thought of her, Francesca, again. My daughter. I had three fine, healthy sons: nine, twelve, and fourteen. I had renounced—my wife and I had, I should say—the prospect of a daughter long ago, without any great pangs. Yet how luscious the idea seemed, now that I had seen her. Had she been in my department I might have invited her over, taken an interest and helped her with her work. Even so, mightn't I befriend her through the translation, ask her over as a kind gesture to a foreign student, make her part of the family? I was aware that faculty wives didn't appreciate their husbands' befriending beautiful students, and in the couple of cases I had observed, their lack of enthusiasm was borne out by the facts. My wife was not particularly suspicious or jealous: I had never given her reason to be. How would she react to Francesca? I might tell her the truth (though not the whole truth): she was the daughter of people who had been hospitable to me in Rome years ago and I wanted to return the favor. But I knew myself. I could not live comfortably with the pretense.

Besides, my wife knows me too, in that unnerving way that wives do. She knows, for instance, that I am less interested in finding a cure for cancer than in charting the erratic paths of the cells, or unraveling the logic that makes them travel and hide, erupt and masquerade. At the university hospital—she is head nurse of the Intensive Care Unit—she sees dying patients every day. She respects my research, yet I have a feeling she finds it somewhat abstract and irrelevant. She finds me abstracted too—though I hope not irrelevant. Maybe, in her plain-spoken way, she sees the same ingenuousness Janet found so amusing. Maybe it has never fallen away with age, only transmuted into what Americans dignify with the term absent-mindedness. I suppose I am absent, in a sense, from my life. I was present with Janet—as who could not be?—and I am present in the laboratory, and often with my sons. Otherwise I suppose I hold myself in abeyance, I don't know why, or for what. I don't mean any harm that I know of. I only feel vague. I am not disappointed with my life; sometimes it feels better than I expected. There was a period, after we had been married a few years and had our first child, when my wife accused me of being disappointed and having cooled, but I denied that, and soon she stopped mentioning it. She finds great satisfaction in her work as well as in the boys, and we get on companionably. I am grateful we never had the turbulence of divorce I have seen disrupt and sometimes destroy the lives of friends and colleagues.

Though the Romance Languages Department is in the building across the lawn from mine, I had never noticed Francesca before. Now I saw her everywhere—lounging on the front steps; in the gym, where I played racketball and she swam; in the local drugstore; in the faculty club, where she was eating with, apparently, some boisterously entertaining young instructors from Romance Languages. Each time, she came up to greet me with her mother's provocative, ambiguous tone. And I responded. She was my daughter—how could I be aloof with her? I was inexpressibly touched to see she liked me, was even drawn to me. I am a pleasant-mannered, nice-looking man, but don't flatter myself that I cut a dashing figure. Something more obscure drew her. I felt as I do in the lab when I draw near to the heart of the mystery—troubled and excited, and though it is where I want to be, I want also to draw back.

I tried to keep a proper distance: I would ask how the translation was going, and she would say fine. Once, coming out of the library, she said she was stopping for coffee, did I want to join her? Naturally I did—I wanted any chance to be near her.

She ordered an espresso and tossed it back in one gulp. She was in her first year of graduate work, she told me. She had gotten her undergraduate degree from Harvard. Harvard! She was studying comparative literature; she had learned French in school and, with her Italian, found Spanish a breeze. German was more difficult. She wasn't sure what she would write her dissertation on—at the moment she was fascinated by the Latin American novelists, but she had a new enthusiasm every month, she said with a self-mocking smile. "Intellectually fickle is what I am, I guess," and she waved regally for another coffee.

I said very little, just basked in her presence. In retrospect, I see I must have appeared entranced, as I truly was. I kept thinking how delightful and eager she was, and how she would never know the truth about herself. Unless Janet had told her, and she, Francesca, was playing some sly game of privileged information. No, knowing Janet, that was inconceivable.

"And what about you, Professor," she said with a droll glance. "I can see from the articles what you're interested in, but what else? Are you married?"

"Yes." I told her about my wife and children. I even pulled pictures from my wallet to show her, and while she said all the proper things —What handsome boys!—she seemed a trifle daunted. I wanted so badly to tell her she was looking at her brothers. Half-brothers. "Are you sure your mother never mentioned me? I know there were lots of students but I—well, I must confess I had a bit of a crush on her."

"Is that so?" Francesca gave her ironic smile. "You were hardly the only one. She was Queen of the Students. She loved it. She was going strong well into her fifties, until the end. Yes, she broke quite a few hearts."

"Oh, but not really—You're not saying that—"

"Of course not!" With all her sophistication, she seemed shocked, as children are invariably shocked at their parents' adventures. "They were kids to her. She and my father used to joke about them after they left. He would guess which ones liked her and she would correct him. I remember them laughing over their coffee. They could never agree on which ones."

"I see."

"What do you mean, you see? What on earth does that mean?"

"I don't know, it's just something to say when you don't know what else to say."

"Don't worry, it wasn't malicious laughter. They loved being around the students. They said it kept them young."

I was newly disturbed when we parted. So close, she had said the very first day. So devoted. But I couldn't lose myself in brooding all over again, at this late date. I would understand no better, only feel more pain. What did it matter now? She was dead. The boy I had been was as good as dead. Except for Francesca, that is.

A few days later she turned up in my office, very businesslike, with the translation. I thanked her and made a note to have the secretary send her a check. She said to contact her if there were any problems with the text, and wrote her phone number on a slip of paper.

"Do you live in the dorms?"

"No, I'm a grad student, remember? I'm too old for the dorms. I have an apartment across campus."

"I see."

"Ah," she laughed, "there you go again. Seventy-four Crabtree Street, if that's what 'I see' meant this time."

"No, it didn't, actually."

"I see," she said, still smiling, taunting. There are countless rules, nowadays, regarding the most tenuous sexual innuendos chanced by professors. One has to be wary, even someone like me who has never chanced anything of the kind. No rules for the opposite, I thought wryly.

"Do you have a boyfriend?" It was fatherly interest—I hoped she would say yes. I could invite them over together. It would be easier for me, as well as for my wife.

To my surprise, her face turned sober. Younger. "There's someone back in Rome I've known a long time, and I always thought . . . But now I'm not sure any more."

"You mean someone from before college? But you were so young."

"Well, yes. We both knew there might be other people. We're far apart and I'm not . . . shy that way—" She paused and gave me the oddest look, half-earnest, half-coy, utterly young, yet I had seen enough of her, not to mention her mother, to know it was also maddeningly canny. Economical as ever, she was accomplishing a great deal at once. "Still, there was some understanding . . . When I went back last fall, when Mother died, we spent a lot of time together. And at a time like that, when someone is close to you and acts kind, you tend to accept what they do for you, and then they think . . . Do you know what I mean?"

"I think so."

"But now I wonder. I feel it would be retreating, in a way. From I don't know what. From life. I see people around and I'm, well, interested, what's wrong with saying it? Everybody is. Why should I have to hold back because I promised things when I was almost a child and didn't know any better? And yet he's a friend of the family, he's—Oh, look, I'm sorry. Why on earth would you want to listen to all this? I've got to be going."

"No, really, I am interested."

"You are? Why?"

"I just am. I guess because I knew your parents, and, well, you're such a lovely young woman."

She mistook my words again, willfully, it seemed, and as easily as slipping out of a dress, she slipped out of her earnest, girlish mode. I was sorry, for I loved hearing it, loved her talking to me as if I might be a father. A father figure, anyway.

"Indeed," was all she said. She sounded like her mother. I could see how she might be irresistible.

"Ah, indeed. That's hardly better than 'I see,'" I teased.

"You're right. What else can I say to a mixed message?"

"Mixed message? Not at all. I meant just what I said. Look, you really must come over for dinner one night, meet my family."

"Meet your family?" She looked dubious. "Well, thank you. That's very kind. Do you want to check it out with your wife first, maybe?"

"I'll see what night is convenient and let you know. She works some nights. And thanks again for getting this to me so promptly, Francesca."

I told my wife about the translation. I told her the almost unbelievable coincidence of the translator being the daughter of a couple who had been hospitable to me in Rome when I was a student. I told her I needed to go over some small points in the articles with the girl, and would like to invite her for dinner one night, partly out of gratitude to her parents and partly to be kind: her mother had died recently. I had never been duplicitous with my wife in this way, but found it remarkably easy. It was what Janet and I had had to do, with her husband, her babysitter, my fellow students. Like riding a bicycle indeed. I even remembered it was not necessary or propitious to add lies, such as that Francesca seemed lonely and found it hard to make friends, and so on. My wife was struck by the coincidence. Okay, she said, how about Friday night?

Ah, she had many guises, my old world young daughter did. She performed graciously the role of foreign student enjoying the hospitality of kind Americans. She praised the food, bantered easily with the boys, helped clear the table, and answered with tact and patience all the usual questions asked of foreigners, comparing life abroad and in the States. After dinner, in my study, we went over a few small points in the translation. I saw I could relax: she was quite professional, as, of course, was I. I remembered how her mother had chilled my caresses when the professor and the students were in the next room.

When we returned to the living room the boys had gone upstairs and my wife was curled up in the easy chair, reading the paper. I said I would drive Francesca home. She and my wife exchanged the customary thank you's and hopes to meet again. They didn't kiss as some women do even on first meeting—neither was expansive enough for that—but the warmth between them seemed genuine.

"Crabtree, was it?" I said in the car.

"Ah, you remembered."

"It's nothing special. I have a good memory for details."

"Oh. Well, you have a very nice family. I enjoyed meeting them. You must be quite pleased with yourself." The lower part of her face was buried in her scarf; she was peering out at me sideways.

"I'm pleased, yes, I suppose so."

"Your wife is a good cook, too."

"Yes."

"Did you accomplish what you hoped from the evening, then?"

"I had no specific hopes. I thought it went nicely. Why, were you disturbed about anything?"

"Not at all, it was lovely." She was silent for the rest of the short ride, except, near the end, to point out the house, an old-fashioned three-story frame house divided into apartments, with an ample porch.

"I'd invite you to sit on the porch for a while, but it's too cold."

"Freezing for this time of year," I said. "Anyway, I should get back."

"Yes, you should. Definitely."

228

"I'm very sorry you're irritated. I can't explain."

"There's nothing to explain. It's not too complex to understand."

"Please don't be angry, Francesca."

"Oh, all right." She gave a bit of a laugh, and again seemed to shake off the mood as easily as a dress. "I'll see you around." And she laid her hand on my arm, just the barest touch.

"Yes. Good night. Thanks again for the translation. You did a terrific job."

"Good night." She leaned over and kissed me very lightly and swiftly on the lips. It was nothing really, no more than a fleeting feathery brush, but then she waited. I was supposed to kiss her back. And maybe it would have been better if I had—just once, and properly, with ardor: then she could have kept her illusion that, like many a timid professor, I wanted her but didn't dare risk my domestic peace. A benign, bittersweet illusion, not one of the noxious kinds. Better than my sitting there unmoving and righteous. Yes, I suppose I did the wrong thing. I suppose it was a disgrace not to kiss her, but I feared the disgrace, in my own eyes, of kissing her even once. Besides, I didn't want to kiss her. I wanted to kiss her mother.

Back home, my wife was still reading the paper in the easy chair. "That was quick," she said.

"She doesn't live far."

"Still, I thought you might take longer."

I threw my coat on a chair and headed for the stairs. I was utterly exhausted.

"There's something between you and that girl, isn't there?"

I stopped on the third stair and faced her. "Nothing of the kind. How could you think that?"

"I'm not wrong. Maybe nothing yet. Maybe you don't even know it yourself yet, but there's something."

"You don't know how wrong you are. It's out of the question. I'm surprised you should even suggest it."

"You should be surprised by me once in a while."

"That may be. That may be. But this is inconceivable."

"All right, never mind then," she said, and turned back to her paper.

She didn't speak of it any more, but she thinks it.

I have never invited Francesca home again. I see her on campus all the time. I watch her from afar and try to avoid coming face to face, for when I do she is cool. To talk to her, to ask her to lunch, which is what I long to do—simply to sit across from her and look at her—would be unfair. In a couple of years, when she finishes her studies, she will go away, and I will be relieved and bereft, never knowing whether she goes home to marry her childhood sweetheart (unlikely, I'd say) or falls in love with someone new, maybe an American. It's not inconceivable that I could run into her somewhere in twenty years, and then will she smilingly, ironically recall how she once had a slight crush on me, very slight, just a vague sense there might be something between us—but I wouldn't give it half a chance? Would it be possible to tell her then? Or even worse than now?

All this might happen, unless something changes erratically in me and I do what she wishes and my wife suspects. I believe I am incapable of that, but I know some organisms are capable of the most unpredictable, riotous, malign behavior. I hope I am not.

POEMS

At the Border

Maybe it was the season, coming again
to the border of the cold time, though the sky
stayed crazy October blue, every tree
preening its last greenness before the turning
and falling. The weather was in ecstasy
while all the women on the bus were weeping
in silence, discreetly. And I was weeping with them—
just from the right eye, it sometimes happens that way—
though I couldn't have named the trouble. Maybe I'd lost
the way or, what's worse, never found one,
or, more likely, come up against an edge,
where weeping was the jumping off, trying to fly.
What does it matter? What matters is how we wept
in unison, tears parading down each smooth cheek
as if for a day of national mourning—war, disaster,
wingless bodies weaving through space threading
a fiery wake. But this grief—if grief it was—
felt undramatic, simply the usual hungers and losses
had crept to the borders of the tolerable
for all of us at once, grief coinciding
with the blue season of fasting and atonement.

The girl's eyes across the aisle, slate pools,
surely dripped for love—the worst part, at her age,
not being the loss, the hollowed-out dungeon in the chest
where the heart crouches alone going wild,
but the not understanding why, why the hunger,
the refusal, why it won't work—while others wept
for death or illness, no money or wayward children,
or all of the above, things imaginable and things
unimaginable, and most of all not understanding,
like the Russian Jews in the hospital where we waited
for my father to finish his dying—this a ways back,
when the Russian Jews were first allowed to come here,
so arrogant, my social worker friend said,
expecting a welfare state and high-level jobs.
They settled on the beach. Leave it to Jews

to find the edge, a beach in a new land:
on the Boardwalk at Brighton I see my ancestors stroll,
those short people who were musical,
with a talent for language and for numbers, transported,
to trudge the boards of Brighton chewing their turgid soul food.
Anyway, we lounged in intensive care: nothing to do
but watch three stocky people around the next bed
who couldn't understand the words the doctor spoke—things
imaginable and unimaginable—about their loved one,
journeyed so far to die where he didn't speak the language,
though maybe that's good, maybe it was good practice
for wherever he was going. I recognized them
and told my mother, Ma, they're Russian Jews.
Go over and explain, they'll speak Yiddish.
And so she did. She wasn't shy, was generous and helpful
even in the midst of grief, and she liked to show off.
She translated for them, whatever tortures the doctor
was telling in English, no easy task, for instance:
We'll take him off the respirator and see if he flies.
As if the machine were his mother's Ukrainian womb.
Yet at the end she spoiled it, for me, at least,
because she couldn't help being nice, she said at the end,
because they were weeping, she murmured, It will be all right,
it will be all right.
And I, when she returned all puffed with charity,
said, Why did you say that, Ma—it will be all right—
since chances are it will not?
Then her face drew back from me, my own mother,
and so we spoiled it for each other.

Our bus rolled past construction sites on the left,
the endless wrecking and building that is civilized life,
with powdered debris sparkling the autumn air, as
mothers and children stumbled through clumps of granite
like an untended graveyard grim with disgrace.
On our right, the ravishing park where I had just walked,
green like the fields of Poland, grown over the bones.

It must have been a lovers' lane, a dark wood
I wandered into unwittingly, I had lost my way,
or what's worse, never known a way to begin with.
There were lovers in front of me and lovers in back.
They make it safe, I thought, this broody lane,
then smiled at the thought that love could make anything safe.
They looked a trifle startled as I passed,
for lovers walk slowly, absorbed, what is their rush,
they glance up at strangers, aggrieved, they pull apart.
Go right on kissing, I wanted to say, or bumping hips and
    shoulders,
whatever it was—I have done it, too, taken all I could,
but just now taking only the common air.
And when I had breathed enough I boarded the bus. Huge,
magnificent, these city buses, their trombone blasts,
the stern fanfare of transport, the darkened, doomed windows.
Ugly and unabashed, they move with spectacular pomp,
great gloomy slugs oozing through more graceful traffic,
past the splintered landscape bordering the green park,
carrying their cargo of weepers, so democratic, welcoming,
anyone with enough coins can climb on for a good cry,
when your legs can't take you another step and you've come
to hate the beggars who don't know when to stop,
who can't tell you're not in the mood for their insistence.
They have no manners or gratitude anymore,
but blink at their blistered palms, the coins you've placed there,
as if saying, It's not enough, it will never be enough.

The weeping women are a silent echo of the baseball players,
in plangent October, season's end, when all has been lost,
and the last batter charges the mound, leaps on the pitcher
wrapping his arms and legs around him like a woman
crazed with love, but here it is rage, a spume of frustration—a ball
barreled into him, maybe, or else a mere show of rage,
a wild urge to fly, and suddenly,
instead of two men fighting, the entire teams
are leaping and heaping together, clawing and thrashing,

amassing a writhing mountain on the field,
having a good manly fight. It is their way.
Later, they will troop in unison to the showers, then fly
off to go duck hunting. The seasons of hunting
and of atonement are the same, before the spiteful frost.

Every weeper has her story and there was a time,
when I loved stories, when I would have been curious
to know each story, would even have made it up for them,
given it grace and shape, made it better.
That girl with the slate pool eyes, oh, what I could make of her!
Lord, I could give them better sorrow than they know,
both imaginable and unimaginable,
the way the fathers used to say, What are you crying about?
You want to cry, I'll give you something to cry about,
though they rarely smacked, so long as we stopped in time.
Crying children are annoying, worse than that, they drive you crazy
till you'll do anything to shut them up, they remind you
of something at the edge, too horrible to contemplate,
of unending and uncomprehended torture
without a moment's respite, with no restraint or fortitude
to bear it. And what happens then?
Like the dogs that barked outside my window at five-thirty
every morning, short, high-pitched, insistent
yelps full of frustration and dismay
as only dogs can feel it. Little black ones,
ratty, with furry tails, I imagined,
as I lay there unwilling to move but raging,
imagining running outside and strangling them
simply to stop the noise. Their owner, I imagined,
maybe the super, maybe the parking-lot attendant,
left them lashed to the gate while he made his coffee.
Let him return to find them dead, and learn
consideration. Then one morning I did get up,
went to the window—not black dogs but paper-bag brown,
short-haired, tethered to the wrought-iron gate.
I saw my visions enacted, yet it wasn't me I saw:

236

my neighbor from upstairs, a steel-haired irascible man
who would shout out his window at passersby picking our flowers,
and now strode to the gate to snap the dogs' necks
one after the other, then strode away
leaving the bodies aquiver, brown bags in the breeze.
Moments later I felt the clomping, his boots over my head,
I heard his roaring throat-clearing, the pent-up phlegm
loosening and rising. And the mornings were quiet.
I'd thought I was at the end of my rope, that I couldn't stand
another instant of the barking, which I imagined
was for something lost or desperately desired,
without which the dogs could not continue, or would continue,
but only in severe and unrelieved pain.
My neighbor made it clear I was not at the end.
He was, while I had rope to spare, to spare.

The weepers are harmless, their stories are turned into brine.
The trouble with grief
is not the having it but finding a place to put it.
It cannot find its niche, it must be turned
into something else. Weeping is the alchemy of grief.
And frankly I am not curious any longer, about the stories,
since they are all the same, no matter where they begin
or end, who are the characters, what mistakes they have made,
what little neglects and calamities, what murders at dawn.
All love stories have unhappy endings, a rabbi said at a funeral,
and my sister turned to whisper, How very true, especially
as who would expect to hear the truth in eulogies?
That struck us most of all, the incongruity.
You expect merely to remember all the others, disposed of
with ceremony and without, in ways imaginable
and unimaginable, and the ones still to come.
You watch the pallbearers who no longer bear any weight
but trail behind, appalled, arms hanging useless,
missing the satisfaction of heavy work.
Civilization has come so far that we are wheeled off.
For this the wheel was invented, for this the shovel.

We roll to our resting place and dig in, just as the bus
rolls us to our destinations, the weepers wipe their cheeks,
and descend to meet what the pitted streets can offer.
Only in the intervals between here and there,
the small respites of travel, of passing through,
can we weep freely, anonymously, among strangers
who are friends in the fellowship of transport, like those other
transports where they did not weep discreetly in unison.
Good God, what a luxury to sit here and be transported.
We are the lucky ones, we the delivered.
Civilization, for all its discontents,
is a sweet notion, really, it is designed
to help us through this fall at the wild western border,
this Central Park West of tears and endless reconstruction.
We have been taken off the respirators, and for a while, we fly.

Looking for the River

Madame La Blue, in exile, stands at the window
laced with ivy, a fretwork of green framing
the view she refuses.
All day long, her stubborn path to the window
on stubborn feet, her eyes blinking back what they see:
fountain of stone, dry branches, sandy bones
of wasted park, gritty litter of lunches.
She cannot get it through her mop of a head
that this is a different window and she is lost.
All day long she is looking for the river,

her native river
thick with ice chunks, sun chips, mucky,
where only the brave fished for treasure, old boot,
or dead pet or drained skin of a heart
that drowned itself for love.
A craving river, it tugged at her girlish eye,
till her vision rocked in the river as love rocks the body.
Her eye became
like a glass-bottomed boat, she saw it all.
She cast her spells like lines, the biting fish
got the blues from Madame La Blue.

Not even so old or past hope, in spirit still moist,
she has a blind spot: she cannot grasp that her house,
her high river view, is burned to the ground.
Too hard,
like quantum physics, where the stars we wish on
have long ago burnt out. Just so, her past
has vaporized, leaving her in the milky cloud
of the present, pulled to the barren window, looking
for the river on the other side of town,
of now.

Letter to Harry in China

Dear,
Since you left me for the Forbidden City
and the city of the hanging gardens
I have been watering all ninety-seven
as you asked.
In your green night forest,
in your hanging gardens,
I murmur oxygenated words of love,
as you asked.
Deprived of you, their enamored caretaker,
they sprouted wistful messages.
I send them on to you,
as they asked:

I am the Golden Peperomia.
In a plant collection I will be noticed
at the first glance. My golden color
makes me a favorite with everybody.
Santo Domingo is my native home.
Keep me warm and moist
and in a semi-shady spot.
I need very little fertilizer.

I am the New Trailing Peperomia.
Besides being a nice houseplant
I grow well in a hanging pot.
Light, but no direct sunlight
is best for me.
Keep me moderately moist and
fertilize me once a month.

Mini White Vein Plant
botanically known as "Fittonia
Argyroneura nana,"
I am the brand new Angel Princess,
right now the newest thing on the market
and come from Europe.

Keep me moist, in a shady location.
Feed me once a month.
My strikingly beautiful
netted, veiny leaves
will attract everybody's attention.

Oh, take a fast boat home
to my shady location.
Keep me moist. The dark is best for me.
I need very little fertilizer but
my strikingly beautiful
netted veiny leaves need your attention.

With love, as ever,
as you asked.

To the Evening Student

Ready to fall in love head first,
they come with open mouths, shy tongues,
thirsty, from hot jobs—cooks, cops, cabdrivers.
They think the teacher's cool.

Front row center nightly,
you alone study my moves as if I were the lesson,
swallow my words and my voice as a chaser,
praise your beloved Wobblies and Jack London,
but scorn Wordsworth—"too self-centered"—
though no more so than you,
your center sealed and ablaze
behind eyes searing like snow in blue light.
You tell me the world is aged and corrupt,
and individualism a Western error,
but your eyes say otherwise.
Listen to me, I see them sometimes in dreams,
floating alone among clouds like billows of cream,
and I open my hand.
I would take you home but for the distance,
and your insistence
that *The Merchant of Venice* is about political economy.

In the twilight, on the street with some girl,
you lap the ice-cream with a boy's avid tongue,
waving and smiling as I pass:
Your smile is a question mark.
Your bleached-out jeans are the color of your eyes.
Your mustache is a joke.
Your hair needs washing—you boys
grow it well enough but can't tend it.
Still, do you know I shuddered?
The sting of vanilla on my teeth.

When I read a poem aloud, again it's you,
my class wonder, rushing to rip the net of silence.
"What he seems to be saying is . . ."

Too prompt, like every boy,
still, something rips in me.
When I say passion is the heart of poetry,
the blue darkens and hides
and I get a premonition
from that sullen inhibition—
I know just how it would be.
So listen—oh, you with the long future—
it's, oh, too bad about you and me.

doctor untangle
is a game the children play
linking arms
legs
necks and torsos
merry in young surrender
in agile, blind serpentine writhing
they fall to the floor in a heap

and doctor untangle comes:
a house call

careful and studious
first he points without touching
this is yours, he says,
and yours and yours
then, jostling flesh over flesh—
his touch is abstracted and cool—
restoring each part to its rightful owner
(modest, miraculous doctor untangle)
he gives them back themselves

Urban Insomnia

Miguel comes at five in the morning to do the chores,
first lugging the bulging squirmy brown bags,
like slick damp animals, up the basement stairs,
lining them up for the truck that comes at eight.
He used to do the garbage the night before,
but local beggars tore open the bags in search
of salvation, leaving a strewn feast
for rats and packs of dogs who erupt from the park,
forcing us, in the morning, to confront
our rotten, forgotten scraps. So now he outwits them,
hauls the trash near dawn, then fetches the shovel
to scrape the sidewalks clear of the day's snowfall,
not deep but rather the perilous slippery kind
on which old people can break a hip, be laid up
for months, never feeling quite right again—
though young or old, the consequences of one misstep
abide in the bones forever.

I know all this because I watch in secret,
roused by the raking sound of shovel on concrete.
Not quite decent to watch those who think they're alone,
yet I feel we labor as one, at the same task—
my hour too to rise and haul and scrape.
Bed is too sweet for the labors of the sleepless,
the scraping of inner surfaces: what I said,
what he said, what we did wrong and wrong and
    wretchedly wrong.
It is a kind of flaying, a raucous peeling
of new wounds grafted on old, layered like snows,
a kind of self-abuse that wants to be done
in the dark, in the cold, while hearts at ease sleep
and we wild ones wake with shovels sharpened.

Now is the warping hour:
each memory a mockery, every dream an incubus.
Now the starving dogs retreat in packs

and night people crawl, bleeding, to the Emergency Room
to wait and bleed and wait.
The consequences of every bungled act
pierce like dogs' teeth drilling down to nerve.
The consequences are what the mystics call Karma—
what I have made possible by my acts
and what I have made impossible. Just so
the Pythagorean brothers asked each day,
In what have I failed? What good have I done,
what have I not done that I ought to have done?
The snow on the inner walls is flakes of remorse,
is being unloved and unloving and cast out,
ruining all by lack of subtlety
and too many words.
May this chill night teach me discretion and cunning,
dealing and subterfuge.

The irreparable has hardened to ice,
resisting the shovel. I must fetch the pick
as my father did in Brooklyn, but in broad light of day,
assaulting the sheen of the surface, his life-long rage
splintering the poor ice.
At the darkened glass, shivering, I watch Miguel
in down jacket, knitted cap and gloves,
gripping the shovel, clearing orderly rows,
making the ragged sound
of metal dragged across unyielding concrete,
the sound that summoned me from sleep to work,
the sound of what I am doing in my head.
Every mistake in the world brings this sound,
not weeping but scraping. Weeping would be music.

When the scraping is done, when discarded despair in mounds
melts down in the dark,
we sleepless return to the hard-earned warmth of bed,
having scraped our fill, having made our grudging
tenuous peace with the errors of today,

made space for the errors and injuries of tomorrow
which will echo the errors and injuries of today,
as the garbage will replace itself with similar scraps.
And at last we sleep, trusting to be reborn
at the eight o'clock sound of the garbage truck,
quite different, a crunching and grinding and pulverizing,
the signal of day. The beggars will be at their posts
on the glittery streets, the prowling dogs in their lairs,
Miguel at his second job, and I at my first,
my only, life, watching new snow pile up,
waiting for night.

On Waiting

I have worn patience like a gown of thorns
have slept with patience my comforter of nails
dined on it daily, straw of the artichoke
patience has left her toothmarks on my shoulder
rat in the night
the tangles in my hair are patience
the ingrown toenail, the mole to pluck in secret
it is the flat-eyed monster
habited like a nun, inhabiting me
squatter imp

My waiting was no virtue
wrung from necessity, but necessity itself
Rule: if we wait long enough
all that we ever wanted will come too late
Exception: it was not too late for you
I was only a novice, I never learned by heart
When you returned
I could still leap with greed, impatient
for you, all sweet and prodigal

Blessed is not the giving but the receiving
not the rough traveling but the arrival
not the waiting but the having
These are the rebel lessons
this is what every child knows
the anti-wisdom wisdom
It must be a devil who teaches patience
who brews piety out of graceless yearning
Lord make me never have to learn again

In Solitary

I used to think I would go crazy
if I were locked up for fifty years,
almost a lifetime, through some miscarriage of justice,
like the pathetic prisoners in books and movies
who, after it was found they were innocent all along,
trudged out shriveled and bent like gnomes,
beards to their chests and angelic wisps of hair,
and mad of course,
sullen or dotty, depending on the plot—
what else could you expect?—
unless they had spent the half-century writing,
in which case it was always a work of genius,
implying they could only have produced it
in solitary.

I pictured my cell: stone, like theirs, and small,
a square cut high on the wall, with a grate
for light and checkered cloud or plaid blue sky,
though never showing the source, the golden ball—
the window was positioned that way on purpose,
sending a bright beam sliding up the wall,
sliding up, finally, out of my stretched embrace;
and a heavy iron door with a barred window
empty but for the mute profile of the guard
pacing the corridor like maddening clockwork,
and a little slot like a mail drop near the floor,
through which the bowls of gruel were slipped,
though I never knew exactly what gruel was—
I imagined a thinnish oatmeal;
and a bucket in the corner for what the books called slops,
which would be removed from time to time and gave off a
    bad smell;
and a lumpy mat on the floor, faintly damp,
that got to smell of me—that was comforting,
to lie down in myself;
and maybe a table and chair, candle, matches,
to read and write by.

There were moments it even seemed homey and bearable,
but mostly I knew I would go mad,
sullen mad, from solitude.

To start with, resentment would make me bitter and cynical,
which is not yet mad, only the first step.
The clincher would be thirsting for the colors
of the world, not seeing what was moving along Broadway,
missing the traffic, the book and sock peddlers,
the Korean fruit families hosing down the lettuce,
the Africans hawking summer dresses dancing on hangers,
and having to make a world inside my head,
a place to live, which I would find impossible,
not being one of the abundant generative souls
like Shakespeare, Mozart or Michelangelo,
who make worlds out of visions.
I would hurtle around in the hollows of my head
like a homemade rattle, pebble in a can,
banging against the walls, knocking on hollow.
I wouldn't have hallucinations, at least diverting.
I would have blankness and disconnection, the ultimate lunacy.
I would not scream but grind my teeth and crouch in a corner,
suffering the caprices of unmediated weather,
breathless and choking in summer, stiff in winter,
praying for death, yearning
for a way to yank out consciousnesss,
like yanking the innards from a slaughtered chicken.
That would be the worst deprivation, not to die.

Fantasies! I tried to shrug them off. This couldn't happen,
yet happens every day, legal loopholes, judicial errors.
Or I might be moved to dismember a bomb or climb
a forbidden fence, as a gesture of freedom
and dissociation from the powers that be,
like certain heroes of our time, who find themselves
in exactly the circumstances I describe.

Or the night I imagined the fire was not quite out
after I left my cabin in the woods,
so I accidentally burned down the artists' colony;
the jury, while recognizing I didn't mean it
(why should I want to kill a colony of artists?),
nonetheless held me responsible.
I wept in the courtroom, but they took no pity.

Or it could be a crime of passion, only a step
from fantasy, where I have committed many.

So it might well happen, but the great thing is,
now having passed my fiftieth year,
I would not go mad
like the old gnomes who rotted in their heads.
No, I'd divide my day in an orderly fashion,
doing exercises at regular intervals,
aerobics for the heart and ballet warm-ups for tautness,
and T'ai Chi for the soul and for the thighs,
and set myself to learning languages, hard ones,
Russian, Greek, Swahili, Chinese, Finnish—
they allow you harmless apolitical books—
and I would make lists of every flower I could remember,
and tree, and animal, like eland and stoat and coati,
and the names of streets in each city I ever visited,
such as Buffalo Speedway or via Accademia dei Virtuosi,
and the names of all the people I knew in school,
from the very first morning—Miss Bradburn and Mrs. Stein:
students, teachers, principals, maintenance staff,
and all my relatives, even the distant and violent long-gone
Russians whose escapades were family legend,
and study maps of the world in giant atlases
till I could trace all the lands on all the six
continents, naming their every river and mountain range,
from the Euphrates to the Carpathian.
I would draw pictures, using a bestselling book

on how to draw for people who can't draw,
and practice arpeggios on an imaginary keyboard and learn
to sight read, and sing very loudly all the arias
of Mozart and lyrics of *Pal Joey* that I could remember:
deprived of cigarettes, I would get my voice back.

Like some notable prisoners, I might even study the law,
not to have my case reopened—by this time
I might not even wish to have it reopened—
but simply to know the spirit and the letter.
I would be very busy, serenely engaged,
sometimes even forgetting to eat my gruel,
running out of candles, begging the silent guard for more.

Every few days I would masturbate, to keep that going.
It would help if they let me have books of high-class porn,
something elegantly written, the French do that best—
I wouldn't mind the gross tortures so much as crude writing—
but if not I could manage well enough on my own,
setting an elaborate scene with silks and velvets,
though maybe as years went by I'd need some weird
implements. I would do it in the dark, in case of the guard.
I like privacy.

And afterwards I would think of all my loved ones
outside in the light, who have not forgotten me,
recalling their every feature, expression and gesture,
the sound of their voices, the varied inflections and accents,
the witty and poignant words of civilized people;
every encounter, every place we ever went, especially
watery ones, the hot tubs, the whirling waters,
the long days at Long Nook and Corn Hill in Truro,
and all the motel beds and the hours of music,
of dancing in the kitchen holding a spoon;
and how the babies' hair thickened to real hair.

I would reconstruct my whole life from the beginning,

from my earliest memory at fifteen months (being chased up the
    stairs
by an uncle who wanted only to bandage my bleeding knee
when I crashed into a glass door, but I was afraid
and hated him ever since, I couldn't help it)
to my most recent memory, a hummingbird hanging in the sky,
batting translucent wings amid bare twigs of birch
sinuous and forking like capillaries—
I am lying on the grass opposite a mountain I am told
has magical powers,
spreading myself out in the sun to catch the magic—
and everything in between the fear and the magic,
my long journey from fear to magic.

Acknowledgments

Essays:

"Taking It Seriously" first printed in the *Barnard Alumnae Magazine*, Spring 1981.

"True Confessions of a Reader" first printed in *Salmagundi* 88–89, Fall/Winter 1991.

"Help" first printed in *The Michigan Quarterly Review*, Spring 1992.

"Rags and Tags and Velvet Gowns" appeared in a shortened version, with the title "Beggaring Our Better Selves," in *Harper's*, December 1991.

"The Tapes As Theatre" first printed as "Lynne Sharon Schwartz on Theater," in *The New Republic*, 1 June 1974.

"On Being Taken by Tom Victor" first printed in *The Threepenny Review*, Winter 1991.

Stories:

"The Melting Pot," "The Subversive Divorce," "What I Did For Love," and "The Two Portraits of Rembrandt" are taken from *The Melting Pot and Other Subversive Stories*, copyright © 1987 by Lynne Sharon Schwartz, reprinted by permission of HarperCollins Publishers.

"Mrs. Saunders Writes to the World," "Grand Staircases," and "The Middle Classes" are taken from *Acquainted with the Night*, copyright © 1984 by Lynne Sharon Schwartz, reprinted by permission of HarperCollins Publishers.

"Francesca" first printed in *American Short Fiction*, September 1992.

Poems:

"At the Border" appeared in *Ploughshares*, Winter 1990–91.

"Urban Insomnia" reprinted from *Prairie Schooner*, by permission of the University of Nebraska Press. Copyright © 1992 by the University of Nebraska Press.

"In Solitary" first printed in *The Literary Review* at Fairleigh Dickinson University, Fall 1992.